Praise for Ginex's
Future of God Amen
A Call to Daughters and Sons of God

- *Nicholas takes facts and figures from Christian, Judaic, and Islamic religions and takes them into a new level where scholars, and professors alike will be mind blown and use this superb work of literature; Collaborating Ginex's controversial piece of literature into their studies for centuries to come. This book is a must read for mystics or anyone who is interested in religious texts and studies!*

Michael G Stone, Poet and Author of five books including; *Forest of Caves: Season's of Heaven and Hell (2005),* and *Forest of Caves: The Darkest Garden (2009)*

- *This is a riveting glimpse into the ancient past where many of our present day beliefs originated and how they have evolved into the contemporary religions and beliefs of today. Whether your beliefs stem from the Islamic, Christian or Judaic beliefs, this book highlights the important roll ancient Egypt played in their creation and where the concept of God has its roots. Nicholas P. Ginex has in my judgment created a masterful, easy to read correlation of well documented and presented historical information, which we can all benefit from. An eye opening revelation for those unfamiliar with the origins of their religious beliefs. A superb addition to anyone's library.*

Canadian Author, Richard Regener

• *A noble effort at religious scholarship that falters under the weight of its too-revolutionary arguments. Ginex's heart is in the right place in this hyper-ambitious book. Recognizing that religious differences often cause strife and violence, the author wants to prove that the great monotheisms—Islam, Christianity and Judaism—share a historical origin and consequently worship of the same god. For centuries, scholars have recognized that a family resemblance links the three traditions—even the Quran identifies Jews, Christians and Muslims as "peoples of the book."*

*Ginex admits that he learned of the genealogical connections linking the three religions when he was just six years old. But he takes the argument to a new level, suggesting that all three can trace their roots even further back, to the ancient Egyptian cult of the god Amen (more frequently transliterated "Amun"). The author also contends that each faith features elements borrowed from its Egyptian spiritual predecessor. Unfortunately, such synthesizing efforts, no matter how well-intentioned, always end up displeasing religionists and scholars. Believers do not appreciate being told that their faith is, at core, no different from their neighbors. And serious scholars recognize that efforts to argue for high levels of coincidence among traditions are often essentializing, that is, they paper over crucial differences in the name of an artificial coherence. Ginex's study risks failing on both these fronts, though he handles the second better than the first, acknowledging significant differences among the three religions. Further, his valiant attempt to produce high-level scholarship ultimately falls short. The proposal most important to Ginex's argument—that Judaism effectively begins in Egypt—was tried decades ago by Freud in **Moses and Monotheism** and dismissed by scholars not long after. Though the author is proud of his bibliography, at a scant two pages, it is too slim to support these radical claims.*

A study without a future.

Kirkus Discoveries, Nielsen Business Media

The above Kirkus review is negatively biased. The reviewer wrote, "*Ginex admits that he learned of the genealogical connections linking the three religions when he was just six years old.*" This is untrue because it was only after he read books by historical authors and Egyptologists that he made the genealogical connection. Also, the statement that scholars have dismissed Sigmund Freud's conclusion—*that Judaism effectively begins in Egypt*—needs to be reevaluated. Freud's conclusion has been substantiated by the many findings presented in this book. The bibliography only cites books used for this work.

The Author

• *Better written and more cohesive than many books on religion, Future of God Amen is scholarly and fleshed out to the point of textbook meticulousness; but it blindsides you with new discoveries and conclusions. Ginex's provocative analysis of theology that we thought was absolute, is unsettling. How much do we really know about God? How much do our religious leaders really know about the beginning of the creation of God? Ginex has conclusively shown that "Amen" is more definitive than "So be it." Muslims use the word "Amin," with the same meaning as in Christianity, and the Islamic use of the word is the same as the Jewish Amen. They all imply an underlining attribute: truth. How stark are the differences? How solid are the similarities? In the drive to reduce everything down to "God is good, Amen," important nuances are lost. Ginex underlines the need for these nuances to be acknowledged by religious leaders of the Judaic, Christian, and Islamic faiths.*

I recommend reading each chapter slowly, and questioning the validity of Ginex's assertions and conclusions. This book is for believers, agnostics, and nonbelievers of God; for those who want a broader perspective of how mankind first conceived God. A recommended read for religious leaders of the major religions; this will unify their scriptures and teach the Word of God—to love one another.

Andrea Borja, Journalist and Author of *Fixing Alicia*

• Ginex has taken on a worthy challenge in "Future of God Amen, A Call to Daughters and Sons of God". His position, that Judaism, Christianity and Islam all find their origins in Egypt, is not a new one, nor without controversy, however, he supports his argument with references, maps and histories, which are quite compelling. His writing style is smooth and is easy reading for an inquiring mind.

The book does not disguise Ginex's personal religious beliefs and education, however. And these views, such as his reference to Jesus Christ, will certainly be points of contention with some of those who do not share his views. His lack of reference to holy books other than the Bible, would be obvious to non-Christians, but for those who take the bible literally and as a historically accurate document will find sufficient proof of his position.

This book would be a valuable addition to the library of any Church, Synagogue or Masjid. Any student of history, civilization and religion would do well to make it required reading.

Artur Zorka, C.H.T.
Astronomer
Author, *"In Search Of Ancient Astronomers"*
Astronomical League Correspondent, Atlanta Astronomy
Club
Recipient of 7 Astronomical Observing Awards

Why this Book?

- Inform people that the soul, righteousness, truth, a hereafter, the God *Amen*, and Son of God, were developed by the religion of Ancient Egypt.

- Reveal that Jesus Christ acknowledged *Amen* in Revelation 3:14 as, *"the faithful and true witness, the beginning of the creation of God."*

- Motivate religious leaders of the Judaic, Christian, and Islamic religions to accept *Amen* as a *common bond* to work together for religious unity.

- Energize religious leaders to eliminate separatism between their religions and prevent the loss of belief in God by a more discerning people.

- Assist Judaic, Christian, and Islamic unification efforts. As an aid, copies of this book have been mailed to 123 religious leaders

- Initiate a *Council for Religious Unity* that provides a forum for Judaic, Christian, and Islamic religious leaders to unify their beliefs with the assistance of Daughters and Sons of God

- Emphasize religious leaders are required to teach our sisters and brothers, from every nation, to love and support one another.

- Base religious beliefs with truth about their beginnings so that religion and science will advance on a parallel path in the quest to know God.

- Encourage religious leaders preserve the spiritual nature of mankind. A silent position will continue bigotry, hatred, violence, and invite terrorism that threatens the very survival of human life and indeed, our planet.

Future of God Amen

A Call To Daughters And Sons Of God

Third Edition

Nicholas Paul Ginex

Library of Congress Control Number: 2009906815
Monochrome, 6 X 9, 373 Pages, 3rd Edition
Trade Paperback: 978-1-4415-5307-2
Trade Hardback: 978-1-4415-5308-9
E-Book: 978-1-4415-7586-9
Full Color, 8 ½ X 11, 272 Pages, 3rd Edition
Trade Paperback: 978-1-4500-3768-6
Trade Hardback: 978-1-4500-3769-3

Nicholas P. Ginex
Future of God Amen
A Call to Daughters and Sons of God

Text includes: Book Reviews, Prologue, Foreword, Epilogue, Table of Contents, 28 Illustrations, 11 Tables, Bibliography, and Index.

1. Religion—Controversial literature. 2. Egyptian religion—Historical development. 3. Judaism, Christianity and Islamic religions—Commonality. 4. Torah, New Testament and Koran-Critique and Recommendations. 5. Resource for history, sociology, theology, philosophy, and humanity studies. I. Title.

Order via: www.xlibris.com/Ginex Or www.futureofgodamen.com

To order large quantities of this book:
Xlibris Corporation
1-888-795-4274
Orders@Xlibris.com
66019 (B&W); 74533 (FC)

To my children
And
To those courageous men and women
Who, throughout the ages,
Have faced adversity and death
In their efforts to
Enlighten us with the truth about God.

*This book has come into fruition only through
the influence of the many wonderful people
who have entered my life. In some small way,
they all had an affect on the thoughts I am
fortunate to impart
to you.*

*I am ever grateful for Diane, my loving wife,
who has been a very constructive editor. My
gratitude is sincerely extended to Margie
Waterbrook for her professional editing and
proofreading efforts. For this 3rd edition, much
love and appreciation is deeply felt for the
editorial assistance given by my
daughter Alisa.*

PROLOGUE

Righteousness was an established concept over 3,000 years before the birth of Jesus Christ. During the 27th century BCE, the Grand Vizier Ptahhotep of Memphis instructed the Pharaoh of Upper and Lower Egypt:

> *"Established is the man whose standard is righteousness,*
> *Who walketh according to its way."*[1]

Throughout the Egyptian ages, righteousness and the moral and spiritual values that sprang from it has influenced the development of the Judaic, Christian, and Islamic religions.

The Egyptians integrated the ideals of truth, justice, righteousness, the soul, a hereafter, and infused them into the belief of God. As far back as 3,000 BCE, the Egyptian Priesthood used these beliefs to institute a morality that has been instrumental in the development of their civilization and enhance the spiritual nature of their people.

This book reveals that ancient Egypt was the first civilization that conceived the concept of one, universal God – *the Maker of all mankind, Creator and Maker of all that is.*[2] His name is announced as *Amen* in temples, churches, and mosques at the end of a prayer, supplication, and expression of thanks. The origin of Amen is unknown by many worshippers and religious leaders ignore or misinterpret

---

[1]   **James H. Breasted,** *The Dawn of Conscience,* **Page vii.**

[2]   **James B. Pritchard,** edited by, *Ancient Near Eastern Texts,* A Hymn to Amon-Re, **Pages 365-367**

Amen. The historical facts provided in this book are confirmed by Jesus Christ who proclaimed *Amen* as,

> *"the faithful and true witness,*
> *the beginning of the creation of God."*[3]

This book appeals to leaders of the Judaic, Christian, and Islamic religions to respect and honor the words of Jesus Christ. When they have accepted *Amen as the beginning of the creation of God,* they will be ready to work together to unify their beliefs and revise their Scriptures with changes our civilization sorely needs.

Future of God Amen was written to one day bring Jews, Muslims and Christians together in a world community where sisters and brothers, from all nations, love and assist one another. It issues a call to Daughters and Sons of God to assist religious leaders with perceptiveness, truth, and love of mankind.

It is an important task for me to try to reveal for you the perceptions and ideas that have added to my understanding of life both on a physical and spiritual plane. The underlying motivation is a search for truth about our past and how it has affected our daily lives. Truth is not, at least in my mind, a fixed concept. It is like everything else in life that is affected by change. As we gain more experience with our world, we refine our concepts and ideas. This is true in the sciences whereby one theory is improved until it may need to be replaced by another more universal theory that takes into account the nuisances that do exist and must be addressed.

By describing how Egypt's spiritual growth led to the formalized religions of today, I believe that there is much for the reader to learn from this book. My research has led me to provide findings,

---

3   **Jesus Christ,** *Holy Bible, King James Version,* **Revelation 3:14**

conclusions, and hypothetical scenarios that are based and grounded with facts that have been surfaced by some of the most respected Egyptologists and historians. A review of the Bibliography will verify that my resources have been provided by exceptionally respected and highly qualified people.

Upon reading this book, if you have found that the linkages of thought have been presented in a fair, straight-forward, and truthful manner, with a tone of respect for the major religions discussed, it behooves you to share this book with others. Ideas, information of value, become lost if they are not communicated. This book was mailed with a letter to 123 religious leaders requesting that they join or support a *Council for Religious Unity*.

My dear readers, because religious leaders have been reluctant to work together, you are needed to pressure them to *Wake Up* and follow the *Word of God*. This book has made it very clear that scripture is not cast in concrete. It has been revised by the Egyptian Priesthood many times until, by the reign of Ramses II, the concept of *Amon As the Sole God* was written. When the major religions:

- agree that their religion is not the only true religion,
- release their hold on the minds of people by allowing them the freedom to explore all avenues of knowledge,
- are willing to agree that they all pray to the same God,
- realize that they all have a common bond verified by Jesus Christ, whereby

Amen "is the beginning of the creation of God",

then - with the help of Daughters and Sons of God, they will be ready to teach our sisters and brothers, from every nation, to love and assist one another.

Foreword

Upon reading the Prologue, there may be some apprehension by very devout believers as to whether or not they should read this book. To these faithful followers of God, I fully respect their desire to shun any information that may weaken their beliefs. This book does not undermine any religion nor does it attempt to change the beliefs of any worshipper. It is written to inform God-loving people that the Judaic, Christian, and Islamic religions have been influenced by the beliefs of the Egyptian religion.

I sincerely do not want to dissuade you from your beliefs in the God you now worship, but to help you appreciate why you do accept your God and that He is the same God worshipped in Temples, Churches, and Mosques.

This book serves to enlighten our young people and generations to come that followers of the Judaic, Christian, and Islamic religions all pray and worship the same God; a God that created all there is throughout the universe. It is the author's hope that through belief in the same God and acknowledgement by religious leaders that *Amen is a sacred bond* between their religions, they will work together to teach our sisters and brothers from all nations—to love and assist one another.

Recommendations are provided in the last chapter of this book to ignite our brightest minds to become proactive with religious leaders. In addition, this book reveals flaws in the Scriptures of the three basic religions that are responsible for weakening the beliefs of many discerning and honest loving people. How these flaws can be resolved by either being revised or eliminated is to be determined by our greatest minds; perceptive and courageous religious leaders, and our wonderful hope for this world—our youth.

Contents

Contents

Contents

Contents

LIST OF ILLUSTRATIONS

Contents

LIST OF ILLUSTRATIONS—CONT.

Contents

TABLES

Future of God Amen

A Call to Daughters and Sons of God

The Ancient Ankh, Symbol of Life
by Taylor Ray Ellison

Symbol of Life is a Misinterpretation.
http://www.touregypt.net/featurestories/ankh.

**Truth. Anubis Presents to the Pharaoh,
Amenhotep II the Symbol of Truth.**

Note: *James H. Breasted in his book, A History of Egypt,
provides Figure 154 which indicates the ankh represents
the Symbol of Truth. As shown on Page 1, many people
have misinterpreted the ankh as the Symbol of Life.
'Truth' was the most highly esteemed quality of the
Egyptians. A Pharaoh would not require 'Life' since he
is guaranteed eternity, but he would nevertheless require
'Truth' to guide him during his reign.*

1.0   Reasons for this Book

The evolution of our belief in one God is a very sensitive topic. For the open-minded reader, this book will take you on a journey that will increase your knowledge of the past and help put into perspective the relationship you may now have with your own personal God. To religious leaders, priests, ministers, rabbis, imams, mullahs and devout worshippers, this book offers a challenge to accept each other's religious traditions and open your institutions to each other with friendship and love, for in reality, we all worship the same God.

Initially, I set out to write this book for my children, Karen Beth, Alisa, Lori Gweyn and Linda Diane. As a father, I felt obligated to leave them with many of my personal thoughts about God. In my youth, I met some young women who harbored a sense of fear and were constrained to react favorably to a kiss. Their religious training was so strict that it was largely responsible for their frigid response. To ameliorate this fear-induced reaction, my wife Diane and I tempered our girls' strict Catholic instruction with a common sense upbringing that prepared them for worldly experiences. Religious instruction that promoted a sense of morality for our girls was important to us and served to reinforce what we taught them. However, we also knew we could not control the spiritual vision of their beliefs because we felt that every individual develops a personal conception of God based upon religious exposure, intellect, sensitivity, and experience.

It did not take long for me to learn that I was on a mission to write not only for my daughters, but to share the knowledge I acquired about the evolution of God with others. Below are the many reasons that have motivated and energized me to write this book. I have no hidden agenda. My desire is to have all people from our different religious institutions, leaders and worshippers alike, accept and honor each other's traditions and beliefs. It is my hope that by acknowledging that we all pray to the same God, we may succeed in putting aside our differences; enjoy each other's traditions; and even attend each other's houses of worship.

The challenge will be hard for many of our religious leaders, who are used to making war against those with different religious opinions than they are used to sitting down and breaking bread with them. However, they have the power to bring together all God's children and thereby truly fulfill their professional mission. This challenge does not stop with religious leaders, for it is the millions of their followers who will ultimately control the direction of their religious institutions and determine the course of our future relationships with one another. The success of this awesome challenge, discussed in the final chapter, will certainly lead to peace among the religious warring factions now responsible for the murder of people throughout the Middle East and other parts of our world.

1.1 The Allegorical Tree, an Acknowledgement

At the tender age of six, I received my introduction to religion. I was sitting in the second seat of the second row of my classroom in PS (Public School) 121, an elementary school in the heart of Manhattan in New York City. To my right, hanging on the wall, was a large 2 by 3 foot picture of a tree. It remained only a tree to me until one morning, Mr. Levy, the principal of the school, visited our classroom.

Mr. Levy, a handsome and charismatic man in his mid-thirties, caught sight of the tree and gave a very intriguing talk about how the Jewish religion was the father of the Christian and Islamic religions. He explained that the trunk of the tree represented the Jewish religion, its two prominent limbs the Christian and Islamic religions, and its branches the offshoots into sects and various denominations. He showed how the major religions branched off into denominations and sects, such as: Catholic, Protestant, Baptist, Episcopal, Methodist, Mormon, Jehovahs' Witnesses, Sunnis and Shi'as. Even Judaism, he pointed out, has several divisions, such as Orthodox, Conservative, Reform and Reconstructionist Movements. I never forgot Mr. Levy and his enthusiastic talk.

After my auspicious introduction to religious thought, several years later I received a formal indoctrination in the Catholic religion. In my later teenage years, I attended the services of other religions and became curious about their beginnings. This interest in various religions encouraged me to listen to rabbis and ministers while serving two active years in the U.S. Army and an additional year during the Berlin crisis. Some years later, after graduating with a degree in Electrical Engineering from the City University of New York, I actively read such anthologies as *Man's Religions* by John B. Noss and, *Man and His Gods* by Homer W. Smith. Upon reading these books, I became fascinated with the Egyptian religion. I proceeded to research the spiritual and moral beliefs of this ancient religion by reading, *The Book of the Dead* by E.A. Wallis Budge.

Egypt's old, tried, and proven religion not only held many of the moral teachings we practice today, but it also provided for the belief in a hereafter and the concept of a soul. I had often wondered where the concept of a soul originated. It was gratifying to find that the Egyptians developed this concept. The Egyptians envisioned two entities that came to be characterized as souls; the ka and the ba. The ka represented the spiritual force of any substance that also imbued its unique characteristics. It formed the individuality and personality of a person or thing. The ba represented a spiritual soul that accompanied the ka to the hereafter for judgment and supported it with food and air within its tomb.

Research revealed that Menes founded the 1st Egyptian dynasty about 3400 BCE.[1] Its religion had multiple gods. An attempt to replace their polytheistic beliefs into one, all-powerful sun-god was made by the pharaoh Ikhnaton (born as Amenhotep IV) who reigned for 17 years between 1375 and 1358 BCE [2]. The Egyptian priests tried to bury this monotheistic belief after Ikhnaton died in 1362 BCE. However, the belief in one all-powerful God was too strong a concept to be denied.

About 108 years after Ikhnaton's death, Moses capitalized on the concept of one God and walked out of Egypt with a religious following surpassing 600,000 people. Moses, brought up in the house of a pharaoh, undoubtedly received the finest education, including education in the Egyptian religion. It would be reasonable to conclude that the sacred writings and prayers of the Egyptian religion indoctrinated Moses and influenced what he taught and wrote. Prior to Moses, the Jews had neither written scriptures nor written words that extolled the belief in one God. In fact, Homer W. Smith in his book, *Man and His Gods*, indicates that the first 5 books of the Jerusalem Bible, or Torah, were not written for use for Israelite worshipers before 750 BCE (500 years after the Moses Exodus from Egypt).[3]

After learning of the above historical events that linked Moses to Egyptian indoctrination, and that the depth of Egyptian spiritual beliefs developed the concept of the soul and its possible entrance into an eternal hereafter, I concluded that the two by three foot picture of the allegorical tree was not completely accurate. I now envision a tree that has become more meaningful and realistic. Below the trunk of the tree, beneath the ground, I see the Egyptian

---

[1]   **James H. Breasted**, *The Dawn of Conscience*, **Page 32**.

[2]   **James H. Breasted**, *A History of Egypt*, **Page 599**, Chronological Table of Kings.

[3]   **Homer W. Smith**, *Man And His Gods*, **Page 92**.

religion as its roots. That is, it was the Egyptian religion that provided for the initial development of the Hebrew religion. It became clear to me that it was the Egyptian concept of an omnipotent and unknowable God, the creator of all things, which became the same God of all the monotheistic religions.

This revelation has been largely responsible for motivating me to share my thoughts with you. You see, I truly believe in giving credit where credit is due. It is a dishonorable and deceitful act when a person or group uses knowledge gained and does not acknowledge its source. However, we may be forgiving, since religious leaders may have unconsciously borrowed from our Egyptian ancestors and many may be simply ignorant of the historical development of the ideas they communicate to their congregations.

The concept of one God, introduced by the unheralded pharaoh, Ikhnaton, was an easy matter for people, be they Egyptians, Jews, or other foreigners to gradually accept as a natural belief. However, the Egyptian priests, except those who believed in Ikhnaton's conception of God, did not eagerly accept this concept. They resisted this new belief by desecrating Ikhnaton's tomb and removing his name from all temples and monuments. This new concept was a threat to their profession. It would nullify the practice of the religious rites and sacred traditions of worship of the many local gods that had already been ingrained in their Egyptian belief system. In spite of this resistance by the Egyptian priests and the failure of religious institutions to give credit to its origin, the Egyptian roots of our belief in one God must be acknowledged.

1.2   The Confrontation Between Science and Religion

Today, we are fortunate to enjoy freedom of expression. It was not that long ago, within my own lifetime, that distinguished authors respected in their fields had to be careful not to offend our religious institutions by ideas that would challenge biblical doctrine.

During the Middle Ages, from about 500 to 1500 CE, the Catholic Church spread its influence in Europe and suppressed the expression of free thought in the arts, sciences and philosophy. Any threat or challenge to the tenets of Holy Scripture was treated severely as heresy with the application of torture and, in many cases, death of the alleged heretic was a likely outcome.

The confrontation between science and religion is a natural consequence of man's search to know truth and define his place in the universe. The scientific approach is based on facts that allow man to use deductive logic and reasoning powers to control his external world. The religious approach is based upon spiritual revelations that tell man how to conduct a moral life in conformance with his God's commands.

Men have accumulated knowledge through the practical application of the three R's (reading, writing and arithmetic), and through them, the arts and sciences. In contrast, the spread of spiritual indoctrination and learning by the Judaic, Christian, and Islamic religions has occurred by the application of intimidation and coercion. The abuse of power by religious and political leaders produced many conflicts during the Middle Ages. These abuses have resulted in the deaths of millions of innocent people.

Over the last century, the Catholic Church has become a more amicable organization that provides for spiritual growth and assists in many worthwhile endeavors to improve intolerable conditions for human beings. However, Islamic extremists, encouraged by the admonitions, warnings, and threats in the Qur'an (Koran), continue to behead nonbelievers and those who do not share their Islamic faith. People that are specifically identified in the Qur'an as unacceptable to their Islamic faith are the chosen people, the Jews; included are Christians who worship three persons incorporated into one God, namely the Father, Son and Holy Spirit.

It is not my intention to visit many of the atrocities inflicted upon human beings by various religious organizations because of resistance to their established doctrines. This history has been well documented and is available in many books. However, I feel it is incumbent upon me to inform the reader of some of the injustices perpetrated on some of our courageous people. Their efforts have motivated me to reveal what I have learned about the origins of our monotheistic religions. Only a brief set of examples are presented below. These examples should remind us of the good fortune we enjoy because of freedom of expression and religion permitted in the United States of America.

1.2.1 Religious Intimidation Is Much Milder Today

James Henry Breasted, PhD, a highly respected professor of Egyptology and Oriental history at the University of Chicago, has contributed greatly to our understanding of the Egyptian culture. He was also Director of the Haskell Oriental Museum and Corresponding Member of the Royal Academy of Sciences of Berlin. You will find his books—*A History of Egypt, Development of Religious Thought In Ancient Egypt*, and *The Dawn of Conscience*—rich in revealing the essence of Egyptian life and thought before Abraham and Moses.

Dr. Breasted was invited to give several lectures at the Union Theological Seminary in New York. They were soon published in 1912 by Charles Scribner's Sons under the title, *Development of Religion and Thought in Ancient Egypt.* Recognizing that he was speaking before a popular audience committed to specific religious training, he tempered some of his statements. Although he emphasizes a point of truth in the following statement, he begins with, "May I venture . . ."; an apologetic beginning that ends with a question mark.

> *May I venture to express the hope that this exposition of religion in the making, during a period of three thousand years, may serve not only as a general survey of the development in the higher life of a great people beginning in the earliest stage of man which we can discern at the present day, but also to emphasize the truth that the process of religion-making has never ceased and that the same forces which shaped religion in ancient Egypt are still operative in our own midst and continue to mould our own religion today?[1]*

In today's climate of intellectual freedom, you can be certain that Dr. Breasted would have felt confident to end the above statement with an affirmative period.

Within our present century, the above instance of a man who found it socially necessary to be careful not to offend his audience is but a mild example of the intimidation he felt from the religious pressures of society. The possible threat to the professional career and respected position that had taken years to earn was no doubt something he considered as he expressed ideas that would challenge a devout public's firmly held beliefs. But this example of intimidation is mild compared to that of other original thinkers who would shake the pillars of religious dogma and lose their lives.

---

[1] **James H. Breasted**, *Development of Religion and Thought In Ancient Egypt*, **Page xix**

1.2.2 Burned At the Stake, A Spirit Surfaces

Weston La Barre, author of *The Ghost Dance*, presents a well-documented exposition of the origins of religion. He was motivated to write his book by his indebtedness to his fathers of the flesh and spirit who posed for him the problems of religious fanaticism. More poignant to his motivation was the death of a relative, Jean-Francois Lefebvre Chevalier de La Barre, who was beheaded and burned at the stake by order of the Roman Catholic Church in Abbeville at the age of eighteen, on July 1, 1766.[1] This teenage boy was convicted of marring a crucifix, singing irreverent songs and wearing his hat while a religious procession passed. He was sentenced to have his tongue cut out, his right hand cut off, and be burned at the stake. None other than Voltaire pleaded for leniency; the clergy's leniency amounted to allowing the youth to be decapitated and his body burned.

1.2.3 A Former Dominican Friar and His Beliefs

Giordano Bruno, an Italian philosopher and a Dominican friar, was another original thinker who wrote books that were judged by the Inquisition in Naples to be heretical to Catholic doctrines. Born in 1548 and burned at the stake in 1600, he expressed in his book *De I'Infinito, Universo e Mondi* (On the Infinite Universe and Worlds) that the universe was infinite, that it contained an infinite number of worlds, and that these are all inhabited by intelligent beings and life forms. His system of thought embodied the concept that the infinite universe consists of many other inhabited worlds, existing in matter and spirit, body and soul, and thereby exists as two phases of the same substance.

---

[1]   **Weston La Barre**, *The Ghost Dance*, **Page vii**. Also link to Internet @: *http://personal.cfw.com/~haught/cincy.html*

Bruno's idea of infinite worlds, far reaching in imagination for his time, has come to be accepted by many people today. Our distinguished doctor of astronomy, Carl Sagan, in his book *Cosmos*, explored the likelihood of advanced technical civilizations that could exist in our own galaxy.

Mr. Sagan estimated that there are about 400 billion stars in our Milky Way galaxy. This number, multiplied by the number of planets ecologically suitable for life, was used to arrive at the number of planets within our galaxy that may sustain life. The estimated planets were then reduced by fractions that presented reasons why such life could not be sustained.[1] For our galaxy, he arrived at the number 10 that would sustain life. This number may be further reduced to 1 if civilizations tend to destroy themselves soon after reaching a technological phase. However, with the possibility that some civilizations learn to live with high technology and might extend their lifetimes, that number could increase to 10 million civilizations.

When one considers the fact that there are billions of galaxies with billions of stars, and some galaxies contain stars numbering ten to a hundred times more than our galaxy, the prospect for other intelligent life is more than a possibility. The limitation to experience alien life is remote when one considers that the nearest star within our own galaxy, Alpha Centauri, is 4.3 light years away. Even if we were to reach this star by traveling at 1/10 the speed of light, it would take 43 years to get there.

The above exercise has been provided to give the reader some appreciation for Giordano Bruno's argument that there are indeed an infinite number of worlds and other life forms created by God. Considered a heretical point of view in his time, it can no longer be denied that life in other worlds is no longer a probability.

---

[1]   **Carl Saga**n, *Cosmos,* **Pages 299-301**

1.2.4   Religious Domination Over Science

Born in Pisa on February 15, 1564, Galileo Galilei became a music scholar, and after his studies at the University of Pisa held their mathematics chair at the age of twenty-five. Highly inventive, some of his contributions to our way of life were the thermometer, compass, a water-lifting machine, improvement of the telescope in 1610, and development of the microscope in 1624.

His use of the telescope led to his supporting the Copernicus argument that the planets revolve about the sun and he published his findings in *Dialogue Concerning the Two Chief World Systems—Ptolemaic and Copernican*. Upon publication in 1632, the book was greeted with praise from every part of the European continent as a literary and philosophical masterpiece.

For this publication, however, Galileo was soon ordered to appear before the Holy Office in Rome, which issued a sentence of condemnation. The Inquisition declared Galileo guilty of heresy and promised mercy only on the condition that he renounce his errors. Galileo begged for mercy, asking his judges to consider his advanced age and take pity on him. His pleas did not forestall his imprisonment. Succumbed by their threats of torture, he declared himself to be firmly convinced of the truth of Ptolemy's system. Publicly kneeling before his tribunal, he declared, "with a sincere heart and unfeigned faith I abjure, curse, and detest the said errors and heresies, and generally every other error and heresy contrary to the . . . Holy Church, and I swear that I will nevermore in future say or assert anything . . . which may give rise to a similar suspicion of me."

The Inquisition had won. Galileo was sentenced to "the prison of this Holy Office for a period determinable at our pleasure". He was first confined in Rome, and then transferred to a friend's house in Siena. Later, he would be allowed to live under house arrest in his own villa outside Florence. Almost totally blind by 1638, he would remain there until his death on January 8, 1642.

The Church in Rome had dealt Catholicism and all of European culture a terrible blow. After Galileo, science and philosophy would lose its Renaissance vibrancy. Although Galileo had been made a martyr, for years later, the division between religion and science intensified. It was now unlikely that these two professions would work together in the search for truth about the universe. For the next few centuries, science continued to be dominated by religion, and the prohibitions of the Middle Ages were extended.

1.2.5 From Religious Heretic To Sainthood

Joan of Arc was born at Domrémy on January 6, 1412. At the age of 13 she claimed to hear the voices of Saint Michael the Archangel, Saint Catherine, and Saint Margaret. At first, her 'Voices' came to her two or three times a week. But by the time she was 18, they visited her daily telling her to go into France to accomplish three objectives: end the siege of Orleans, conduct the Dauphin Charles of Ponthieu to Reims (became King Charles VII) for his crowning, and drive the English from the land.

After being accepted and approved by a Church council headed by the Archbishop of Reims, Joan was allowed to lead the Dauphin's army. In March of 1429, she received approval of the Church scholars at Poitiers and granted titular command of an army, which quickly lifted the siege of Orléans on May 8, 1429. She went on to capture the cities of Jargeau, Meung-sur-Loire, and Beaugency in mid-June, and defeated an English army at Patay on June 18. After accepting the surrender of the city of Troyes and other towns, the army escorted Charles to the city of Rheims for his coronation as the King of France on July 17.

The crowned king granted her noble status along with her family on December 29, 1429. However, from this time on, the king no longer valued Joan's advice and guidance. She had always told him that God had given her 'a year and a little longer' to accomplish His will but the king seemed to take no notice of it. For almost a year he wasted what time remained to Joan. In frustration she left the court on another campaign only to be captured at the town of Compiegne on May 23rd, 1430.

As a prisoner of the Burgundians she was treated fairly, but that all changed on November 21st, 1430 when she was handed over to the English. She was placed on trial in Rouen by a selected group of pro-English clergy, many of whom nevertheless had to be coerced into voting for a guilty verdict. The English not only wanted to kill Joan, but they also wanted to discredit King Charles as a false king by having Joan condemned by the Church as a witch and a heretic. To obtain this goal the English used those Church authorities whom they knew to be favorable to them; the staunchest being Bishop Cauchon.

The fault of bearing false witnesses and creating deceitful accusations against Joan was not totally due to the fanatical efforts of the church; the English were eager to prove that Joan could have defeated them only by using witchcraft. They brought her to trial for sorcery and heresy (the act of challenging the authority of the Church). The representatives of the Church who tried her believed that God would speak only to priests. They wanted her to deny that she heard voices of saints and to remove the soldiers' or mens' clothes that she wore, since this was a violation of Church rules. Joan, always honest and true to her convictions and belief in God, refused to do what they wanted and courageously faced a horrible death as opposed to agreeing to their false accusations.

At the tender age of 19, she was convicted and burnt at the stake in Rouen's market square on May 30th, 1431. However, shortly after the English were finally driven from Rouen in 1456, another Inquisition review declared her innocent. This review resulted in a ruling that the original trial be declared "null and void". It had been tainted by fraud through use of illegal procedures, intimidation of the defendant and many of the clergy who had taken part in the trial. The Inquisition then revered Joan as a martyr 478 years after her death. She was declared to have attained the blessedness of heaven on April 11, 1909 and eleven years later, she was canonized as a saint on May 16, 1920.

1.3 The Mutual Benefits Between Church and State

The trial of Joan of Arc reveals that a mutual coexistence of the spiritual and material world, namely, the Church and a Kingdom of England, had fostered a conspiracy that led to her death. Powerful rulers have always known that they can benefit from the moral and spiritual values taught by the Church. They know that such values enhance order and harmony within their country. History has shown that efforts to establish harmony and peace with a secular view that denies the existence of God only results in a moral breakdown of a people. A lesson learned has been demonstrated by the Russian people who, to retain their spiritual beliefs and improve morality, attended their churches in greater numbers after the fall of the Iron Curtain.

As both religious and political leaders encourage belief in a religion, they must keep a clear separation between the functions of religion and functions of the state. The trial of Joan of Arc teaches us that justice was overwhelmed by the collusion between Church and State as spiritual fanaticism and politics dominated over truth and reason.

1.4 Monotheistic Religions Worship the Same God

The control of a people's behavior through spiritual beliefs within any country is not necessarily a bad thing. It *is* necessary, however, that its adherents should be able to benefit and grow from those beliefs. The desire for power and expansion by religious leaders of the Judaic, Christian, and Islamic religions have caused constant conflicts with each other.

The religious conflicts stem from the desire of one religion to extend its power and growth over others. An exception appears to be Judaism, which may be due to the complete destruction of the Jewish nation throughout all of Syria and Palestine in 70 CE by the Romans. Religious leaders have neglected to teach their followers that they all pray to the same God. These leaders, in their efforts to extend control over their own people, have caused deep divisions between their people and those that follow another religion.

An omniscient and merciful God does not change the rules for one religion over another. Still, there are incompatibilities in these religions' Holy Scriptures and commandments. Worse yet, because these religions developed to serve the interests of a unique group of people with their own vision of God, they do not honor each other's beliefs and respect each other's house of worship.

Blinded by their own beliefs and traditions, religious leaders have failed to apply common sense and see that God could only spread His influence gradually. Moses used righteousness, spiritual concepts, and commandments first developed by the Egyptians for God's chosen people to follow. Through the development of the Hebrew religion, belief in one God was extended to the pagans by Jewish holy men that believed in Jesus Christ and his teachings. Finally, the Arabs, who were a disorganized people with their independent sheiks, princes and tribes, found the ability to unite themselves through the God of the Hebrews. This was made possible by the revelations of the archangel Gabriel[1] to their prophet Muhammad and accomplished by *"a party whose business is to invite goodness, enjoin equity and to forbid evil."*[2] In Subsection 9.3.1, the author reveals that the Qur'an uniquely identifies this party as *"We"*, an Islamic group of religious leaders responsible for instructing and directing their followers.

The monotheistic religions are linked to each other by revelations and intercessions of the same God. It is therefore incumbent upon the religious leaders of these religions to encourage love for all humanity by teaching their followers to love one another, respect each other's religious traditions, and be humble enough to pray in each other's house of worship. Since these monotheistic religions follow the same God, it would follow that He has purposely given His worshippers a challenge to follow His commandment proclaimed by His surrogate, Jesus Christ—*to love one another*. However, continued separatism among believers, pride in one's own religion, and the taking of life in the name of God, has shown God's creations to be dismal failures in following His Word—*to love one another*.

1.5 To Bury the Past is a Dishonest Act

Although there is an overwhelming amount of literature, be it history and books dealing with critical analyses of our relationships between ourselves and the world, there are a few number of men that would challenge what many people gullibly ingest as true. There have been exceptional attempts by many courageous thinkers, such as Giordano Bruno, Galileo Galilei, Arouet de Voltaire, James H.

---

[1] **Muhammad Zafrulla Khan,** *The Qur'an,* **Chapter (Sura) 2, Verses 98-100,** published 1997 by Olive Branch Press, ISBN 1-56656-255-4.

[2] **Muhammad Zafrulla Khan,** *The Qur'an,* **Sura 3:105.**

Breasted, Sigmund Freud, and Homer W. Smith. These men have influenced, or otherwise supported, my thinking; for which reason they are referenced in this book.

In addition, some of our great thinkers have become so educated and erudite, that the average reader finds their messages complex and even boring. Great minds have addressed the falsehoods of the past, but they have also missed some obvious and common sense findings that the average reader could readily understand and accept. It is these findings that this author wishes to share with you in the following chapters.

1.6 A Father Seeks to Reveal Truths to All

It would be derelict of this father not to reveal the truths learned by extensive reading and research; and by the exchange of ideas with the many people that have entered my life. Truth can be elusive and may take many years to comprehend based upon real life experiences. This author has been fortunate to have come upon truths by accident and, in many cases, by simply connecting the dots through the application of common sense. It would be a foolish gamble to wait for somebody else to present the findings acquired in my lifetime. Our lives are made up of too many different events that shape our thoughts. Be they on an educational, social, and personal level, these events combined with our intellect and sensitivity will always present a different color of the way each of us see, interpret life, and develop our thoughts for others to hear or read.

This father feels a deep responsibility to educate and prepare his children for the world they live in. They were the initial motivation to write this book. As a father who desired to inform his children of the traps and deceptive ideas propagated around us, he felt obligated to share thoughts that may enable others to get closer to the truths that he has earnestly tried to surface. It is the author's nature to be grossly offended when he or others have been made a fool of by means of lies and deceptive ramblings. However much it hurts, he prefers to always know the truth. He will not knowingly stand by and let his children made to be fools. This author writes for all those who have the courage to examine new avenues of thought. They will benefit by getting to know their own God and be less likely to end their spiritual quest in disillusion and separation from God.[1]

The spiritual quest this author alludes to may simply be love for mankind. However you may conceive your God, you may be assured that He would rather have you love the people around you than to focus your love on Him. My responsibility as a father is to educate and prepare my daughters to make their own way in life. They need not bow down, prostrate themselves in a submissive manner, and humble themselves as if their father was a God. They need only to respect me for the love and precious time invested to help direct their lives, develop their potential, and become strong individuals who can stand on their own two feet. God may be present, but He cannot do what a father and mother can do for them. That is, to have them carry on the legacy of raising wonderful children in this world.

As mere mortals, we may never be able to know the whole truth about God. We have had our share of prophets and righteous men who endeavored to show their fellow beings how they can lead moral lives. We shall see in the forthcoming chapters that some have made mistakes in their zeal to impart knowledge about God. We should not fault them for trying to have us inherit a belief and way of life received through their revelations. Only by consistently trying to seek

---

[1]   God may be your own personal god that is not bound to a particular religious faith. God is therefore not conceived in the same way by each person and is formed by one's own sensibilities, intellect, acquired beliefs and knowledge.

the truth, will we be able to have a clearer understanding of the lives we lead and, a more positive and healthy outlook for the future.

Many of us have some doubts about the existence of God. Others find themselves with a desire to believe in God but unable to accept many religious teachings and traditional mores. There are others who feel that the concept of God is simply another form of philosophy that tries to find answers to questions of morality and the possibility of an eternal life. Then there are those who do not want to deal with the concept of God at all. They may follow the rule that is most equivalent to, "Thou shalt love thy neighbor as thyself."[2] Stated more simply, "It's nice to be nice."[3]

This book is not written to deceive my children and my readers. You will find that every conclusion and assertion made has been grounded in facts and references that have come from reliable sources. This author will not waste time on gobbledegook to prove a point. It is love for the truth that gives him the stamina to share his research efforts with you. There is no other agenda in this book than to open your eyes, widen your perceptions, and bring you closer to understanding yourselves and the God in which you believe.

---

[2] **Holy Bible**, *King James Version*, **Matthew 22: 39**

[3] Anonymous

2.0 An Overview of Egyptian History

Before we examine how the monotheistic religions are interlinked and owe much of their beliefs and traditions to the culture of the Egyptian civilization, it would be useful to review the significant periods of Egypt's history. By having a mental picture of the periods in Egypt's history and how certain events had much to do with the formation of religious concepts, we can arrive at very plausible and common sense conclusions. Figure 2-1 is provided to give an overview of Egypt's history, starting with dwellers in small localities as far back as 5500 BCE, and ending with control by the Romans in 30 BCE.

In Figure 2-1, the left page shows Egypt is in control of its territory, whereas the right page shows Egypt undergoing several upheavals, beginning with an internal struggle for power by the pharaoh Menes. During the 1st Intermediate Period, Egypt's social order changed as the local governors challenged the pharaohs and took control. In the 2nd Intermediate Period, a Semitic people from Syria and Palestine invaded Egypt. This was the first time that a foreign people seized control of the Nile Delta and most of Lower Egypt. More unrest and transfer of power occurred during the 3rd Intermediate Period and the remaining periods that followed.

Figure 2-1 is intended to give a relative understanding of the events that changed Egypt's social structure and grant insight into the numerous exchanges of power from both internal and external forces. The purpose of this book is to reveal those events that affected Egypt's culture and religious beliefs. To acquire a detailed account of each period that includes two hundred illustrations and maps, refer to James H. Breasted's, *A History of Egypt.*

5500-3400 BCE. Predynastic Period

Dwellers of each locality worshipped their own gods. After many centuries of internal conflict circa 3400 BCE, these local principalities united to form a state. Society became governed by the need for justice and ethical qualities, which became fixed with the development of their state gods. The 365-day calendar was invented in 4241 BCE. ➤

▲ **Great Pyramid of Gizeh, circa 2580 BCE.**

2980-2475 BCE. Old Kingdom

- The first pyramid, in step form, was engineered by Imhotep, vizier for King Djoser (Zoser), about 2660 BCE. Another vizier, Ptahhotep, wrote proverbs and maxims that reveal the level of moral conduct and wisdom attained.
- Great achievements in art, architecture, engineering, medicine, and literature.
- By the 5th dynasty, pharaohs revered the Sun-god Re and attached to the title of their name, "Son of Re".
- The priests at Heliopolis had become so powerful they were able to maintain that the pharaoh was the physical son of the Sun-god by an earthly mother.

2160-1788 BCE. Middle Kingdom

- During the 11th and 12th Dynasties, the pharaohs solidified their rule over all of Egypt and restored order in the land. Control expanded into Northern Nubia and Western Asia. The 12th Dynasty pharaohs were blood related (Amenemhet I-IV and Sesostris I-III), checked the power of the local rulers, centralized government, refurbished temples, improved irrigation systems, and erected fortifications.
- In the East, the Egyptians traded with and influenced Syrian and Palestinian states.
- Foreign trade increased to the Island of Crete. 12th Dynasty reigned 213 years.

▲ **Ikhnaton ascends throne in   ▲ Moses leads Hebrew Exodus**
    1375 BCE. Reigns 17 years   about 1250 BCE.

1580-1090 BCE. New Kingdom

- Ahmose, pharaoh of the 18th Dynasty, repels the Hyksos from Egypt, unifies the land, extends Egypt's empire into Syria, and reestablishes control in Nubia.
- Followed by the leadership and campaign successes of Pharaoh Thutmose III against the Hyksos, Egypt became the greatest power in the ancient world. Colossal statues and magnificent temples were built, via international commerce new ideas were accepted, and art and literature achieved a brilliance that surpassed the Old Kingdom.
- The Pharaoh Ikhnaton introduced the concept of one God during his reign, 1375-1358 BCE. By 1250 BCE, at Mount Sinai, Moses communed with his God Yahweh and wrote *The Book of the Covenant.*

Figure 2-1. Significant Periods of Egyptian History.

3400-2980 BCE. Early Dynastic Period

- Menes united Upper and Lower Egypt.
- Memphis became the capital of Egypt.
- Hieroglyphics were developed and paper from dried papyrus reeds facilitated communication.

2475-2160 BCE. 1st Intermediate Period

- The Old Kingdom gradually declined as land barons and nobles challenged the restraining power of the Pharaoh.
- By the 6th dynasty, after the death of Pepe II, the barons gained their independence and the Old Kingdom fell. Temples were vandalized and destroyed.
- The Theban pharaoh, Mentuhotep II, conquered lower Egypt, united the two lands, rebuilt the nation's army, imposed law and order and renewed trade.

▲ Semitic tribes from Syria and Palestine invade Egypt.
Abraham enters Egypt around 1680 BCE.

1788-1580 BCE. 2nd Intermediate Period

- Around 1675 BCE successive invasions by the Hyksos and tribes of Shepherd Kings established control of the Nile Delta and most of Lower Egypt.
- Hyksos leaders appointed themselves pharaohs over Lower Egypt during the 15th and 16th Dynasties and adopted Egyptian customs.
- In Upper Egypt, the Theban pharaohs continued to exist as vassal states and paid tribute to the Hyksos pharaohs in Lower Egypt (Nile Delta). After 100 years, the Theban pharaoh, Ahmose I drove the Hyksos back into Palestine and Syria.

▲ About 900 BCE the 1st   ▲ Death of Jesus
Hebrew Scripture (J)   Christ in 30 CE

1090-663 BCE. 3rd Intermediate Period

- Upper Egypt controlled by the Priests of Amon; Lower Egypt under Nubian rule. Assyrians rule in 670 BCE.

663-525 BCE. Saite Period

- Egyptians expel Assyrians. Saite pharaohs usher in a golden age of art and literature.

525-332 BCE. Persian Period

- Persians conquer Egypt in 400 BCE.

332-30 BCE. Ptolemic Period

- Macedonian commander, Alexander the Great conquers Persian empire including Egypt. Greek Ptolemy family rules.

30 BCE-395 CE

- Egypt comes under Roman rule.

2.1 We Use the Egyptian Calendar Everyday

Before we review significant concepts in the religious development of Egypt, it is noteworthy to recognize that the Egyptians in the Delta region, referred to as Lower Egypt or the North or Upper Delta, had already become an advanced civilization as early as 4200 BCE. Their technical ability was demonstrated during the Predynastic Period by the development of the calendar in 4241 BCE.[1] They were the first people to invent a calendar by dividing the year into 12 months, each with a length of 30 days. It is this calendar that, although altered by the Romans, has survived over 6,000 years and is still used by us today.

With the invention of the calendar, time became a relevant element in the consciousness of the Egyptian people. The same tool that allowed them to count days and years that receded into the past, also allowed them to extend their imagination to wonder about the future and what could possibly happen to dear departed relatives. As early as the Predynastic Period, Egyptians believed in an afterlife. To retain the comforts of his earthly life, the king had his wives, concubines, nobles, couriers, servants and slaves buried with him in his royal cemetery. This finding has been verified in the tombs of Abydos, just North of Thebes. The splendor displayed by these tombs indicated that these people had already conceived the idea of life after death many years prior to the 1st Dynasty. That such a belief would exist at the time of, or even prior to, the invention of the calendar, at least 4200 years BCE, is remarkable.

---

[1]   **James H. Breasted**, *A History of Egypt*, **Page 32**

2.2 Development of Spiritual Beliefs

It was within Egypt that human beings, for the first time in the history of the world, developed concepts of a soul and a hereafter. These concepts developed only after thousands of years of man's struggle to tame the environment around him. Before we explore how these and other Egyptian concepts developed, it is necessary to learn who the Egyptians were and where and when their notions of an afterlife began. Therefore, a brief history of the African people and their development as one of the first civilizations must follow before venturing into how they developed their religious beliefs.

2.2.1 From Nomad Hunters to Civilized Communal Life

A slow process of communal development began over 250,000 years ago when all of Africa was a region of plentiful rains and rich vegetation. Prehistoric surveys have discovered flint weapons of African hunters far out in the Sahara region thousands of miles west and south from the Nile. These hunters had an abundant supply of animal, fowl, and sea life. Evidence has revealed that these prehistoric hunters migrated northward from as far south as the southern tip of Africa. The mental ability of prehistoric man was advanced sufficiently not only to adjust to the changes in climate by finding areas where water was more abundant, but also to portray life around them through the art drawn within the caves in which they lived.

Around 100,000 years ago, these people showed evidence of symbolic reasoning with remarkable drawings engraved with ocher pigments. Figure 2-2 illustrates the ability of the artist to portray abstract thought by representing what appears to be two different ethnic or racial groups living together as shown by the two distinct colors, red and black, employed on half the bodies of two figures.

Figure 2-2. A Symbolic Drawing Dated 70,000 BCE.
http://www.homestead.com/wysinger/badarians.html

This drawing was found in the Blombos Cave located on the southern coast of Africa and is dated around 70,000 BCE; over 30,000 years before anything equivalent in Europe.[1]

Evidence of hominid occupation also existed in northern Africa. In Algeria, early remnants of hominid occupation have been found in Ain el Hanech (near the city Saida), not far from the Mediterranean Sea around 200,000 BCE. In the north-eastern corner of Algeria, excavation at the Bir el Ater site (south of Annaba near the Wadi Seybouse River), tools dated about 30,000 BCE, exhibited a high standard of workmanship.[2]

---

[1]   Internet @: http://www.homestead.com/wysinger/badarians.html

[2]   Internet @: http://en.wikipedia.org/wiki/Annaba_(city)

During the prehistoric era, there is no doubt that regions above, below, and even within the Sahara Desert, teemed with human life. The Sahara, once a region of extensive shallow lakes watering large areas, became arid as plentiful rains subsided forcing its inhabitants to venture northward, southward and eastward towards the Nile. Lost were the streams that allowed travel into deeper reaches of the Sahara region. Memory of this ability was carved onto the rocks of the Nubian Desert behind Abu Simbel where drawings of Nile boats were found.

Figure 2-3 illustrates a recent photograph of the northern portion of Africa and the countries that have been affected by the immense dry areas of the Sahara Desert. This desert is 2.5 million years old and so large that the entire land area of the United States of America would fit inside its borders.

Inspection of Figure 2-3 shows that the Sahara Desert uniquely isolates Egypt with arid land and extends east into the Arabian Desert. Together with the Mediterranean Sea to the north and Red

Figure 2-3. A Physical View of the Sahara Desert.
http://ecrc.geog.ucl.ac.uk/qarun/map.htm

Sea towards the east, Egypt truly became a unique laboratory for the development of a civilization along the Nile River. Egypt was influenced by foreign intruders only after it had reached an advanced state of community and religious life.

As their land increasingly dried up, the influx of nomads to the Nile area greatly accelerated, and many lingered long enough to become permanent inhabitants. The earliest of these settlers were the Tasians of Deir Tasa.

2.2.2 The Earliest Settlers, the Tasians

Evidence of the earliest settlers in Egypt has been excavated on the west side of the Nile River in the Faiyum region. This region, just below the Nile Delta, contains a large body of water, located at the Faiyum, called Lake Qarun. Figure 2-4 shows this lake lying west to east and over a few thousand years has decreased in size to about 27 miles long and ten miles wide. For those nomads who traveled east to avoid the arid conditions of the Sahara Desert, it had to have been a most welcome sight. It provided a site where they could find food; fishing with hooks and harpoons, and hunting with bows and arrows.

The Tasians also settled at two other sites: one a six-acre site west of the lower Delta named Merimde, and the other, Deir Tasa, midway between Thebes and the Faiyum. The Tasian culture was characterized by a great variety of polished stone implements and by the development of new social forms based upon primitive techniques of weaving, spinning, pottery making, and the introduction of agriculture whereby they grew emmer wheat and barley. They devised an old form of hand mill for grinding grain and they domesticated pigs, cattle, sheep and goats.

Tasian art was distinguished by geometric patterns closely resembling that of basket weaving, and their earthenware pots were decorated

Figure 2-4. Early Egyptian Communities from Predynastic Times.

with incised lines. They painted their eyes and faces with ocher and malachite and adorned themselves with perforated shells from the Red Sea. No graves have been found at the Faiyum, whereas the peoples of Tasa and Merimde buried their dead apparently without grave offerings. They wore cylindrical beads, carved ivory into female figurines and pierced stone axes, and used them as charms on their necklaces. These amulets appear to indicate their concern with magic, protection, and fertility.

All three Tasian sites were abandoned about 10,000 BCE.[3] Many Egyptologists have estimated that the Tasians started their settlements around 8,000 BCE and were absorbed by other nomad cultures. It is more likely that in the following 2,000 years, they gradually intermixed with the Badarians, another group of people that entered the area just below Deir Tasa [4] (refer to Figure 2-4).

2.2.3 Ancestors of the Predynastic Egyptians

The Badarians settled at Badari about sixty miles south of Deir Tasa on the east side of the Nile. Some historians speculate that they may have ventured from the coasts of the eastern Mediterranean Sea from Greece and western Egypt. If this was true, surely there would have been many more settlements starting from where the Nile enters the Mediterranean and down the west side of the Delta, but no such evidence has been found to exist. Instead, it appears that they entered Egypt from the Sahara Desert near the Sudan region. Figure 2-4 illustrates this possibility, since the Badarians also settled in Hierakonpolis and Armant below Abydos about 100 miles from the first cataract. Settlers then appear to have traveled towards the Delta, evidenced by findings of Badarian objects excavated at Badari,

---

[3]   **Homer W. Smith**, *Man and His Gods,* **Page 11**.

[4]   Internet @: http://www.theology.edu/egypt1.htm, Neolithic Period, Pg 1

Deir Tasa and Matmar.[1] With reference to Figures 2-3 and 2-4, it does appear that this conjecture offers the more likely possibility. Even if the order of travel towards the Delta is not exact, it may be logically concluded that the Badarians entered Egypt from the Sudan region and not the Levant.

Although there is no firm agreement among historians, it seems likely that the Badarians entered Egypt from the Sudan region around 8000 BCE. When considering the transformations required for individual nomes to progress to villages and begin communicating, working, and planning together, it appears that the Badari people intermixed with the Tasians in the following one to two thousand years. They used malachite as a cosmetic and had discovered, probably by accidentally dropping this substance into the fire, how to make copper beads. They created their pottery without a potter's wheel, yet still created artifacts with a delicacy and simple perfection never exceeded; even at the height of Egyptian civilization. The vases and bowls, fired to produce a brown or red body with the rim and interior blackened, were extremely thin and decorated with an exquisite ripple effect.

The Badarians used the boomerang to capture small game. They wore necklaces of copper tubes and glazed quartz, bracelets and rings of ivory, and pottery nose plugs. Their concern with magic had increased to the point where amulets were made in the shape of the antelope and hippopotamus. Objects from the Badarian culture were found well into the 5th millennium BCE and these people are considered to be the physical and cultural ancestors of the so-called 'Predynastic' Egyptians.[2]

The Badarians gave their cattle and sheep ceremonial burial and placed their dead in graves lined with straw matting. The dead were

---

[1]   Internet @: http://www.egyptorigins.com/prehistory.htm

[2]   **Homer W. Smith**, *Man and His Gods,* **Page 11.**

usually buried with their bodies lying on their left side in a crouched position with their heads pointed to the south. Their hands were placed in front of the face or under the cheek with the face looking west. In many of the graves the dead body was accompanied with female figurines carved from ivory or molded in clay. It appears that some religious significance of facing the body in the direction of the setting sun had begun to take form.

It is believed by many Egyptologists that the evolution of Egyptian society from the Tasian-Badarian groups to dynastic times was extremely rapid. But this conclusion is not realistic when one considers the achievements of these Predynastic Egyptians. If we look back at the Egyptians' development of the calendar as occurring in 4241 BCE, then we can extrapolate that it had to take several centuries for the settlers to first observe the consistent behavior of the Nile that rose once a year and begin to establish some relationships of the sun continuously setting at predetermined positions during the year. For this to happen, there had to have been some way of recording their observations, which implies that they had already begun to develop the rudiments of writing.

To estimate a reasonable period in which these first nomads interbred, we must account for: their advances in agriculture, growing barley and wheat; their domestication of swine, cattle, goats and sheep; the integration of several nomes whereby the more advanced in leadership dominated to facilitate organization of local and religious control; and the technology to irrigate the land by controlling water derived from the Nile. Such advances would require a common level of communication between the emerging societies of nomes. It would be necessary that the people living on the land be able to set boundaries and measure off distances not only to determine the extent of land ownership, but also to work and plan together in connecting and designing the irrigation systems. Truly, these accomplishments did not occur rapidly, but had to have developed as nomes became villages over some 2,000 years. Considering the coordination required to integrate their irrigation systems, the development and learning of measuring and writing skills, and the gradual acceptance of dominant leaders and emerging local religions, it would be reasonable to estimate that they settled along the Nile around 8,000 BCE. It may be concluded that these people initiated the early beginnings of the Predynastic Period no later than 6,500 BCE.

2.2.4 Development of the Predynastic Period

Located halfway down the Nile, a people named the Amratians, after El Amrah, occupied the Naqada site. Figure 2-4 shows this site lying on the west side of the Nile not far from the renowned burial grounds known as the Valley of the Kings and the cities that would later become Karnak and Thebes. Based upon these initial settlements that also include Abydos, it would appear that they also originated from the Sudan region. Findings of excavated sites associated with the Naqada people have led Egyptologists to conclude that they started as a parallel culture with the Badari. But as the Badari-Tasians and Amratians began to interbreed and merge their cultures, it was the Amratians that eventually superimposed their culture and dominated the Predynastic period. It was this combination of African people, the Badari-Tasians and Amratians, that became the race thought of as the first 'true Egyptians'. It would take another millennium for these groups to interbreed and give birth to the Predynastic Period around 5500 BCE, a period which would end with the accession of Menes (Narmer) around 3400 BCE—the start of the Dynastic Period.

A noticeable change began to be reflected in their pottery. The simple bands of paint were replaced with clever geometric patterns and the world around the inspired artist began to be reflected with pictures of animals and plant life that were painted and carved onto their vessels. Decorative clay and ivory objects became more varied and aesthetic in portraying dancing figures that exhibited movement with upraised arms. The development of architecture is shown in several clay models of houses which resemble the rectangular clay brick homes of the Old Kingdom. The design of individual dwellings that began to form towns and reflect urban planning started around 5000 to 4500 BCE.[1] Like the Badari (inbred with Tasian blood), the Amratians lived in villages that eventually grew into towns. They also learned to cultivate the fertile Nile valley, supplementing their hunting with agriculture.

At excavated sites, amulets and pendants carved as female and bearded male figures appeared in greater numbers and had a magical or spiritual significance for the user. Religion became a greater part of their lives, and in its infancy, took the form of worship of animal deities. This form of worship, known as totemism, involves reverence of various animals that exhibit strengths and attributes people lack, fear, or desire. Each nome had its own animal deity. The use of a clan or group emblem to identify residence in, allegiance to, and protection of a local nome, is similar to gangs that develop in deprived sections of a city to mitigate their fears and offer protection to their members. Such totem forms of animal worship must have begun many years prior to settlements along the Nile.

Regional differences were distinguished by worship of particular animal deities, with twenty nomes in Lower Egypt (the Delta region) and twenty-two nomes in Upper Egypt. Kings gradually assumed leadership of these nomes; the stronger kings often merging with the weaker. The kings were closely aligned with the Priests, the leaders who established the clan's totem god. The Priesthoods not only supported the nomes' spiritual beliefs, but in many cases, influenced the appointment of its king. It was reverence of these animal gods that set the stage for development of the dynastic pantheon of Egyptian gods.

---

[1]   Internet @: *http://www.touregypt.net/ebph5.htm*, Prednyastic Period

In the Amratian graves, the deceased were buried with miniature mummy-form figures to protect and/or serve them in the afterlife. Along with these figures, the dead body was buried with food, weapons, amulets, ornaments and decorated vases. The funerary vases and slate palettes were decorated with vivid scenes that would later be depicted in the tombs of later kings. Amulets included diverse animal, bird, fish and human figures. With this abundance of religious artifacts and belief in an afterlife, it would follow that a Priesthood would develop, along with the craftsmen and artisans that would be in demand for the villages that would soon emerge.

A period ensued whereby one nome would try to dominate another and the symbolic emblem of their animal god would supplant the weaker nome's emblem. From either a victorious show of force or through peaceful integration, leaders would surface who formed the initial villages that led to the development of simple irrigation systems. A stable environment that lasted for hundreds of years served as the backdrop for agricultural, technical, and artistic development. As the Egyptian people began to appreciate the wonderful bounty of their lives, they had sufficient leisure time to reflect on a hereafter. With time to reflect on a spiritual afterlife, the Priesthood became a growing entity. The Priests assisted and nurtured each nome's unifying belief in its totem's deity, and more importantly, supported the spiritual belief that its leader was empowered with the attributes of its god.

2.2.5 The Gerzean Culture Dominates

The Amratian culture was absorbed by the Gerzean culture in the middle of the fourth millennium, leading to the 1st Dynasty. The Gerzeans were originally Amratians from the Naqada area and spread northward just east of the Faiyum to the site known as El-Gerza, shown in Figure 2-4. By this time, through the experience already gained as Amratians, they had mastered the art of agriculture and established advanced irrigation systems. The people no longer needed to hunt for food, as they had learned to store fruits, grain, and seeds in large vats and granaries. They became farmers as they discovered how to plant seed and furrow it in continuous rows by pulling a plow and then training oxen to ease the task. The necessity for keeping track of the seasons would lead to the invention of the calendar by 4241 BCE.

Hieroglyphic writing became a form of communication as the Gerzeans learned to barter and negotiate trade transactions. They traded for copper and gold outside the localities of their Nile settlements, exceeding the distances traveled by the previous two cultures. From Asia they brought silver, lapis lazuli, lead and other foreign commodities. The ability to count and measure became a necessity to keep tallies of transactions, map their fields, estimate areas for farms and homes, and to appraise their value. Metal implements and weapons at Gerzean sites indicate that they had mastered the art of casting metal. Long distances of arid desert made interaction with other peoples infrequent. Boats had not yet been designed for transportation on the Mediterranean Sea, although there were boats navigating the Nile. Society was going through an agrarian, technological, economic, social, and religious evolution as the Nile watered their lands and kept them productive.

The Gerzean people continued to expand their artistic skills, creating new styles of decorative pottery, replete with highly realistic depictions of animals, people, birds and plants. Unusual animals such as ostriches and ibexes, not found to be near the Nile, were also painted on their pottery, confirming that they formerly hunted these animals in the subdesert.[1] Their palettes for mixing paints and cosmetics took on the shapes of animals and evolved into a shield-shaped form that became

---

[1]   **David C. Scott,** Internet @: http://www.touregypt.net/ebph5.htm, Egypt: History- Predynastic Period

the ancestor of the ceremonial palettes used in the early Dynastic Period. They were proficient working with metals, creating copper knives, and casting metal into farm implements and weapons.[2]

All along the Nile, villages started to grow into densely populated towns, as there was only desert and mountains on either side. These constraints caused people to settle at desirable locations and not move about too freely. In addition, the vats and granaries in which they stored their supplies of fruit, grain and seed were too large to be dragged from place to place. Having acquired valuable stores of food, seed and livestock, farmers were more likely to keep a permanent residence and gain the advantage of joining together to defend themselves against lazy neighbors and robbers. There was now a need for greater dependence upon one another; not only to protect their permanent homes but also to participate in the community and defend it with military force.[3]

Like the scribes who learned to write in hieroglyphic form and become a valuable source for documenting trades and preserving literary and spiritual ideas, craftsmen also became an honored trade in demand for creating new homes, temples, and statues of their gods. In this Predynastic era, the wealthy leaders of the developing towns built estates and palaces. The Gerzaeans developed the town of Hierakonpolis, where they built a cult center for Horus, son of the earth god Osiris and his faithful sister-wife, Isis. In the ritual precinct of Nekhem, evidence was found of a complex of buildings with a large oval courtyard. These structures were forerunners of the royal ritual precincts of the early Dynastic Period.

---

[2]   **Caroline Seawright**, Internet @ http://thekeep.org/~kunoichi/ kunoichi/ themestream/egypt_predynastic.html, article titled, Upper Egyptian Neolithic and Predynastic Religion and Rulers.

[3]   **Homer W. Smith**, *Man and His Gods,* **Pages 12-14**.

As greater numbers of people enjoyed ownership and prosperity, villages became towns. The wealthiest leaders vied for power within their clans that held allegiance to a totem deity. As a clan grew, increased credibility and power was attributed to its local god. Leaders became committed to their local animal deities and were supported by the local Priesthood, who fostered the perception of the deities' power in order to enhance their own positions. The combination of strong leaders and a strong Priesthood became a core component of stability of the growing towns. As the communities grew, it was these two components that nurtured the concepts of truth and justice. These two attributes became the basis for the evolution of morality within the Egyptian civilization. The concept of an afterlife, promoted by the Priesthood, added support to man's desire to lead a righteous life. The following subsections attempt to trace the development of this spiritual concept.

2.2.6 Nubians, the Stimulus for Egypt's Unity

This section would not be complete without some discussion of the Nubians who settled in Egypt's upper boundary. They were the catalyst that eventually caused the Egyptian kings to unite Lower and Upper Egypt. It is believed that in the fifth millennium BCE, the Nubians, as the groups of people before them, trekked out of the Sahara region towards the Nile valley and settled below the 2nd Cataract within an area that came to be known as Qustul. Hunting became less important as they learned to farm and domesticate cattle, goats and sheep. They were able to mine gold, and it is reputed that they were the first to learn how to melt and cast iron. As Egypt grew wealthy and its culture expanded into Nubia, the Nubians actively traded incense, copper, gold, shells from the Red Sea, ivory, hardwoods, semiprecious stones, and cattle in return for manufactured articles and probably agricultural produce.

Research by Egyptologists has determined that a line of kings lived in Qustul (its location is shown in Figure 2-4), a town estimated to have developed around 3800 BCE, preceding Egypt's 1ˢᵗ Dynasty. An independent people, the Nubians fought against being subservient to the Egyptians from Predynastic through dynastic times. Although the Nubians constantly fought Egypt's pharaohs from the north, they compliantly provided amounts of gold as tribute. They had no need to leave their home in order to find food or employment in the major towns of Egypt. During this time, the Egyptians knew Nubia as "Ta Seti", interpreted as 'Land of the Bow'. The fame of the Nubian archers sustained reluctance by their Nubian kings to join the unification of Lower and Upper Egypt. The often quoted phrase in Egyptian literature, "enemy of the nine bows" refers to the Nubians.[1] Their desire for independence was supported by the skill of their Nubian archers who forestalled the conversion of Nubians to Islam until 1400 CE.[2]

The oldest tombs of a pharaonic type that precedes the Dynastic Period have been found in Qustul at Cemetery L. Excavators have found thirty-three tombs that were unusually large and, at Cemetery L-24, there was a considerable amount of wealth. L-24 has been dated as being four generations before King Ka (introduced in Subsection 3.4.1) and the wealth was vastly superior to any contemporary tombs in Nubia or Egypt including the Royal Cemetery at Abydos, which contains the tombs of Ka, Narmer, and Iry-Hor. At the Qustul tomb was found a thousand painted bowls, a hundred stone vessels, twenty-two storage jars, and local objects in unusual numbers and quality.

A remarkable find was the Qustul incense burner, illustrated in Figure 2-5. Once part of an incense burner, this decorated stone fragment presents an astonishing scene of three boats that advance towards a facade of a palace. The royal procession depicted on the burner

---

[1]   **James B. Pritchard,** *Ancient Near Eastern Texts,* **Page 3, Note 6.** The Nine Bows were the nine traditional, potential enemies of Egypt.

[2]   Internet @: http://www.homestead.com/wysinger/badarians.html

has led many archeologists to conclude that it provides evidence of the world's first monarchy. Its motifs and symbols would later be embraced by many of the kings and pharaohs who came to rule Egypt. A few hundred years later, King Ka adopted the symbol of the falcon within his serekh.

On the stone burner, the first boat carries a prisoner held onto a seat by another individual; the central boat carries the king, sitting and equipped with a long robe, flail and white crown; and the king faces towards the last boat, as does the falcon on the serekh, which is just in front of his head. The following object is a rosette with nine slender petals. Before the last boat we see a harpoon, a rampant antelope, and a man capturing a kind of sawfish and a big fish. We may infer that the occupant of the last boat is an animal deity, half bull and half lion, because it is followed by a falcon-topped standard.[3]

The evidence at Qustul of royal tombs, wealthy rulers, and victories as commemorated on an incense burner described above, has been dated about four generations before Kings Iry-Hor and Ka.[4] This has led to the premise that one or several powerful Nubian kings may have initiated warfare with their neighbors at Abydos, Naqada, and Hierakonpolis to control important resources of their territory, expand their ideology, and monopolize the commercial trade routes that existed towards the Nile Delta. These initiatives eventually failed as Abydos, under the leadership of such able rulers as King Ka, defeated the Nubians at Qustul and took control of Upper Egypt. It would be generations later that Narmer would successfully unify both Upper and Lower Egypt.

---

[3]   Internet @: http://xoomer.virgilio.it/francescoraf/hesyra/dynasty0.htm

[4]   Internet @: http://www.homestead.com/wysinger/badarians.html

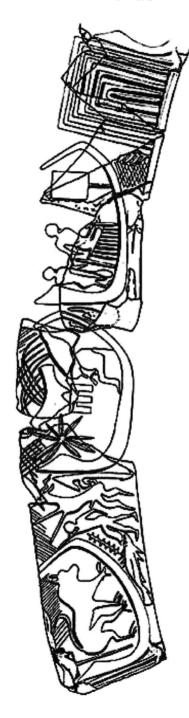

Figure 2-5. The Qustul Incense Burner Shows a Royal Procession.

Meanwhile, the rulers at Abydos acquired the warrior instincts of the Nubians to defend their territories and acquire control of Qustul. Tombs excavated at Badarian, Amaratian and Gerzean cemeteries clearly denote the stratification of people all along the Nile into distinct social classes. The increasingly larger funerary offerings in certain tombs, the presence of larger tombs and wealthy burials for children, express two important factors: the acceptance of specific mortuary beliefs and the formation of a ruling class that no longer shared the same destiny in life or in death with the common people. The earlier practice of equal social, political, economic rights and privileges by the people eroded as their developing communities evolved into large low-density farming villages.

Initially, people lived in small villages sparsely scattered along the Nile. As climatic conditions were more favorable for life along the river, small populations concentrated there to enjoy the advantages of farming and domesticating animals. But as increases in population continued and land became a premium, the earlier settlers with greater portions of land were able to capitalize on the labor of those who came later and had little or no land. The disparity in ownership, wealth, and skilled workers among the people led to classes of distinction consisting of rulers, the elite, craftsmen, and most certainly, the Priesthood.

The rulers exploited the lower classes, which were forced to produce for them. An increasing population afforded the rulers and elite classes to extend their land ownership to meet the larger need for cultivation and breeding to sustain themselves and their workers. This expansion gave rise to a class of craftsmen to produce farm implements; build houses, temples, and estates; and procure particular materials. In addition, the elite and ruling classes needed their workers to defend them from inner and outer dangers. The large quantities of farm products required storage vats that were easy prey for ravagers.

Occurring on a larger scale in Nubia, class distinctions became more apparent and the clan chieftains needed some mechanism to maintain order. The natural component to sustain the ruling classes was the Priesthood. This class promoted morality through their articulation of spiritual beliefs. The spiritual beliefs of all the settlements along the Nile, as we have reviewed above, had a common set of burial customs that may have been wide-spread for many ages throughout the Sahara Desert. This common tie of spiritual beliefs had developed into common conceptions of totemism and the evolution of animal gods all along the Nile.

The more powerful communities during the Predynastic period were those towns extending from Abydos (Thinis) to Hierakonpolis (Nekhen), which included Dendera, Ballas, Naqada, Armant and Gebelein. As these towns grew and class distinctions became the norm, competition for resources, gold, and trade of luxury goods caused military conflicts between the towns. Eventually the weaker towns succumbed and were absorbed into fewer centers called city-states. The three principalities that prevailed and controlled larger sectors of the Nile were Abydos, Naqada and Hierakonpolis. Meanwhile, the Nubians at Qustul also advanced economically with even greater class distinctions, and would repeat the above scenario.[5]

The Nubian chiefs looked to strengthen their position by monopolizing long distance trade and spreading their religious ideology.

History has shown that they were defeated by the kings that ruled just north of them. It is very likely that King Ka of Abydos conducted a successful campaign to subjugate Qustul. However, the powerful influence of the Nubian Priesthood had a profound affect that not only emboldened their kings to believe in a spiritual empowerment provided by their gods, but caused Egypt's northern city-states to adopt

---

[5]   Internet @: http://xoomer.virgilio.it/francescoraf/hesyra/dynasty0.htm

this theology. Exactly when this concept of *godly empowerment* was introduced will cause interesting speculation by our foremost Egyptian historians. Based upon the evidence of godly support illustrated on the Qustul incense burner, it is reasonable to conclude that the Nubians first promulgated this belief. The existence of widespread belief in their kings having godly powers has proved to be validated by the number of pyramids built in the Nubia-Kush region. Through the years of rule by kings and pharaohs, this region had built a total of 223 pyramids; double the number of pyramids in Egypt [6].

---

[6]   Internet @: http://www.homestead.com/wysinger/badarians.html Number of pyramids stated under Subsection: 7000 BCE, South Nubia.

3.0 Religious Concepts of the Egyptians

Now that we have some knowledge of where the people of Egypt came from and how they evolved into city-states with class distinctions, we will examine the spiritual beliefs that caused the people to accept the dogma advocated by the Priesthood. This examination will show how the Egyptians logically developed the concept of one god. As we review these concepts, we will find some fundamental patterns emerging:

- *Man learns through the knowledge acquired from the past* and uses it to advance his conceptions and theories about his world in the present. This process applies to the spiritual as well as the pragmatic side of man's nature.
- *Religions have and will continue to undergo changes* to keep pace with the intellect of the people and knowledge gained about their world.
- *There will be changes to today's religions* to cleanse the myths and falsehoods of the past.
- *Mankind's faith in and worship of god is increased when religion and science are compatible and based upon truths* established by real-life experiences and scientific facts.

In the final chapter of this book, recommendations are provided to assist perceptive and courageous religious leaders to implement changes that will unify the beliefs of worshippers of the Judaic, Christian, and Islamic religions. A religious reformation is needed to assist man's understanding of himself and his God, thereby ushering in an age when,

> *'Man to man shall be a friend and brother and*
> *all Earth's family love one another!'* [1]

---

[1]   **Gerald Massey**, *Poems by Gerald Massey,* **Page 355, & Figure 6-1.**

3.1 Commonality of Mortuary Beliefs

Each community of people that entered Egypt had spiritual beliefs. Long before they settled along the Nile, the African people had an affinity for the belief in spirits and some idea of life after death as attested by the artifacts, food, and weapons left in their graves and tombs. The priests, being the most educated in their ability to read, write, and articulate spiritual matters, influenced both the leaders and people of their community (clan) through religious doctrine.

As the community grew into small towns and progressed into city states, the need for communication through the written word became an important tool in providing the mechanism for documenting trade transactions; measuring land ownership; building houses, estates and palaces; planning and implementing irrigation using the Nile source; establishing and enforcing laws of moral conduct; and eloquently writing and articulating the spiritual dogma that would harness the spiritual energy of the people. The need for an organized Priesthood would become a natural consequence of the spiritual beliefs felt and practiced by the people.

As the leaders of the community gained more power and wealth, there came a greater need for control and protection of their assets. A society of people that depends upon one another requires honesty and truth. The application of truth, expressed as *maat* by the Egyptians, therefore became an essential part of their morality. Both the clan leaders and priests of the community recognized this attribute as essential to their interests. The task of establishing truth as an honorable trait became an imperative necessity. We will explore how the Priesthood implemented truth and righteousness with their religious concepts and within their religious doctrines. The clan leaders embraced the spiritual code articulated by the Priesthood because it provided a moral and practical code of conduct for their people.

3.2 Early Influence of the Priesthood

Evidence of the Priesthood's effectiveness has been depicted on the Qustul incense burner introduced in Subsection 2.2.6. As depicted on a fragment of the Qustul incense burner, the Nubian Priesthood had already articulated the belief that their leader was empowered by their animal deity. The royal procession revealed the victorious return of a white crowned leader to his palace, and in the third boat, their clan god. This idea of being protected and empowered by the totem god was only a step away from the Priesthood conceptualizing their leader as the offspring of such a god. This concept became established after the Priesthood had articulated their beliefs about how their god created all things.

3.3 The Creation Concept and the God Atum-Re

The development of the concept of creation intrinsically involved the concept of a god. The Egyptians had a sense of kinship with life all around them, be it animal life, plant life, or those elements that affected their lives if not in substance but in wonder—like the sun, moon, sky, earth, and water. They began to venerate these elements as gods during Predynastic times and soon formulated the concept of creation that would lead to the concept of one god responsible for the creation of all things. The inquiring minds and spiritual nature of the Egyptians led to the creation of concepts that explained their existence. That spirit continues today; it is one of wonder about the outer limits of our universe and also about God being responsible for all the galaxies that exists.

Just when the Priesthood first formulated the concept of creation by their deity cannot be precisely dated; but it was defined prior to the founding of the 1st Dynasty. It was not until the 6th Dynasty, around 2540 BCE, that this profound concept was carved inside the pyramids of Merne-Re I and Pepi II (Nefer-ka-Re). The hieroglyphic text, *"The Creation by Atum,"* provided below, describes how Atum, god of Heliopolis, created the gods essential to life. Atum was also knows as Atum-Kheperer, a compound name that contained two ideas: Atum, who represented the sun-god Re that advances in age to an old man as the sun completes its journey from east to west; and Kheprer, the morning sun-god rising in the east.[1]

The Creation by Atum [2]

O Atum-Kheprer, thou wast on high on the (primeval) hill; thou didst arise as the ben-bird of the ben-stone in the Ben-House in Heliopolis; thou didst spit out what was Shu, thou didst sputter out what was Tefnut. Thou didst put thou arms about them as the arms of **ka***, for thy* **ka** *was in them.*

(So also), O Atum, put thy arms about King Nefer-ka-Re, about this construction work, about this pyramid, as the arms of **ka.** *For the* **ka** *of King Nefer-ka-Re is in it, enduring the course of eternity. O Atum, mayest thou set thy protection over this king Nefer-ka-Re, over this his pyramid and this construction work of King Nefer-ka-Re. Mayest thou guard lest anything happen to him evilly throughout the course of eternity, as thou didst set thy protection over Shu and Tefnut.*

O Great Ennead which is in Heliopolis, Atum, Shu, Tefnut, Geb, Nut, Osiris, Isis, Seth, and Nephthys, whom Atum begot, spreading wide his heart (in joy) at his beginning (you) in your name of the nine bows,[3] may there be none of you who will separate himself from Atum . . .

---

[1] **James H. Breasted**, *A History of Egypt,* **Page 59**.

[2] **James B. Pritchard**, ed. by, *Ancient Near Eastern Texts,* **Page 3**.

[3] **James B. Pritchard**, ed. by, *Ancient Near Eastern Texts,* **Page 3**. The Nine Bows were the traditional, potential enemies of Egypt. There is a play on the "Nine (Gods)" and the "Nine (Bows)" here. The magic of the spell protects against the potential enmity of these gods.

The concept of the first creation was developed in the city of Heliopolis. This city is located at an advantageous focal point of the Nile Delta, where it branches out towards the Mediterranean Sea. There, the Priesthood was a dominant entity as they advanced the idea that it was their city god Atum-Kheprer who, on a small hill that rose out of the waters of chaos (Nun), brought the first gods into being. This was a very perceptive concept that recognizes Atum as emanating from two very important elements: the heat of the sun, associated with Kheprer; and water, associated with Nun. While on the primeval hill, Atum spat out Shu, god of air, and Tefnut, goddess of moisture. The Egyptian mind was resourceful and reflective; for without the elements of air and moisture, life could not be sustained.

At the time the above hymn was created, the Priesthood recognized that the sun was the source that sustained life, and so it came to be identified with their local god as Atum-Re. Within the same text, the Great Ennead was identified as originating in Heliopolis. The first four gods that make up the Great Ennead were created by Atum. It was Nut (Heaven) and Geb (Earth) who created the children: Osiris, Isis, Seth, and Nephthys. The nine gods are listed below.

(1) Atum, the creator

(2) Shu, god of air.   (3) Tefnut, god of moisture.

(4) Geb (Keb), god of earth.   (5) Nut, goddess of the sky.

Following are the sons and daughters of Nut and Geb:

(6) Osiris, god of grain, the Nile and afterlife.
(7) Isis, Osiris beloved sister-wife, divinity of the fertile black field of the Nile, goddess of love, maternity and magic.
(8) Seth, (Set) Osiris's brother, god of wind and storms, warrior of Egypt, the great hunter and ruler of northern Egypt.
(9) Nephthys, goddess and Osiris's sister.

Figure 3-1 captures the strong belief in the creation. It shows the sky-goddess Nut as a nude woman arched as the heavens over the earth. She is supported by the upraised arms of the air-god Shu, who is represented in human form, with the symbol for 'year' crowning his headdress. At his feet lies the earth-god Geb, with his left arm stretched out along the ground. A ram-headed god, symbolizing strength and fertility, stands on each side supporting one of Shu's arms. Watching are several gods and the deceased owner of the Papyrus.

There is question as to whether the gods of the Ennead had been conceived before the creator god Atum-Re. It is very likely that gods that represented the elements: air, moisture, sky, grain, wind and storms; as well as the bodies of water, the earth, and sun, had already been identified many generations before the 1st Dynasty. It was man's nature to appreciate his surroundings and feel that spirits exist in every living and non-living thing, be it a tree, hilltop, birds, or creatures like himself. When man was not able to explain events, he attributed them to the power of magic, which was a gift of their personal god Isis, Osiris's wife. Another personal god, Horus, the son of Osiris and Isis, was worshipped during the Predynastic period. He was loved by the people for assisting in the resurrection of his father. Prior to *The Creation by Atum-Re* by the Priesthood, Osiris and his son Horus played a strong part in two principle doctrines: the concept of an *Afterlife* and the concept of the Pharaoh as the *Son of God*. These concepts will be presented in subsections 3.5 and 3.7, respectively.

Many religious leaders, historians, and biblical scholars have referred to the creation as conceived by the Egyptians as a myth. And many people today tend to regard the beliefs of primitive religions as myths. But we must not forget that the religious beliefs conceived by Egypt's Priesthood and followed by their people were not myths—they were beliefs that were fully accepted and that furnished food for their

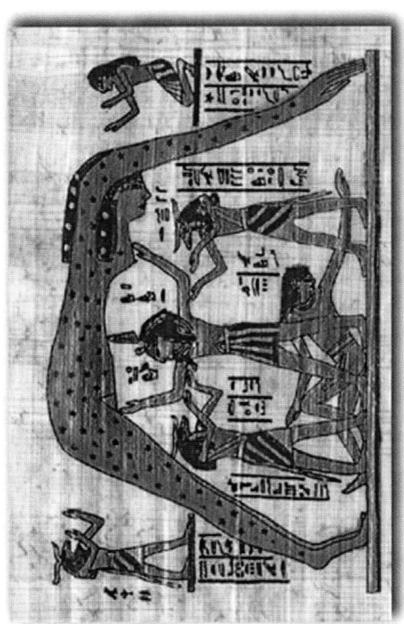

Figure 3-1. The First Generation of the Great Ennead.

spiritual needs. A myth is a story that we tell and retell because it provides joy or a theme that serves as a lesson we might utilize in the future. One such myth is the Christmas story of Santa Claus. This is a myth nobody believes but the story is retold year after year to ignite the joy and happiness in children. The Egyptian religious beliefs were not myths—they were a set of beliefs that have been infused into the monotheistic religions of today.

3.4 Concept of a Soul

The Egyptian civilization developed the concept of a soul. Many people have assimilated this very complex concept as a natural part of their spiritual beliefs. However, very few people know where and when this powerful concept evolved. *The Creation by Atum* described Atum's *ka* as being imbued into his creations. It is fair to reason that the concept of a soul, called the *ka*, came into existence with the concept of creation.

It appears that the idea of a *ka* had emerged before or during the life of King Ka, who existed a few generations before the start of the 1st Dynasty. By the 6th Dynasty, the Priesthood had over 800 years to merge the concept of *the ka* with *the creation* by Atum.

3.4.1 The Ka, the Living Soul of an Entity

The creation hymn reveals that all created things are protected by the *ka* of Atum-Kheprer. Let us revisit the lines that state that the creator god, Atum, put his own vital force into his first creatures: [1]

> *"Thou didst put thy arms about them as the arms of a ka,*
> *for thy ka was in them."*

---

[1]   **James B. Pritchard**, ed. by, *Ancient Near Eastern Texts*, **Page 3**. The *ka* was the guardian spirit or vital force of a personality. The creator-god Atum put his own vital force into his first creatures.

To be endowed with an internal force or spirit called the *ka* from the creator god Atum must therefore have had extreme importance. This vital source must be what gave the created object its unique characteristics and/or its special force. Scholars of Egyptian history believe that the *ka* represents the alter ego, a guardian spirit, or the vital force of personality.[2] Since the god Atum puts his *ka* into his creations, it identifies their unique characteristics and attributes. That is, the *ka* provides those attributes that uniquely form the totality of a living or material substance. In essence, the *ka* represents the total makeup of glandular, physical, and mental functions that defines humans and their personality.

As applied to human beings, E.A. Wallis Budge defines the *ka* as an "abstract individuality or personality which possessed the form and attributes of the man to whom it belonged, and though its normal dwelling place was in the tomb with the body, it could wander about at will; it was independent of the man and could go and dwell in any statue of him. It was supposed to eat and drink, and the greatest care was usually taken to lay abundant supplies of offerings in the tombs lest the *kas* of those who were buried in them should be reduced to the necessity of leaving their tombs and wandering about, eating offal and drinking filthy water."[3]

The word *ka* seems to have surfaced through the recognition of an Egyptian ruler, King Ka, who governed a generation prior to the 1st Dynasty, around 3500 years BCE [4], and in whose tomb the symbol

---

[2]   **James B. Pritchard**, ed. by, *Ancient Near Eastern Texts,* **Page 3**, Note 4

[3]   **E.A. Wallis Budge**, *The Book of the Dead,* **Page lxvii**

[4]   Internet @: http://www.mazzaroth.com/ChaptFour An Egyptologist, W. F. Petrie, dated the First Dynasty of Menes as commencing in **4777 BCE**; another named James H. Breasted around **3400 BCE,** the middle of the age; some others suggest **2850 BCE** toward the end. For consistency of dates used throughout this book, the Breasted dates have been used.

for the *ka* was first found on broken pottery. Figure 3-2 shows the symbol as two raised arms, and is placed on the head of King Hor who reigned from 1783-1633 BCE. One may intuitively conceive that the two arms represent the proud acknowledgement of the unification of the two lands referred to as Upper and Lower Egypt.

King Ka takes us back before the reign of King Aha Menes (also known as King Narmer) who is attributed with unifying the two lands of Egypt, marking the start of the 1ˢᵗ Dynasty. King Ka was buried in a double tomb at Abydos (just above Thebes), where he is considered to have preceded King Narmer as king of This (or Thinis) which was the old capital of or city near Abydos). He may have been the father of Narmer, whose tomb was built in a similar style and size, and placed just 30 meters away.

King Ka is the best-documented Predynastic King prior to King Narmer. It is conceivable that King Ka may have ruled over Upper Egypt prior to its unification by Narmer. This king had the symbol *ka* written within a "serekh" shown as Figure 3-3. It is a box within which the names of early Predynastic Kings were written. He was one of the first kings to adopt this sign with the falcon on its top, accompanied with the plant symbolizing Upper Egypt.

It is significant that the symbol of a falcon was used long before that of a ka, as revealed on the stone fragment of a Qustul incense burner (Figure 2-5). The ka and falcon symbols would later accomomdate the more advanced theological concept of a hereafter, a place where the soul of the king would join his god Atum-Re for eternity. It is very likely that King Ka was a strong supporter of the Priesthood and the religious beliefs they advocated. In commemoration of his father, it may be that King Narmer introduced the *ka* symbol to indicate the unification of Egypt; for the *ka* already was venerated as a vital force existing within any living or non-living thing.

French archaeologist De Morgan at Dashur found this fine wooden statue in the tomb of the 13th Dynasty King Hor I, who reigned from 1783-1633 BCE. This life size sculpture is a masterpiece of its kind among the objects in Egypt's Cairo Museum.

The statue represents the king's *ka*. The *ka* is symbolized by the two upraised arms on the head of the statue. It is the hieroglyph used to signify the word *ka*.

The eyes of the statue are inlaid with stones and crystals, giving them a realistic and lively appearance. They are outlined with bronze. The nose of the statue is narrow and the slight smile on its face shows that it is pleased.

The body is represented in a striding pose, with his left foot forward. His left arm is pushed forward as well, suggesting that the statue once held a staff that reached the ground. The right arm has a hole in its fist, which indicates that there used to be a *kherep* scepter (or ankh) in this hand.

Aside from a wig and a belt around the hip, this figure is represented naked. Some holes in the belly, however, suggest that the statue may once have been clad with a loin cloth.

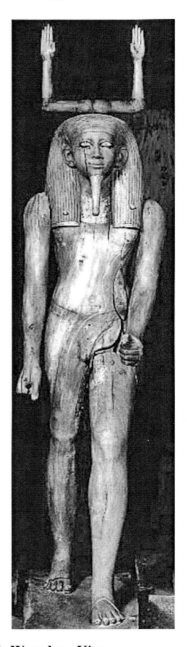

Figure 3-2. Symbol of a *Ka* Worn by a King.

http://www.ancient-egypt.org/kings/1314_hor_i/wooden_statue.html

Note: The first mnemonic symbols and semi-cursive hieroglyphics used to identify an Egyptian King appeared within a box called a serekh and was superceded by the cartouche during dynastic times.

Figure 3-3. Cursive Hieratic Script that Identifies King Ka.
http://www.nemo.nu/ibisportal/0egyptintro/2aegypt/

The interpretation of the *ka* representing both a vital force within an entity and a symbol for the unification of the two lands also implies the *'arms of the Ka'* as a protective spirit. This protective attribute is implied in the lines quoted from "*The Creation By Atum*" whereby Atum's *"arms of a ka'* were put around his creations Shu and Tefnut. The idea of the *ka* as a life force and protector was shown in a bas-relief group of Amenhotep III in the Great Temple of Karnak. This relief shows the Pharaoh followed by his *ka,* which stands behind him in human form. The *ka* carries the "ankh," the symbol of Truth, in one hand, and in the other the customary staff terminating in a bust of the King. Over his head is engraved, "The ***Royal Ka***, Life of the Lord of the Two Lands."

The bas-relief of Amenhotep expresses that the *ka* was envisioned as the life force of the king and also his guide as he protected Egypt. By the time Amenhotep III reigned, the belief in the *ka* had already found its acceptance by the nobility and common man. This is verified by the common man's belief of sustaining the *ka* after the death of a loved one with food until it is united with the ba.

3.4.2 The Ba, the Soul After Death

The *ba* came into existence only after death. It was normally represented in the form of a bird, sometimes with a human head. It would visit the tomb wherein the mummy lay bearing air and food to the *ka* to whom it belonged. It could move about, but always returned to the body to which it belonged. Spells enabled the *ba* to *assume any shape it wished.* It partook of the offered nourishment and seems also to have had creative powers.[1] Figure 3-4 shows the ba of Tutenkhamon, son-in-law of Ikhnaton (Amenhotep IV) who had a short reign towards the end of the 18th Dynasty.

It was the local priests, and in some cases the survivors of the deceased, who accomplished the transformation of the dead person into a soul that would live in the hereafter. In particular, it was the mortuary priest who performed indispensable ceremonies to win the favor of the gods for the deceased. The ka, which constituted the individual's uniqueness and provided protection during life, passed into the hereafter under the guidance and protection of the ba. Initially, the *ka* was the exclusive possession of kings but eventually, through the priest's role in performing elaborate ceremonies witnessed by the public, all Egyptians came to believe they too, possessed a *ka.* [2]

---

[1]   Internet: @ http://www.reshafim.org.il.ad/Egypt/religion/body_an_soul.htm

[2]   **James H. Breasted**, *The Dawn of Concience,* **Page 49, 50**.

Figure 3-4. The Ba of the Pharaoh Tutenkhamon.
http://www.reshafim.org.il.ad/Egypt/religion/body_an_soul.htm
Courtesy of Jon Bodsworth

3.4.3 The Heavenly Being and Spiritual Body

The soul, in the Egyptian's mind, was conceived as being separate
and distinct from the body. By the 18th Dynasty (1580-1350 BCE),
the more affluent and nobles who could arrange for the maintenance
of their dead bodies in a tomb, had utterances performed by mortuary
priests to assist in their journey into the hereafter. By this time, the
concept of the soul evolved into a more complex form consisting
of the ka, ba, khu and sahu. From the Papyrus of Ani the Scribe
(British Museum, No. 10,470, sheet 17), there are references made
to the ba and khu. The *ka* and *ba* was believed to become a united
soul called the *khu* that resided in the spiritual body called the *sahu*.

This spirit body would rise to live with the gods for eternity as *'one of the shinning ones'* with the stars. [1]

The *sahu* is an advanced concept that provides for the habitation of the soul. It sprang from the material body through the prayers said and the ceremonies performed over the dead body by duly appointed and properly qualified priests. *Sahu* is a lasting and incorruptible spiritual body which attained the knowledge, power, and glory needed in the afterlife. This spiritual body could converse with the soul and ascend into heaven to dwell with the beautified. In it, all the mental and spiritual attributes of the natural body, the *ka*, were united with the *ba* and *khu*. [2]

The following text from the Papyrus of Ani the Scribe (British Museum No.10,470, Sheet 18.) illustrates how the Egyptians used the various entities of the soul, such as the sahu and khu.

The Chapter of Coming Forth By Day After Having Made the Passage Through the Tomb.

Saith Osiris Ani:—Hail Soul, thou mighty one of strength! Verily I am here, I have come, I behold thee. I have passed through the Taut (underworld), I have seen [my] divine father Osiris, I have scattered the gloom of night. I am his beloved one. I have come; I have seen my divine father Osiris. I have stabbed the heart of Suti [3] [I] have performed [all] the ceremonies for my divine father Osiris, I have opened every way in heaven and in earth. I am the son who loveth his father Osiris. I have become a **sahu***, I have become a* **khu***, I am*

---

[1]   **E.A. Wallis Budge,** *Book of the Dead,* Introduction by David Lorimer, **Page lxviii**.

[2]   **E.A. Wallis Budge,** *Book of the Dead,* Introduction by David Lorimer, Page lxx and Note 1 on **Page 47**.

[3]   Set (Seth), the mighty antagonist of Horus, by who he was slain.

*furnished [with what I need]. Hail, every god, hail every **khu***! *I have made a path [for myself, I] Osiris, the scribe Ani, victorious.*

To further illustrate the liberal use of various aspects of the soul, such as the ba and the khu, another excerpt from the Papyrus of Ani the Scribe (British Museum No. 10,470, Sheet 17) is provided.

The Chapter of Causing the Soul to Be United to Its Body in the Underworld [4]

*[Hail,] great God! Grant thou that my soul may come unto me from wheresoever it may be, . . . Let me have possession of my **ba** (soul), and of my **khu**, and let me triumph therewith in every place wheresoever it may be . . .*

Hail, ye gods, who tow along the boat of the lord (Re) of millions of years, who bring it above the underworld and who make it travel over Nut (earth), who make souls to enter their spiritual bodies, . . . And behold, grant ye that the soul of Osiris Ani, triumphant, may come forth before the gods and that it may be triumphant along with you in the eastern part of the sky to follow unto the place where it was yesterday; [and that it may have] peace, peace in Amentet (hereafter or underworld). May it look upon its material body, may it rest upon its spiritual body; and may its body neither perish nor suffer corruption ever.

It is apparent that the component parts of the soul did not all exist at the same time, but took on more advanced roles over several generations. After the development of the *ka* concept, it did not take very long for the priests to enhance and give greater meaning to the soul. The desire to transform the material body of the deceased into a spiritual body that could live in the hereafter was satisfied by

---

[4]   **E.A. Wallis Budge**, *Book of the Dead*, **Pages 279-281**.

uniting the spiritual entity of the *ka* with the *ba*. Eventually, these components of the soul merged with the heavenly attributes of the *khu*, and finally, all parts of the soul resided in the *sahu*.

The more advanced vision of the soul developed as a consequence of the expanded religious belief that encompassed the idea of there being a reward after death for those who had lead a righteous life. From a practical standpoint, the concept of a hereafter served to accommodate the Priesthood and the organized State to establish order throughout the many communities by emphasizing the attributes of truth, morality, righteousness, and justice. One can easily see how useful these qualities would be in helping the Priesthood and their ruling king to maintain power and order.

3.5 Concept of a Hereafter

Two of the oldest gods that ignited the imagination of the Egyptians were linked with the phenomenon of day and night. The sun-god Re, sailing in his celestial barque on a sky of sea, brought in the morning as Kheprer. Towards evening, Atum the sun-god, settled in the west and entered the Nile beneath the earth. Through a long dark passage with successive caverns, the celestial barque traveled through the night to arrive in the east at early morning. It was in this gloomy part of the netherworld that the Egyptians believed the dead resided. Their god was Osiris. As the grain-god, Osiris succeeded the sun-god Re as king on earth. He was regarded as the benefactor of men and beloved as a righteous ruler. But as recounted below, Osiris was craftily misled and slain by Seth, his brother. A popular story, a variant of this brother conflict has been repeated in the Bible, under Genesis 4:8, where Cain killed his brother Abel.

The love between Osiris and Isis was consummated in the womb of Nut. This brother and sister marriage represented the union of the Nile and the fertile land and was repeated annually when the river rose and the earth became green and fruitful from its embraces. This yearly union of Osiris and Isis emulated the epitome of human desire, satisfaction, and subsistence. From the valley, softly caressed by the Nile, this union became the source of food, providing nourishment of seed into bread and fruit, fish, fowl, and a haven for animals that quenched their thirst in its waters. The Egyptians were constantly reminded of the grain-god's power to revitalize the seed after its growth and harvest. Year after year, seeds would burst into grains, fruits, and vegetation by his living spirit embodied in the Nile. As the god of grain and crops, he passed into the bodies of all who consumed the fruits of the earth.

The worship of Osiris as the spirit of the Nile and grain made him thought of as Lord of the Underworld and Ruler of Eternity. In the Osiris story that follows, his resurrection led to the concept of eternal life, which intrinsically involved the concept of a hereafter. The Egyptian Priesthood originated this concept to promulgate the belief that, based upon the judgment of the Osiris court, the pharaoh could join the gods after death. The reader is reminded that the gods of the Great Ennead—and Horus, the son of Osiris and Isis, had long existed in the hearts of the Egyptians several generations before the 1st Dynasty and the reign of the pharaohs. As the kings became more powerful and ruled greater Egypt, they began to embrace the concept of immortality. This vision would place them among the gods and extend their lives on earth into the realm of eternity.

3.5.1 The Osiris and Seth Dichotomy

The antithesis to Osiris was his brother Seth. Cruel and treacherous, Seth was likened to the spirit of the forbidding desert that borders both sides of the Nile. Ever jealous of his brother, he married his sister Nephthys to mitigate his feelings of inferiority caused by the fruitful marriage of Isis to Osiris. Isis and Osiris were loved by the people for her reputation as a devoted wife and able manager and for his fertile power to fill the country with abundance. To Seth's disappointment, Nephthys could not bear a child. For like the sterile desert, Seth brought barrenness to all he touched and she sought fertilization from another source. It was rumored that Nephthys made Osiris drunk, had drawn him to her arms without his knowledge, and borne him a son. The child of this furtive union was the jackal, Anubis, who prowled along the edges of the desert, and who stood as sponsor for the dead in the Judgment Hall. This embarrassing invasion of Seth's domain by Osiris ignited an open strife between the brothers.

With such an embarrassing event, the dichotomy between Osiris and Seth became even more transfixed in the minds of the Egyptians: one stood for all goodness and life, laboring to produce abundance; the other came to be associated with evil and death, striving only to destroy. It would be this dichotomy that would later define a sharp line between good and evil in our contemporary religions. Seth long remained respected as god of war and during the 13th to the 17th Dynasties, was perhaps the national god of the Delta. But by the 19th Dynasty, his name met with such disdain that it was stricken from all monuments. Shortly thereafter, the nicknames, "Evil One" and "Stinking Face" were applied to him. However, even as a prime liar, breeder of mischief and murderer of Osiris, Seth was envisioned as an evil god and not the god of evil.

The association of evil with a god or fallen angel was not a belief originated with the Egyptians.[1] The concept of an evil entity that caused human beings to become the offspring of sin was conceived by the Christian Priesthood. From Genesis (2:16,17) of the Hebrew Testament, original sin became Christian dogma based upon Adam and Eve disobeying God's command not to eat of the tree of knowledge of good and evil. A belief that human beings are born into sin is

---

[1] **Homer W. Smith**, *Man and His Gods,* **Pages 23, 35-36.**

an unfortunate concept. Such a theological precept psychologically demeans and belittles the creation and dignity of human beings.

Seth's jealousy and dissatisfaction with the contrast between himself and Osiris angered him so greatly that he devised a plan to eliminate his brother. While Osiris was in Asia teaching men the arts and agriculture, Seth obtained the measurements of Osiris's body to construct a richly adorned chest. Seth then gave a banquet in Osiris's honor to which he invited seventy-two of his conspirators. When Seth produced the chest at the feast, all rejoiced at its beauty. In response, he promised to give the chest to the one whom it would fit exactly. All who tried could not meet the true fit of the chest until Osiris at last got into it and laid down. Quickly Seth and his conspirators closed the cover, nailed it firmly shut, soldered it together with melted lead and threw it into the Nile, which carried it out to sea.

The oldest record of this event, the Memphite Drama, says that Osiris drowned, while the Pyramid Texts simply relate that Seth murdered him at Nedyt, which may have been the ancient name for Byblos. The grief stricken Isis cut her hair, put on mourning robes and fled to the Delta in search of the body of her lord. In the Pyramid Texts, it is said that she found his body there, and the spirit of Osiris visited her secretly so that she bore a son Horus, whom she hid in a basket of rushes.

In the Pyramid Texts legend, Nephthys accompanied Isis, and in the form of birds they engaged in a long search for Osiris. The lamentations of the two sisters were the most sacred expression of sorrow known to the Egyptians. It was told that the waves had washed the chest ashore off the coast of Byblos, where a tree suddenly sprang up and enclosed the chest in its trunk. The king of that country, having admired the tree, had it cut down and placed it as a pillar beneath his house. Isis entered the service of the king as a nurse and drew the chest out from the pillar. She then took it to Egypt where she hid it in the Nile and rejoined her son Horus.

While hunting in the moonlight, Seth discovered the chest and opened it. Recognizing Osiris, he cut the corpse into fourteen pieces and scattered them widely. Isis once more set out on a woeful pilgrimage to recover the body parts of her lord. She was able to collect all the parts of Osiris and bury them where they were found except his phallus, which had been devoured by the great Nile catfish. Ever after, men revered each of the spots as the grave of their benefactor: at Busiris his backbone was buried; in Abydos his head was enclosed in a small chest; and at Athribus he was honored with his heart. It appears that his divine parts multiplied, as Memphis also claimed to be the repository for his head, and the number of legs claimed to be his would have sufficed for several ordinary mortals. The innovated Isis used her magical powers to construct a model of the lost phallus. Thereafter, the Egyptians celebrated the feast of Pamylia, which is commemorated by a procession of a phallic statue and pitchers of water carried from the Nile in Osiris's honor.[2]

3.5.2 The Concept of Resurrection

A theological innovation of the Egyptian Priesthood was the concept of resurrection. It was an idea that developed as a natural consequence of the rebirth of the beloved god Osiris, who was reborn year after year providing sustenance for the people. The resurrection of Osiris enhanced the stature of his son Horus, who already had begun to be revered by the kings of Upper Egypt even before the establishment of the 1st Dynasty. It is the god Horus that is associated with the symbol of the falcon. Because he was the son of the most beloved god of Egypt, the people could identify themselves with him on a personal level. The idea that Horus and his falcon symbol existed prior to the 1st Dynasty is confirmed in subsection 2.2.6 (Nubians, the Stimulus for Egypt's Unity), where it is noted that the falcon was well established as the standard or banner of the Nubians.

---

[2]   **Homer W. Smith,** *Man and His Gods,* **Pages 36-37.**

When Horus had grown to be a man, he left his hiding place in the rushes to avenge the death of his father. His encounter with Seth immediately initiated a gruesome fight, and the outcome left Horus with only one eye. Seth was rendered impotent, and the vanquished warrior acknowledged Horus as the new monarch of the earth. Fortunately, Thoth, the god of wisdom replaced the eye of Horus and restored sight to it by spitting upon it. Horus then set about reassembling the dismembered parts of his father's body, which Isis had buried. Completing this task, he prepared a mummy skillfully made under the direction of Anubis, who invented the art of embalming. This effort fell short of bringing Osiris back to life as a warm, breathing body, spontaneous in movement and capable of thought and speech. Instead, he was an immobile, cold, blackish mass, adequate only to assure the continuity of the *ka*.

The inert state of Osiris's body condemned him to vegetate in the darkness of the tomb without pleasure and barely enough consciousness to exist. To bring Osiris back to life again, it took the combined efforts of Isis, Horus, Anubis and Thoth. Thoth played a prime role. As the inventor of magic words and writing, he showed how to inscribe protective bandages with the proper figures and formulas; how to decorate the body with amulets of special efficacy for its different parts; and how to draw on the boards of the coffin and the walls of the sepulchral chamber scenes depicting Osiris's glorious adventures both in this world and the hereafter. The performance of magic rituals by the resourceful Isis successfully enabled Osiris to open his mouth, his eyes and ears, loosen his arms and legs, restore his breath, and start the movement of his heart. Under Thoth's direction, they joined the severed phallus to Osiris's body and empowered him to perform its natural function. The final step to Osiris's resurrection was performed by Horus—he gave his father his eye to eat. This act fully resurrected Osiris to life as a living god.

3.5.3 Heaven On Earth In the NetherWorld

A common disagreement reflecting the discord between the peoples of Upper and Lower Egypt since Predynastic days involved the question of who ruled both lands. This political discord was cast into the religious realm and became part of the Osiris legend. The issue was so critical to both lands that the priests, and very likely the ruling king, disseminated a resolution with the use of their gods. By using the Great Ennead, they had the gods' rule that Horus inherit his father's ownership of the Two Lands.

After the Great Ennead delegated Osiris as ruler of the underworld, there were several contests between Seth and Horus as to who was the rightful ruler of the two lands. Not long after the resurrection of Osiris, Seth proceeded to file a charge that Horus was not the son of Osiris but a bastard whom Isis had conceived after the death of her husband. This case was brought before the Ennead, a tribunal of nine gods at Heliopolis, to settle the dispute. Thoth, acting as Osiris's advocate, completely cleared both father and son. In this instance, the Ennead was presided over by Re, the 'All Lord', and Horus was made king of Upper and Lower Egypt.

To appease Seth, Re had him join him in the heavens as a thunder-god to live as his son and to speak out in the sky so that men may be afraid of him.[1] In another folk tale, the gods decided that Osiris be made king of the netherworld and be 'justified' by the gods.

---

[1]   **James B. Pritchard**, ed. by, *Ancient Near Eastern Texts,* **Pages 14- 17**, A folk tale entitled, 'The contest of Horus and Seth for the Rule', section XIV. This tale was written in Thebes in the 20th Dynasty around the 12th century BCE.

Thereafter, the word 'justified' was applied to the dead to mean innocent, triumphant, assured of immortality, while the resurrected dead were called, 'justified of Osiris'.[2]

Osiris was loved by all Egyptians and was constantly remembered for his goodness in satisfying their needs with abundant food; his resurrection after overcoming death by the treachery of Seth; the lamentations of Isis and Nephthys that expressed the depths of sorrow felt by the people; the devotion of his son to avenge his death and restore him to life with one of his eyes; and the Ennead trials that proclaimed the favorable outcomes on behalf of Osiris and his son Horus. These are all human instances in their religious teachings that were close to life's realities and comprehensible to the humblest people. They could relate in both substance and destiny to the grain that died upon bearing fruit, and with each new season came to life again. The concept of never-ending life became a belief that was possible for the worshippers of Osiris—for if the love of Isis, the sacrifice of Horus, the wisdom of Thoth and the preservation knowledge of Anubis could give life to Osiris, could these gods do the same for them?

By the end of the 5th Dynasty, the worship of Osiris spread among the people and later would advance solar theology. For by this time, religious literature revealed Osiris as capable of climbing up the sun's ladder or being ferried in the sun-god's bark. It is the oldest religious literature ever found, and it was fortunately preserved in the pyramid of Unis (5th Dynasty, 2655-2625 BCE). With the help of dedicated Egyptologists much of it has been deciphered and has formed the collection called the Pyramid Texts. Ascension by Osiris to the solar heaven where the gods resided, was an effort by the Priesthood that would later elevate the netherworld to the heavens. However, at this time, the common people, including the kings, still thought of their

---

[2]   **Homer W. Smith**, *Man and His Gods,* **Pages 37, 38.**

dead as either dwelling in the tomb, or at best, inhabiting the gloomy realm of the West; the subterranean kingdom ruled by Osiris. The *Taut,* or netherworld, was not actually subterranean, but lay far to the west beyond the 'Mountain of the Sunset'.

The Egyptians envisioned Taut as an extension of the world in which they lived. It was conceived as a paradise where wheat grew to three cubits in height and there was never any hunger. In this land of happiness, they could go fishing or fowling among the reeds, lounge under the trees which were perpetually green, or retire into their lovely pavilions to tell amusing tales and to play at draughts. But their lives were not entirely carefree. They had found work a necessary function for idle hands, especially when they participated in projects to plan and design the irrigation systems, and build temples, palaces, and pyramids along the Nile. Their exposure to the arts was extremely gratifying, as they created paintings, pottery, and statues that aroused admiration in their ability to capture beauty and relate the significant events of the life of their pharaoh. Therefore even in the netherworld they simulated their real world and protected it by building walls around their kingdom to defend themselves against the followers of Seth. In the hereafter, they continued to be productive by maintaining their canals and dykes, tilling the ground, planting and reaping the grain, and enjoying their next life without pain, want, or misery.

Since Taut was now available to the poor, they entered it well equipped with *ushabti* figures, and statues of farmers, soldiers, bakers and the like made of wood, clay or other inexpensive materials. It was possible that these miniature servants would come to life and take up their responsibilities by the citing of proper incantations. The Priesthood had made great strides in devising the chants, litanies, and prayers that would safely bring the departed into the netherworld and stimulate servants to do mundane yet essential work. This collection of magic incantations had been ascribed to Thoth in a collection known as

The Book of the Dead, but a correct reading of the hieroglyphic title read as, *Coming Forth into the Day.*

The Book of the Dead had been in use since 3000 BCE or earlier. Here we find that the deceased spirits, the *ka* and *ba,* are given the spells to protect their journey to, and in, the netherworld. It is evident that the distinction between the ka and ba is that: at birth the person is associated and imbued with the spirit of the ka, which defines one's person; and the ba upon one's death serves as its guide and protector.[3]

Prior to the 6th Dynasty, the incantations of The Book of the Dead were confined to kings buried in pyramids. Thereafter and well into the 11th Dynasty (2160-2000 BCE), they were written upon the coffins of commoners, frequently with great haste and carelessness. By the start of the New Kingdom (1580 BCE), the texts were written on long rolls of papyrus, partly because they were too numerous to be placed on the coffin and partly because they had to be written inexpensively and quickly in order to meet the great demand.

Upon leaving the tomb, the *ba* guides the deceased and his *ka* by following the prescriptions of The Book of the Dead to the letter. They head west into the desert and cross the land of the sacred sycamores. They bypass many dangers as they ascend the mountains that surround their world. A great river is then crossed with the assistance of a ferryman who transports the deceased with his *ba* and *ka* to the further shore. There the gods and goddesses of the court of Osiris meet them. Together they enter the Judgment Hall, and at the further end, the Lord Osiris sits in mysterious twilight.[4]

---

[3]   **Homer W. Smith**, *Man and His Gods,* **Pages 39 and 40**.

[4]   **Homer W. Smith**, *Man and His Gods,* **Page 42**. Note: Homer only refers to the *ba* on the journey to the west and over the river to the Judgment Hall of Osiris. Yet, as portrayed in Figure 3-5, it is the deceased double or *ka* that stands in judgment before Osiris with the ba close by. Therefore the ba does accompany the ka.

The judgment scene was always painted on the walls in the tombs of the deceased pharaohs, nobility, and persons who had attained sufficient wealth, or those revered for their contributions, such as scribes. The common elements of these scenes give us insight into the values of the Egyptians at this time. Over the hundreds of years from its inception, there are many slight variations of the theme that illustrated the weighing of the deceased's heart. The heart is symbolic of the deceased's conscience that is weighed in the balance against the feather, which symbolizes Right and Truth. Figure 3-5 illustrates the judgment scene with three panels that present the key parties participating in the momentous occasion of judging the deceased. Judgment of the deceased will result either in entering into eternal life in the realm of Osiris, or being eaten and ceasing to exist.

In the upper register of Figure 3-5 are fourteen gods who sit in judgment. They are not uniquely identified due possibly to the haste in which it was painted. In another scene from the Papyrus of Ani the Scribe and his wife Thuthu, there are twelve gods who are presented with their individual characteristics. They are: Harmachis, the great god in his boat, Temu, Shu, Tefnut, Geb, Nut, Isis, Nephthys, Horus the great god, Hathor the lady of Amenta, Hu, and Sa.[5] Beginning in the upper left-hand corner, the deceased appears before the 14 judges to make an accounting for his deeds during life. The ankh, the key and symbol of Truth, appears in the hands of seven of the judges.

---

[5]   **E. A. Wallis Budge,** *The Book of the Dead,* Volume I, **Pages 21, 22.** The Judgment Scene was contained in papyri of the 18th, 19th, and following Dynasties.

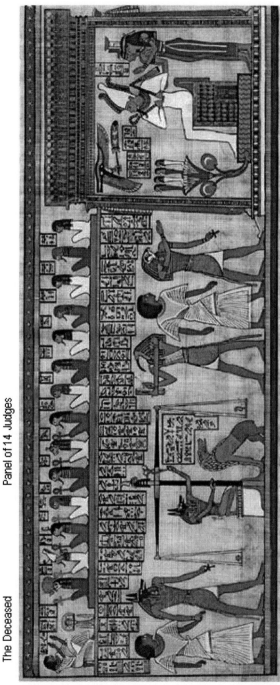

The Deceased   Panel of 14 Judges

The Deceased   Heart   Anubis   Ammit   Feather   Thoth   Deceased presented   Ba   Osiris, Isis and Nephthys
led by Anubis   of Maat   by Horus   Horus's Four Children

Figure 3-5. The Weighing of the Heart of the Dead.

Below, in the second register, the jackal god Anubis, who represents the underworld and mummification, leads the deceased before the scale. Note again that the ankh, a revered symbol, is held in the hand of Anubis. Anubis then weighs the heart of the deceased against the feather of Ma'at, goddess of truth and justice. In other variations, the goddess Ma'at, not just her feather, is shown seated on the tray. The significance of Justice and Truth are emphasized by the placement of Ma'at's head, crowned by the feather, at the top of the fulcrum of the scale. If the heart outweighs the feather, then the heart of the deceased contains evil deeds, and Ammit the monster will devour the heart. However, if the feather remains stationary or outweighs the heart, then the deceased has led a righteous life and may be presented before Osiris to join his realm of everlasting life. Thoth, the ibis-headed god of wisdom, stands ready with his reed pen and palette to record the outcome.

The weighing of the heart is an appraisal of the character of the deceased. Central to this ceremony is the Negative Confession, cited in the 125th chapter of the Book of the Dead. This chapter consists of three parts: the Introduction, the Negative Confession and a concluding text. The Introduction, which consists of a hymn of praise to Osiris, was said when the deceased arrived at the Hall of double Maati, [6] and it includes a number of denials to Osiris. The Introduction is followed by a Negative Confession that was recited by the deceased before forty-two gods in the hall. The hymn, denials spoken to Osiris, and the Negative Confession, spoken to each god, are presented in the next subsection. The extensive set of

---

[6]   **E.A. Wallis Budge,** *The Book of the Dead,* **Page 355, Chapter CXXV.** Note: This is the hall where the goddesses Isis and Nephthys who symbolically represent Right and Truth are seated. Also present are the 42 gods, to each of whom the decease must address a prescribed negative statement

denials illustrates the depth of Egyptian morality and their respect for human life.

In the lower right panel of Figure 3-5, Horus, with the revered symbol of Truth (some historians believe it symbolizes life, but life is determined by the scales of Truth and Righteousness) leads the deceased to Osiris, lord of the underworld. Above the four children of Horus is the *ba* with out-stretched wings, the soul of the deceased, which accompanies his *ka*. Osiris, represented as a mummy, sits on his throne. On his head is the white crown of Lower Egypt (the north or Delta region). He holds the symbols of Egyptian kingship in his hands: the shepherd's crook to symbolize his role as shepherd of mankind; and the flail, to represent his ability to separate the wheat from the chaff. Behind him stands his wife Isis (in red), and her sister Nephthys. Together, Osiris, Isis, Nephthys, and four children welcome the deceased to the underworld. Another symbolic notion is imparted: Horus represents the personification of the pharaoh during life; and diametrically, his father, Osiris, represents the personification of the pharaoh after death. The Egyptians believed that the gods could grant everlasting life to all Egyptians who had led lives of righteousness and truth.

The belief in life beyond the grave gave rise to an extensive set of mortuary incantations, prayers, and litanies that extended the duties and need for the Priesthood. The priests embalmed the bodies to preserve them, assisted the dead with embalming techniques to preserve the body, maintained offerings at the deceased's tomb, and performed the religious ceremonies to permit the deceased to enter the hereafter safely. The Egyptians also held the belief that the deceased's next life would be in the body given him from birth. An eternal life with a body that would bare the trials of pain and enjoy the most wonderful moments of life was conceivable to the Egyptians; this belief may be just as true for human beings living today.

Before burial, the embalmed body was subjected to several elaborate ceremonial incantations relating to the resurrection of Osiris. One chant the priests performed envolved opening the deceased's mouth and ears so that he might hear and speak in the hereafter. A short extract from The Book of the Dead, Chapter 23, "Of Opening of the Mouth of the Deceased" is provided below:

The scribe Ani (the deceased), triumphant, saith:—

"May the god Ptah open my mouth, and may the god of my city loose the swathings, even the swathings which are over my mouth. Moreover, may Thoth, being filled and furnished with charms, come and loose the bandages, even the bandages of Seth which fetter my mouth; and may the god Tem hurl them at those who would fetter [me] with them, and drive them back. May my mouth be opened, may my mouth be unclosed by Shu with his iron knife wherewith he opened the mouth of the gods . . ." [7]

In summary, this subsection provided a brief history of how Osiris became the Lord of the Underworld; the settlement of a bitter dispute over who inherited the Two Lands that was once the domain of Osiris; the Egyptians conception of the netherworld; how the deceased was led by his ba into the sanctuary of Osiris; the judgment of the deceased; the type of ceremonies performed by the priests to safely guide the deceased to the hereafter; and a description of the hereafter where the Egyptians envisioned the joys of eternal life.

---

[7] Note the reference made to Thoth. It emphasizes the beliefs that: he was the great master of the use of magical names and formulae; he gave the word which resulted in the creation of the world; and he supplied Isis with words of magical power that enabled her to effect the resurrection of Osiris (she also resurrected her son Horus after he had been stung to death by a scorpion).

3.6 *Egyptian Morality and the Ten Commandments*

This section emphasizes the social law and morality of the Egyptian people that was observed during the worship of the predynastic god, Osiris. It lists the denials of guilt to Osiris taken from a portion of the 125th Chapter of the Book of the Dead.[1] This literary work illustrates that the Egyptians had defined moral principles more than 2000 years before the Ten Commandments. For instance, although the deceased addresses his god from a negative perspective, the social values of human conduct are explicit. To read about the Egyptians' sense of morality in a positive framework of wisdom literature, the reader may consult any of the following texts: [2]

- *The Instruction of the Vizier Ptah-hotep.* He was the vizier to King Izezi of the 5th Dynasty, about 2450 BCE.
- *The Instruction for King Meri-Ka-Re.* Represents the advice given by a king to his son and successor.
- *The Instruction of King Amen-en-het.* The first Pharaoh of the 12th Dynasty offers advice to his son and successor.
- *The Instruction of Ani.* A father gives instructions to his son towards the end of the New Kingdom around the 3rd Intermediate Period, which starts with the 21st Dynasty in 1090 BCE.
- *The Instruction of Amen-em-Opet.* The instruction and words of wisdom given by Amen-em-Opet has been found to be closely related to the Hebrew Testament, Book of Proverbs. This instruction is given in 30 Chapters and differs from the earlier Egyptian books of wisdom in its humbler, more resigned, and less materialistic outlook. The date of the manuscript is estimated some time after the New Kingdom of the Egyptian Empire, between the 10th and 6th centuries BCE.

---

[1]   **E.A. Wallis Budge,** *The Book of the Dead,* **Pages 355-378.**

[2]   **James B. Pritchard,** *Ancient Near Eastern Texts Relating to the Old Testament,* **Pages 412-425** provides the miscellaneous texts.

The following is a brief extract taken from 125th Chapter of the *Book of the Dead*. It is an Introduction that begins with the deceased addressing his god, Osiris, with the following words of respect before denying guilt for possible crimes and shortcomings.

Homage to thee, O Great God, thou Lord of Double Maati (Right and Truth). I have come to thee, O my Lord, and I have brought myself hither that I may behold thy beauties,' [i.e., experience thy gracious clemency]. 'I know thee, and I know thy name, and I know the names of the Two-and-Forty gods who exist with thee in this Hall of double Maati, who live as warders of sinners and who feed upon their blood on the day when the lives of men are taken into account in the presence of the god Un-Nefer [i.e., Osiris] . . . In truth I have come to thee, and I have brought Maat (i.e., Right and Truth) to thee, and I have destroyed wickedness for thee.

These words are followed by a statement of the offenses that he had not committed; they are presented in Table 3-1 below:

Table 3-1. Part A of the Protestation of Guiltlessness. [3]

A1 I have not done evil to mankind.

A2 I have not oppressed the members of my family.

A3 I have not wrought evil in the place of right and truth.

A4 I have had no knowledge of worthless men.

A5 I have not wrought evil.

A6 I have not made to be the first [consideration] of each day that excessive labor should be performed by me.

A7 [I have] not brought forward my name for [exaltation] to honors.

A8 I have not ill-treated servants.

A9 [I have not thought scorn of God].

A10 I have not defrauded the oppressed one of his property.

---

[3] **E.A. Wallis Budge**, *Book of the Dead*, **Pages 360-362**.

A11 I have not done that which is an abomination unto the gods.

A12 I have not caused harm to be done to the servant by his chief.

A13 I have not caused pain.

A14 I have made no man to suffer hunger.

A15 I have made no one to weep.

A16 I have done no murder.

A17 I have not given the order for murder to be done for me.

A18 I have not inflicted pain upon mankind.

A19 I have not defrauded the temples of their oblations.

A20 I have not purloined the cakes of the gods.

A21 I have not carried off the cakes offered to the *khus* (blessed dead).

A22 I have not committed fornication.

A23 I have not polluted (defiled) myself [in the holy places of the god of my city], nor diminished from the bushel.

A24 I have neither added to nor filched away land.

A25 I have not encroached upon the fields [of others].

A26 I have not added to the weights of the scales [to cheat the seller].

A27 I have not misread the pointer of the scales [to cheat the buyer].

A28 I have not carried away the milk from the mouths of children.

A29 I have not driven away the cattle which were upon their pastures.

A30 I have not snared the feathered fowl of the preserves of the gods.

A31 I have not caught fish [with bait made of] fish of their kind.

A32 I have not turned back the water at the time [when it should flow].

A33 I have not cut a cutting in a canal of running water.

A34 I have not extinguished a fire (or light) when it should burn.

A35 I have not violated the times [of offering] the chosen meat-offerings.

A36 I have not driven off the cattle from the property of the gods.

A37 I have not repulsed God in his manifestations.

I am pure! I am pure! I am pure! I am pure! . . .

Part B of the deceased protestation is referred to as the *Negative Confession*, and is an extension of Part A. In Table 3-2, the deceased addresses each of the forty-two divine jurors by name.[4] Some of the names defy translation; some show fear, while others apply to the judgment scene rather indifferently. He presents his protestations of guilt with the hope of convincing the posthumous court that he is worthy of eternal happiness.

Table 3-2. Part B of The Protestation of Guiltlessness. [5]

B1   Hail Wide-of-Stride, who comes forth from Heliopolis, I have not committed evil.

B2   Hail Embracer-of-Fire, who comes forth from Babylon,[6] I have not stolen.

B3   Hail Divine Nose, who comes forth from Hermopolis, I have not been covetous.

B4   Hail Swallower-of-Shadows, who comes forth from the place where the Nile riseth, I have not committed theft.

B5   Hail Dangerous-of-Face, who comest forth from Re-stau, I have not killed men.

B6   Hail O Ruti, who comest forth from heaven, I have not damaged the grain measure.

B7   Hail O His-Eyes-Are-of-Flint, who comest forth from Sekhem (the shrine), I have not caused crookedness.

B8   Hail O Flamer, who comest forth *backward*, I have not stolen the property of a god.

B9   Hail O Breaker-of-Bones, who comest forth from Suten-henen (Herakleopolis), I have not told lies.

---

[4]   Knowledge of the name of each divine juror was important in regards to courtesy and influence.

[5]   **James B. Pritchard**, ed. by, *Ancient Near Eastern Texts,* **Pg 35.**

[6]   Egyptian Babylon, near modern Cairo.

B10   Hail O Commander-of-Fire, who comest forth from Het-ka-Path (Memphis), I have not taken away food.

B11   Hail O Dweller-in-the-Pit, I have not been contentious.

B12   Hail O White-of-Teeth, who comest forth from Ta-she (the Faiyum), I have not trespassed (attacked no man).

B13   Hail O Eater-of-Blood, who comest forth from the execution block, I have not slain the cattle of the god.

B14   Hail O Eater-of-Entrails, who comest forth from the Thirty (*mabet* chamber),[7] I have not practiced usury.

B15   Hail O Lord of Justice, who comest forth from Ma'ati, I have not stolen the *bread-ration*.

B16   Hail O Wanderer, who comest forth from the city of Bast (Bubastis), I have not *gossiped*.

B17   Hail O *Aadi*, who comest forth from Annu (Heilopolis), my mouth has not gone (on unchecked) [against any man].

B18   Hail O *Djudju-serpent*, who comes forth from the nome of Ati (Busiris), I have not argued with *someone summoned because of* his property.

B19   Hail O *Wamwmti-serpent*, who comes forth from the place of judgment, I have not committed adultery.

B20   Hail O *Maa-Intef* who comest forth from the Temple of Amsu (Min), I have not defiled myself (committed any sin against purity).

B21   Hail O Superior of the Nobles, who comes forth from *Imau* (the city of Nehatu, a city of the sycamore in Upper Egypt), I have not caused terror (struck fear [into any man]).

B22   Hail O Wrecker, who comes forth from the Lake of Kaui (*Saite Nome)*, I have not trespassed (encroached upon [sacred times and seasons]).

B23   Hail O Mischief-Maker, who comes forth from Urit (a sanctuary), I have not been (over) heated (angered).

---

[7]   A law court of Egyptian magistrates.

B24 Hail O Child, who comes forth from the Lake of Heq-at (13th nome of Lower Egypt, Heliopolitan), I have not been unresponsive to a matter of justice.

B25 Hail O *Ser-kheru* (disposer of speech), who comes forth from *Wensi,* the city of Unes (19th nome of Upper Egypt), I have not stirred up strife (been quarrelsome).

B26 Hail O Bastet, who comes forth from the sanctum, I have not winked (made no [man] to weep).[8]

B27 Hail O His-Face-Behind-Him, who comes forth from the *Tep-het-djat* (dwelling), I have not *been perverted*, neither have I lain with men (or boys).

B28 Hail O Hot of Leg (of Fire), who comes forth from the twilight, I have not swallowed my heart.[9]

B29 Hail O Kenemet (Dark-One), who comes forth from the city of darkness, I have abused [no man].

B30 Hail O Bringer-of-His-Peace, who comes forth from the city of Sau (Sais), I have not been over energetic (violent).

B31 Hail O Lord-of-Faces, who comes forth from the city of Tchefet (Heroonpolite Nome), my heart has not been hasty.

B32 Hail O Plan-Maker (thou who givest knowledge), who comes forth from *Utenet*, I have not transgressed my color (interbred with a foreigner?); I have not washed the god.

B33 Hail O Lord-of-Two-Horns, who comes forth from Siut, my voice is not too much about matters (have not multiplied my speech overmuch or was boastful).

B34 Hail O *Nefer-tem*, who comes forth from Memphis, I have not committed sins, and I have not done evil.

B35 Hail O *Tem-sep*, who comes forth from Busiris, I have not been abusive against a king.

---

8 Distress possibly due to injustice.

9 Appears to imply not being evasive or over-secret.

B36   Hail O Acting-with-His-Heart, who comes forth from the city of *Tjebu*, I have not fowled water.[10]

B37   Hail O Flowing-One, who comes forth from Nu,[11] my voice has not been loud (haughty).

B38   Hail O Commander-of-the-People, who comes forth from Sau [*his shrine*], I have not been abusive against a god.

B39   Hail O *Neheb-nefert*, who comest fort from the Lake of Nefer (*Saite Nome*), I have not made puffings-up. [12]

B40   Hail O *Neheb-kau*, who comes forth from the town, I have not made discriminations for myself (sought for distinctions).

B41   Hail O High-of-Head (whose head is holy), who comes forth from the cavern, my portion has not been too large, *not even* in my (own) property.

B42   Hail O *In-af* serpent, who comes forth from Aukert (the underworld or cemetery), I have not blasphemed against my god who is in my city.

Following the above protestation on behalf of the deceased, which was also inscribed on his sarcophagus, a priest addresses the gods for the deceased with words from the Book of the Dead. Typically they read, "Homage to you, O ye gods who dwell in your Hall of double Maati, I, even I, know you, and I know your names . . ."

What is significant about the above protestations is that their social constraints had to have been in practice even before the 1st Dynasty, over 2,000 years before they were engraved on the temple walls of the 18th Dynasty (1580-1350 BCE).[13] We already know that the

---

[10]   The deceased denies polluting the waters of the Nile or canals.

[11]   The abysmal waters of Nun.

[12]   Been insolent, boastful, proud or vain.

[13]   **James B. Pritchard**, *Ancient Near Eastern Texts Relating to the Old Testament,* **Page 34**. The text of the 125 Chapter of the Book of the Dead were gathered from the 18th to the 21st Dynasty.

deceased Egyptian had to pass an ethical test at the close of life in order to enter the hereafter of Osiris. This test was an examination of one's moral character while alive. Below are a number of extractions taken from Breasted's *A History of Egypt* (pages 65, 66) that further confirms the conscious belief in righteousness and virtuous actions by the Egyptians.

A noble of the 5th Dynasty had inscribed within his mastaba the following words:

"I have made this tomb as a just possession, and never have I taken a thing belonging to any person . . . Never have I done aught of violence toward any person."

Another Egyptian citizen states:

"Never was I beaten in the presence of any official since my birth; never did I take the property of any man by violence; I was doer of that which pleased all men."

An Egyptian noble, who governed a district called Cerastes-Mountain, was even more positive about his virtues stating:

"I gave bread to the hungry of the Cerastes-Mountain; I clothed him who was naked therein . . . I never oppressed one in possession of his property, so that he complained of me because of it to the god of my city; never was there one fearing because of one stronger than he, so that he complained because of it to the god."

It would be instructive to compare the Ten Commandments that Moses received from his god to the moral codes observed by the Egyptians. Upon review of the above protestations, it becomes evident that the Egyptian pharaohs and Priesthood imposed such rules in order to enforce social behavior. Table 3-3 presents the Ten Commandments in the first column and Egyptian laws in the second column. Comparing these two columns shows that the Ten Commandments are not new. Social laws of conduct extremely similar to them existed in Egypt before the 1st Dynasty (3400 BCE).

A review of the Ten Commandments against Tables 3-1 and 3-2 reveals that the Egyptians had practiced all but two of the commandments given to Moses by God since the 1st Dynastic Period. Recall that the rules were set down by the Egyptian kings and Priesthood in order to respect the gods. These rules included not performing an abomination that would degrade their beliefs or fear of god, not resorting to blasphemy, not interfering in the procession of a god, not stealing property belonging to the temple of a god, and not using abusive language against the god and king.

Table 3-3. The Ten Commandments and Egyptian Law.

Ten Commandments: *Exodus 20:3-17*	Egypt Law
1. Thou shalt have no other gods before me.	
2. Thou shalt not make unto thee any graven image, or any likeness *of any thing* that is in heaven above, or that *is* in the earth beneath, or that *is* in the water under the earth: Thou shall not bow down thyself to them, nor serve them: for I the Lord thy God *am* a jealous God, visiting the iniquity of the fathers upon the children unto the third and forth *generation* of them that hate me; and shewing mercy unto thousands of them that love me, and keep my commandments.	A11
3. Thou shall not take the name of the Lord thy God in vain; for the Lord will not hold him guiltless that taketh his name in vain.	A9, B38, B42

Ten Commandments: *Exodus 20:3-17*	Egypt Law
4. Remember the Sabbath day, to keep it holy. Six days shalt thou labor, and do all thy work; But the seventh day *is* the Sabbath of the Lord thy God; *in it* thy shalt not do any work, thou, nor thy son, nor thy daughter, thy manservant, nor thy maidservant, nor thy cattle, nor thy stranger that *is* within thy gates: For *in* six days the Lord made heaven and earth, the sea, and all that in them *is*, and rested the seventh day: wherefore the Lord blessed the Sabbath day and hollowed it.	
5. Honor thy father and thy mother: that thy days may be long upon the land which the Lord thy God giveth thee.	A1, A2, A3, B17
6. Thou shalt not kill.	A14, A17, B5, B12, B21
7. Thou shalt not commit adultery.	B19
8. Thou shalt not steal.	A20, A22, A24, A25, B2, B4, B6, B8, B10, B15,
9. Thou shalt not bear false witness against thy neighbor.	A1, A3, B9, B24
10. Thou shall not covet thy neighbor's house, nor shall thou covet thy neighbor's wife, nor his manservant, nor his maidservant, nor his ox, nor his ass, nor anything that *is* thy neighbor's.	A19, B3, B7, B34

As land became a priority and nomes grew into towns and cities, the Priesthood included moral and social codes that became necessary to maintain stability. The adherence to fairness and truth became essential as the Egyptian people became more integrated with each other in setting land boundaries, planning canals for the control of water from the Nile, growing crops, raising herds of animals, and building temples, sanctuaries and pyramids.

The Egyptians could not have had the first and forth commandment of the Ten Commandments for two main reasons:

a. Their religion had not yet advanced to the belief in one god; not until Ikhnaton made an initial attempt in 1370 BCE. It was during the ruling period of Ramses II that the Priests of Amon embraced the conception of a universal god by extolling *Amon As the Soul God*. It is clear however, that the sole god concept was developed and implemented by the Egyptians before Moses left Egypt and received the Ten Commandments.

b. The Sabbath observance occurred after the Moses Exodus and was dedicated to the Israelite God to celebrate His six days of creation. It should be noted however, that the concept of creation was already written by the Egyptian Priesthood by 2625 BCE, in the hymn, *The Creation by Atum*.

In summary, the Ten Commandments did not originate from the Israelite God. Eight commandments were conceived and written before Moses received and recorded them in the *Book of the Covenant*. It seems dishonest to advocate that the Ten Commandments are revelations from God when, eight of the ten commands are a restatement of the Egyptian code of conduct. The Egyptian people followed the code that was set in stone by the Priesthood more than 2000 years (3400 BCE-1250 BCE) before Moses.

The Egyptian code of conduct was more encompassing than the Ten Commandments. It must be acknowledged that the Egyptian was mindful **not to**:

Commit evil acts against men, use violence on a poor man, cause anyone to get sick, make somebody weep, cause anyone to suffer, have sexual relations with a boy, defile or degrade one's self, increase or diminish the measure of grain, falsify the measurement of land, add weight to the balance, take milk from the mouths of children, cut off water supplied to another, neglect offerings to the gods, cause crookedness in others (to be cheaters), tell lies, be contentious, practice usury, gossip, be overly boastful, cause terror in others, be angry, be unresponsive in matters of justice, be abusive, act hastily, be abusive against the king, yell at others, be a showoff (overly proud), make discriminations (prejudice and bigotry) towards others.

To pray to their gods and state the sins and injustices they did not commit against others reflects a high level of social consciousness. The social and moral codes of conduct that the Egyptians observed in their daily lives are to be admired. The code, "I have not taken milk from the mouths of children," is highly humane. The goodness in man, practiced at a high level of morality by the ancient Egyptians, gives this author, and I'm sure others, a sense of pride.

It is conceivable that God was at work from the very beginning by first introducing Himself to the Egyptians as the god of creation, Atum. This god, venerated as two phases of the sun, Atum and Kheprer, later became Atum-Re. As the Priesthood developed a high moral code of conduct that offered the promise of eternal life, Atum-Re became Amon-Re, the principle god of Egypt. By 1270 BCE, the Priesthood of Amon proclaimed, *"Amon As the Sole God"* of all creation. Today, many worshippers are unaware that they revere Amon as they announce his name as Amen in temples, churches, and mosques. They have been misled by religious leaders who continue to ignore the words of Jesus Christ stated in John's *Revelation* 3:14. There, Jesus proclaimed Amen as, *"the faithful and true witness, the beginning of the creation of God."* Rather than reveal the truth, religious leaders have taught their worshippers that Amen means, "So be it."

3.7 The Son of God Concept

Before introducing the most audacious belief agreed to by the Priesthood—that the king upon death becomes the creative and ruling god of the heavens and earth (Section 3.8)—we need to examine how the king came to be worshipped as a god. In Chapter Two, we learned that the Egyptians, as with people in other emerging civilizations, possessed a natural desire to interpret their surroundings and the skies above them. The beauty of nature and the objects that impacted and controlled their lives—the sun, water, vegetation, animal life, and the air they breathed developed an appreciation based upon wonder and awe. When reason could not be applied, fear and respect caused them to envision gods to which they could appeal. This interpretation of the world developed a spirituality within many of the early peoples on many parts of our earth. The Egyptians were unique because they developed their spiritual faculties in an isolated region, free from interference from other cultures.

At least three thousand years of spiritual growth blossomed as their prehistoric nomes grew into local towns. Through several periods of stress where the more powerful rulers expanded their territories through internal warfare, Upper and Lower Egypt finally merged into one united state around 3400 BCE. This union was controlled by two entities: the kings, who provided leadership; and the Priesthood, who advanced religious doctrine within each principality. As the priests articulated their beliefs in writing, a new form of communication was mastered. After many iterations, before the centuries that led to the Mosses Exodus, the priests refined and shaped the many concepts that are now incorporated in our monotheistic religions. In this section, we will explore how the concept of the king as the *Son of God* developed.

3.7.1 Horus, a Principal, Primeval God

The earliest surviving writings, *The Creation by Atum* and *The Pyramid Texts* (much of which appear in *The Book of the Dead*), reveal that the two objects of nature that had the greatest impact on the spiritual development of the Egyptians were the sun and the Nile. The sun came to be worshipped as a prime god who took on personal form with the name Re. He was imagined as two phases of the sun with the names of Kheprer and Atum. And, as previously discussed, the Nile was glorified in their earthly god, Osiris.

Prior to the Thinite family of kings being supplanted by the Memphite kings, the primeval god Horus was associated with the sun as a newborn child at dawn called Horus-of-the-East. He would then be praised as a hero in his prime of life at noon, and would later become an old man named Temu tottering with feeble steps into the sunset.[1] By the 3rd Dynasty, in the Delta city On (Heliopolis), Re became known as Khepri (represented by the beetle) and became personalized as Atum emerging, as did Horus, in youthful vigor upon rising. Like Horus, he assumed the role of hero during the noonday hours, and towards evening, also became an old man entering the western horizon.[2] In the past, when individual nomes were asserting dominance over others, Horus from Upper Egypt provided protection and success for the warring kings in battle. He was perceived as having the physical attributes of a man and the features of a falcon. Later, the Priesthood announced that Horus was the progenitor of their king and established the belief that he, the king, was the *Son of God*.

The other object of nature, the waters of the Nile, inspired the concepts of creation and rebirth into eternal life, which gave rise to the god of the people, Osiris (Refer to Section 3.5).

---

[1] **Homer W. Smith**, *Man and His Gods,* **Page 9**.

[2] **James H. Breasted**, *A History of Egypt,* **Page 46**.

Originally, Egyptians from different nomes associated Re with their own local symbols, but the vision of a falcon dominated, as the idea of a bird flying high into the heavens easily conjured thought that it was the comrade of the sun. The falcon was given the name Hor or Harakhte, which meant "Horus of the Horizon." The remarkable find of the Qustul incense burner, a fragment of which is provided in Figure 2-5, illustrates that this symbol existed around 3800 BCE and earlier. In Nubia, near the 2nd cataract just below Abu Simbel, the symbol of the falcon was introduced and gravitated to Edfu and then to Abydos where King Ka was buried in a double tomb (just above Thebes). We have noted in subsection 3.4.1 that this king had the symbol *ka* written within a "serekh" (Figure 3-3), and he was one of the first kings to include the falcon accompanied with the plant symbolizing Upper Egypt.

Therefore Horus was already a recognized god even though he was not described as one of the first gods of the Great Ennead in Heliopolis as cited in *'The Creation of Atum.'* Heliopolis, located in Lower Egypt, just below the Delta, was where the Priesthood authored the text of the Atum creation. In this document, carved inside the pyramids of Mer-ne-Re and Pepe II (6th Dynasty kings), we find that the sun-god Re is addressed as Atum-Kheprer and no reference is made to Horus. Atum became the prime entity of the ancient text as creator of the gods and it can be concluded that it was this name that later took on the forms of Amon and Amen, each associated with Re, such as Atum-Re and Amon-Re.

3.7.2 The King Becomes Son of Horus

The kings of Predynastic and early dynastic periods were known as the followers of Horus and were believed to be the incarnation of Horus. Remembered for avenging the death of his father Osiris, Horus became the god of strength, order, and justice. By assuming a divine kingship with Horus who inherited both Upper and Lower

Egypt, the king ruled all of Egypt. Table 3-4 reveals seven of the eight rulers of the 1st Dynasty who demonstrated their reverence by prefixing Horus to their names.

Table 3-4. First Dynasty Kings Named after Horus.

1	Horus Aha[1]	5	Horus Den
2	Horus Djer	6	Horus Anedjib
3	Meretneith (Djer's mother)	7	Horus Semerkhet
4	Horus Djet	8	Horus Qa'a

Because Horus had been known from Predynastic times as the god who provided protection and strength on the battlefield, the king assumed his name. More importantly, the king promulgated the belief that he was the son of Horus through the support of the Priesthood. This contention is based upon two facts: first, that the king acquired great power upon controlling the Upper and Lower regions of Egypt as the son of Horus who inherited both territories in the Osiris legend; and second, the king expressed his authority through doctrine and scripture written by the Priesthood, which created and advocated the beliefs accepted by the people. This was a symbiotic relationship between the shared authority of the king and Priesthood. As revealed in utterances carved within their tombs, some Egyptian kings used their authority to place them above the gods. Surely, the Priests supported the king by agreeing to inscribe on the walls of his tomb utterances that will safely secure everlasting life. In the following subsections, the reader will see that the kings of Egypt had become so powerful that they even claimed to be Lord of the Gods.

---

[1] **Marie Parsons**, http://www.touregypt.net/featurestories/earlydyn2.htm. Aha, probably the son of Narmer and his queen was Nithotep. It is thought that he may be King Narmer and his tomb is in Abydos.

3.7.3 Power Exerted by the Kings

Soon after the initial victories of unification by King Ka, he was succeeded by King Narmer (Menes). Historians have credited King Narmer with successfully unifying Upper and Lower Egypt and they use this momentous event to identify the start of the 1st Dynasty. This event has been commemorated with one of King Narmer's own gifts to his god, a 23-inch high, dark-green crystalline stone, which has been named the Narmer Palette. This carved stone illustrates the unification of Egypt by showing the king wearing the White Crown of Upper Egypt on one side and, on the reverse side, the Red Crown of Lower Egypt.

Figure 3-6 shows both the front and back of the palette. The front palette shows the king wearing the White Crown, and to infer strength and power, a bull's tail. The top level, on both sides of the stone, provides the king's name in a serekh which is flanked on each side by a cow's head that identifies one of the oldest known goddesses, Hathor.

Figure 3-6. The Front and Back of the Narmer Palette.
Http:/www.ptahhotep.com/articles/Narmer_palette.html

The lower left (front) palette of Figure 3-6 shows the king with a mace in his right hand and appears ready to smash the face of a kneeling man who may have been an important leader, as his name in hieroglyphics is written to the right of his head. Above the victim's head is the falcon symbol of Horus sitting upon the plants of a personified papyrus marshland. Each papyrus blossom represents the numeral one thousand, which signifies that the king had killed six thousand enemies. Below the feet of the king are two naked, fallen Deltaic enemies lying helplessly on the ground.

The reverse side shows the king wearing a Red Crown and holding a mace in his left hand. His right hand holds a flail, which symbolizes royalty. He is accompanied by his vizier and a female holding a scepter in her left hand. They are represented on a much smaller scale as they walk toward ten decapitated bodies. The central scene shows the elongated necks of two feline animals being tied together by two persons, symbolizing unification of the two parts of the country. The bottom level shows a bull trampling an enemy of the Delta to represent the king's strength and power.

Figure 3-6 shows the symbol of the falcon which illustrates: the king's reverence for Horus as the god of warfare; and the powerful association of Horus as the father of his success. This religious belief caused the kings to conceive themselves as the reincarnations of Horus, making them his sons. The veneration of Horus began long before the establishment of the Thinite line by King Ka and King Narmer. King Ka levied taxes in the Nile Delta, which indicates his successful conquest of Lower Egypt before King Narmer's reign. The sway of power demonstrated by King Narmer has been recorded on an ivory cylinder found in the temple of Hieraconpolis. It commemorates his victory over the Libyans, who consistently entered Egypt west of the Delta. The Narmer Palette described above is a testament of the Libyan nomes conquered in the western Delta. On this campaign, Narmer took 120,000 captive, killed 6,000, and plundered 1,420,000 small and 400,000 large cattle.[1]

The Narmer conquests did not stop the entry of Libyans from the west or the Bedouins and Palestinians from the east, nor did it end the constant uprisings from the Nubians south of Egypt. The kings of Egypt went to war repeatedly to demonstrate their authority and power over these invaders. Following Narmer, King Neterimu smote the northern cities of Shemre and the "House of the North." Late in the 3rd Dynasty, King Khasekhem named a year of his reign as the "Year of Fighting and Smiting the North." In this war, he took captive 47,209 rebels and commemorated this victory in the temple of Horus at Hieraconpolis with a great alabaster vase bearing his name and two remarkable statues of himself.

The authority and power that the Thinite Kings demonstrated as they vanquished their enemies made them rulers over the conquered peoples and their material resources. The expansion of towns and cities invigorated trade both within and outside of their borders; and created a remarkable growth of engineers, craftsmen and artisans, including administrators for their courts and accounting of their wealth. Soon, new structures were built, conceived by the marvelous imagination of man. As each new city came under the rule of the Egyptian king, its citizens added to the numbers of people who venerated the gods revered by the king. As a result, the Priesthood, which supported belief that the king was the *'Son of God,'* became stronger and more organized. This power of the state and organized religion created the perfect breeding ground for vanity, pride, and arrogance often found to coincide with power. The king, through the belief system advocated by the Priesthood, came to desire not just the hereafter on earth

---

[1] **James H. Breasted**, *A History of Egypt,* **Page 47**.

envisioned by the Osirian faithful, but to reach the heavens and reside with the gods.

The vision of becoming a celestial being, one with the gods, caused the king to attempt to insure that his royal existence would be perpetuated in heaven. He imagined his heavenly life to be an extension of his earthly one so that upon ascending to the throne, he would amass a fortune to erect a tomb equipped with all the appurtenances of royalty. He not only furnished his tomb with fine wines, maintenance, offerings, cattle, and his favorite objects of art and gold, but would eventually sacrifice his queens and servants to accompany him into eternity. In former times, the king did not place himself above his follow men and was buried with only his favorite objects; now he took other humans to the grave with him. The Priesthood advocated and supported this practice because it was consistent with the concept of the king as a *Son of God*. This religious belief that elevated the king to a God catered to his vanity, causing him to place himself above his fellow man.

Shown in Table 3-5 are the numerical mix of wives, concubines, nobles, couriers, servants, and slaves that the kings of the early dynastic period sacrificed in the belief that they were taking them into the other world. Some kings also immolated cattle for their journey. The taking of innocent lives upon one's own death is an example of fanatical thinking caused by religious beliefs. Beliefs developed by the Priesthood with good intentions, became compromised by their support of inhuman practices. The practice of sacrificing human life to accompany the king into the beyond continued into the Middle Kingdom. Homer W. Smith, in his book, *Man and His Gods*, indicated that Hepzefa of Suit was buried with 300 Ethiopians while Mentuhotep sacrificed six princesses.

Table 3-5. Inhuman Deaths by the Kings and Priesthood.

King[2]	Deaths	Comments
Aha	33	
Djer (Zer)	334	70 were from the royal harem.
Meretneith	41	
Djet (Zet)	174	
Den	?	
Anedjib (Enezib)	64	
Semerkhet (Semti)	137	
Qa'a	?	

3.7.4 The Kings as Gods in Heaven

As belief in eternal life became more formalized by the dogma advocated by the Priesthood, the king and affluent nobles developed a safer repository that evolved from a simple burial in the ground to a tomb vast in size and made of stone that eventually rose high above the ground. The height of the tomb depended upon the desire to be renowned by the people and/or gain acceptance of the gods; but this required wealth, raw materials, time, and the supply of skilled craftsmen, artisans, and workers.

By the 4th Dynasty, the greatest mortuary structure ever built was through the organizational skills of Khufu (2900-2877 BCE); known as the Pyramid of Gizeh, it lies in the city of Giza located near Cairo. This able king had the ability to mobilize his human and

---

[2]   **Marie Parsons**, http://www.touregypt.net/featurestories/earlydyn2.htm. Also, **Homer W. Smith**, *Man and His Gods*, on **Page 31** listed the four kings that the author has identifi ed within parenthesis and assumed their relationship to the names given by Marie Parsons

material resources to erect a vast, impenetrable, and indestructible resting place. For such an enormous project, much credit has to be given to the government under Khufu to support the construction of his pyramid. It was built with over 2,300,000 limestone blocks, each weighing about two and a half tons. Quarrying, transporting, and assembling these immense and burdensome blocks must have severely taxed the treasury. The Greek historian Herodotus has written that the pyramid required the labor of 100,000 men over a period of 20 years. The excellence of engineers and craftsmen that constructed the pyramid to a height of 481 feet, retain a length of 755 feet at each side of its base, and maintain an error of less than ten thousandth of a foot, is remarkable.[1]

By the 6th Dynasty, the impact of the belief in Osiris's resurrection and in life after death had already begun to encourage the common man to improve his resting place with the religious scenes, articles, and incantations that were once reserved for their kings. Tombs of the nobility began to be grouped around the colossal pyramids and their masonry structures had become so immense that a King, just a few centuries before, would have been proud to own them. Such a tomb of the noble class was built for the vizier of Pepe I (2591-2570 BCE). It contained no less than thirty-one rooms, and was a rectangular structure with its sides slanted at an angle of seventy-five degrees with the ground. With the exception of its rooms, it was solid throughout and reminded the natives of the 'mastaba,' which formally served as a terrace or bench before taking on greater height to accommodate the rooms within.

The more simple mastabas for the common man had no rooms within, only a false door on the east side by which the deceased, dwelling in the west, might enter the world of the living. This false door was finally incorporated into a chapel chamber within the masonry

---

[1]   **James H. Breasted**, *A History of Egypt,* **Pages 117, 118**.

and was placed on the west wall of the chamber. The walls of this chapel bore scenes carved in relief of the servants and slaves of the deceased at their daily tasks on his estate. They were shown plowing, sowing, and reaping the harvest of the fields; tending the herds on the pastures and slaughtering them for consumption; creating stone and alabaster vessels; building boats for the Nile; and producing all types of necessary items for the lord's welfare in the hereafter. These scenes would show a towering figure of the noble supervising and inspecting their labors as he had done before his death.[2] Such illustrations depicted the hereafter as an extension of their lives on the banks of the Nile and thereby provide us with a source of knowledge of their lives and customs.

It is noteworthy to observe that the Egyptians' view of the hereafter reveals a constructive and industrious life that emulates their earthly activities. In sharp contrast, the last monotheistic religion to have evolved, Islam, presents a conception of heaven that caters to the sensual appetites of men. As a review of the Judaic, Christian, and Islamic religions are presented in the later chapters, the reader will find in Chapter 9.0 that the Qur'an describes a god that rewards righteous men with a blissful life in heaven.

3.7.5 Pharaoh Becomes God of the Heavens and Earth

The realm of the heavens ruled by Re, Lord of the Gods, and the realm of the hereafter ruled by Osiris, Lord of Eternity, were in constant rivalry for the status of supreme god of the Egyptian religion. Both gods were worshipped by the Egyptian people. Although eternity in the heavens was at first reserved for the gods and pharaohs and eternity in the hereafter on earth was provided for all by the Osirian faith, the concept of a hereafter on earth was elevated to the heavens as the solar gods took precedence. Heaven became the realm of

---

[2]   **James H. Breasted,** *A History of Egypt,* **Pages 68, 69.**

everlasting life and has become a source of hope for monotheistic believers even in today's world. The Egyptians did not conceive the additional concept of a hell to provide punishment for the rest of eternity, as advocated by most monotheistic religions of today.

Noted in Subsection 3.5.3, Horus, son of Osiris, was acknowledged as the god that prospered and united the Two Lands. This honorable recognition given to Horus was widespread during the 1st Dynasty. However, with the establishment of Egypt's capital at Memphis, by the end of the 2nd Dynasty, the Memphite family replaced the Thinite family. The Priesthood in the Delta region began to emphasize the Solar faith, and by the end of the 6th Dynasty, the text of *The Creation By Atum*, carved inside the pyramids of Mer-ne-Re and Pepe II (Nefer-ka-Re), made no mention of Horus. With the ascension of Zoser of the 3rd Dynasty, a transition from Horus-Re to Atum-Re became a reality.

King Zoser (Djoser) ruled during the 3rd Dynasty (2980-2900 BCE) for almost two decades and through the ingenuity of his chief advisor, Imhotep, he had the first stone pyramid built for his mortuary tomb. It was designed by Imhotep initially as a mastaba that was nearly 38 feet high, about 227 feet wide and a bit longer in length. During Zoser's reign he continued to add additional levels until it consisted of six steps that rose to a height of 195 feet. It is believed to be the first large structure made of stone, and was encased with beautiful white limestone. This structure was followed by King Snefru (or Senefru), who built two tombs: one located between Memphis and the Faiyum (called the Red Pyramid); and the other at Dashur (called the Bent Pyramid), an isolated place just south of Giza. The Red Pyramid is the third tallest at 344.5 feet and is exceeded by the pyramids built during the 4th Dynasty (2900-2750 BCE) by Khufu (Cheops) and Khafre (Chephren), 481 feet and 447.5 feet, respectively.[1]

---

[1] **James H. Breasted**, *A History of Egypt,* **Pages 111-124.**

The magnificence of the pyramids was intended to recognize the power, leadership, and administrative control of the pharaohs from the 2nd through the 4th Dynasties. This was a period of unprecedented splendor in Egypt's history, during which the nine pyramids of Giza were built. One of these pyramids has survived and is recognized as one of the Seven Wonders of the World. By the end of the 4th Dynasty, the king transferred his allegiance from being the 'Son of Horus' to being the 'Son of Re.' This transition was successfully accomplished by the Priests of Heliopolis (Delta region); the same priests who were progressive enough to author *The Creation By Atum*.

In the vicinity of Memphis, the kings of the 5th Dynasty invariably added Re to their coronation name. The old Horus title continued to be used but receded into the past as the new designation, *'Son of Re,'* became the official pharaonic title for the reigning pharaohs throughout Egypt's history. The pyramid became the symbol of Re, and the devoted pharaohs envisioned the heights of these structures as bringing them closer to heaven. However, as the vast amount of resources required to build pyramids became scarce, sanctuaries consisting of a large forecourt with cultist chambers on each side were built. Included was a huge altar, and in the rear, a tall obelisk that rose from a mastaba-like base. The obelisk was the practical substitution for the pyramid, for at its peak sat a pyramid pointing to the heavens.

The discussion above reveals how powerful the pharaohs had become as they elevated their stature above the common man. Supported by a powerful Priesthood capable of directing the religious beliefs of his people to worship him as a *'Son of God,'* the pharaoh's vanity grew until he was no longer satisfied with monuments that reached the heavens. Vanity was replaced by arrogance. By the end of the Old Kingdom, some pharaohs not only claimed to be the *Son of God,* but the God of all creation. Below are some utterances that demonstrate such arrogance. The utterances illustrate that their desire for eternal life was no longer satisfying enough; now they sought to take even the place of Atum-Re as the universal God of all creation. In the Old Kingdom, the texts appear in the pyramids of Kings Unis, Teti II, Pepe I, Mernere I, Pepe II and Ibi (of 1st Intermediate Period). The utterances extracted below are from *Development of Religion and Thought in Ancient Egypt,* [2] and the *Pyramid Texts.* [3]

Utterances 173-4 and 273 are Similar

Extract 1: Clouds darken the sky, the stars rain down, the Bows (a constellation) stagger, the bones of Aker (hell-hounds) tremble, those beneath them flee in terror at seeing King Unis rise as a Ba (soul), *a god who lives on his fathers and feeds on his mothers*.

Extract 2: King Unis is lord of wisdom whose mother knows not his name. The honor of King Unis is the sky, his might is in the horizon, like Atum his father who begat him. *When he begat him, he was stronger than he*.

Extract 3: *King Unis is the Bull of the sky, who shatters at will, who lives on the being of every god, who eats their entrails*. Even of those who come with their bodies full of magic from the Island of Flame.

Extract 4: The protection of King Unis is before all the noble (dead) who dwell in the horizon. *King Unis is a God, older than the eldest*. Thousands revert to him, hundreds are offered to him. Appointment as 'Great One' is given to him by Orion, father of the gods. *King Unis has dawned again in the sky, [shining] as Lord of the Horizon*.

---

[2] **James H. Breasted**, *Development of Religion and Thought In Ancient Egypt*, **Pages 123-139**.

[3] **Taylor Ray Ellison**, http://touregypt.net/featurestories/pyramidtext.htm

Extract 5: The lifetime of King Unis is eternity, his limit is everlastingness in this his dignity of: 'If-he-wishes-he-does, if he-wishes-not-he-does-not', *who dwells in the limits of the horizon forever and ever.*

Extract 6: Lo, their (the gods) souls are in the belly of King Unis; their Glorious Ones are with King Unis. The plenty of his portion is more than (that of) the gods . . . *Lo, their souls are with King Unis.*
Utterance 274

(Since the utterances are typical, the name of the king is omitted.)

Extract 7: He has revolved around the whole of the two skies. He has circled the two banks. *For Pharaoh is the great power, that overpowers the powers. Pharaoh is a sacred image, the most sacred image of the sacred images of the great one. Whom he finds in his way, him he devours bit by bit.*

Extract 8: Pharaoh's place is at the head of all the noble ones who are in the horizon. For Pharaoh is a god, older than the oldest. Thousands revolve around him, hundreds offer to him. *There is given to him a warrant as a great power by Orion, the father of the gods.*

Extract 9: Pharaoh has risen again in the sky. *He is crowned as Lord of the horizon. He has smashed the backbones, and has seized the hearts of the gods. He has eaten the Red Crown. He has swallowed the Green One. Pharaoh feeds on the lungs of the wise, and likes to live on hearts and their magic.*

Extract 10: Pharaoh's dignities will not be taken away from him. For he has swallowed the knowledge of every god. Pharaoh's lifetime is eternity. His limit is everlastingness. In this his dignity of: 'If-he-likes-he-does. If-he-dislikes-he-does-not.' *He who is at the limits of the horizon, forever and ever. Lo, their Ba is in*

Pharaoh's belly. Their Khu's are in Pharaoh's possession, as the
surplus of his meal out of the gods, which is cooked for Pharaoh
from their bones.

The above extracts combine two powerful beliefs: (1) that the resurrected
king exceeds the power of even the creator God, Atum-Re, and (2)
the king lives off the bodies of the gods, absorbing their wisdom
by eating their hearts (thought to be the mind by the Egyptians)
and assimilating their khu's (souls) by eating their flesh. Emphasis
on eating the gods was the Priesthood's solution to sustain the king
once in heaven. The solar theology of Atum-Re was exclusive to
the pharaohs and the gods. Consequently, food that was formally
provided by the people who attained the hereafter on earth in the
Osirian theology, was not available for the heavens.

By the 6th Dynasty, the priests resolved the dilemma of obtaining
food in the solar heavens by resorting to clever assistance from the
gods. In the Pyramid Texts, Utterances 128-130, divine nourishment
is provided for the king: "Bring the milk of Isis for King Teti, the
flood of Nephthys, the circuit of the lake, the waves of the sea, life,
prosperity, health, happiness, bread, beer, clothing, food, that King
Teti may live therefrom."

The findings that the kings of Egypt became so powerful that they
believed they could attain immortality among the stars and even
replace the creator God, should be considered. Is the king to be
blamed for becoming so arrogant in believing that he was greater
than his creator? Or is religion, as taught by the Priesthood, to blame
for leading the king into a world of fantasy? It is obvious that the
indoctrination of a theology by the Priesthood was responsible for
shaping the views and conceptions that formed in the mind of the
king. In fairness, both the king and Priesthood may have shared the
authority to carve the utterances on the tomb walls. Although the
priests were subservient to the king, they had him believing from

early childhood that he was the *Son of God*, which inflated his vanity and gradually lead to the development of a distorted illusion of himself and his gods.

In summary, theology, like a scientific hypothesis, is constantly revised and updated in order to serve a useful purpose in society. Throughout Egypt's history, the Priesthood found it necessary to change their theology. This observation serves to reveal that as man's intelligence evolves to better understand the world and his relationship to it, his conception of God will also change.

Theology, taught by any religion is subject to change. Change is good, not because of mistaken ideas, but because it is necessary in order to make improvements. Man has learned that to survive we must adapt as technology continues to push the limits of our abilities. So too, religion must change and evolve to keep pace with the knowledge man obtains in his world. The Egyptian Priesthood, in the course of many generations, revised their theology and successfully blended the Osirian and Solar faiths. Later, by 1375 BCE, the Pharaoh Ikhnaton, initiated a change that reduced the multiple god concept to one god. The Priesthood finally got the message, and by 1270 BCE proclaimed *"Amon As the Sole God"* of all creation. This concept was borrowed by Moses in 1250 BCE and written in the initial writings of the Hebrew Testament around 950 BCE.

4.0 Father of the One God Concept

The greatest period in Egypt's history was during the New Kingdom. The Egyptians had ousted their foreign intruders back into the Asiatic lands of Palestine and Syria and subdued the Nubian kings in Upper Egypt. The start of the New Kingdom began with the Pharaoh Ahmose, who was the first to successfully run the Hyksos, a Semitic people that invaded Egypt in 1675 BCE, out of Egypt. From Thebes came a succession of powerful leaders who established Egypt's empire, illustrated in Figure 4-1. The Thebean pharaohs responsible for this successful growth ended after 205 years, with the reign of Amenhotep III. He was the father of the first pharaoh to conceive, develop, and implement the concept of one god.

After the death of Amenhotep III, his son Amenhotep IV succeeded to the throne in 1375 BCE and remained pharaoh for 17 years. He inherited the kingship at a time when the nation was being confronted by uprisings in the Asiatic regions, and his country sorely needed a military leader with the leadership qualities and aggressive nature of his grandfather, Thutmose III. Lacking his grandfather's military strengths for decisive action proven over 17 successful campaigns through Palestine, Syria, and as far north as the Euphrates River, Amenhotep IV inherited the sensitive and congenial traits of his father who was inclined to use diplomacy as opposed to being embroiled in battle.

4.1 Amenhotep IV Becomes Ikhnaton for His God

It is instructive to have some idea whether Amenhotep IV became pharaoh as a young boy or as a mature young man. Since Amenhotep III inherited the throne at the age of ten in 1411 BCE, we may estimate that the birth of Amenhotep IV occurred about six years later in the year 1405 BCE. Knowing that Amenhotep IV ascended to the throne in 1375 BCE, it is likely he was around 30 years old (1405-1375). He was not a boy, as was his father, but was a young man who had already formulated many ideas about the world around him.

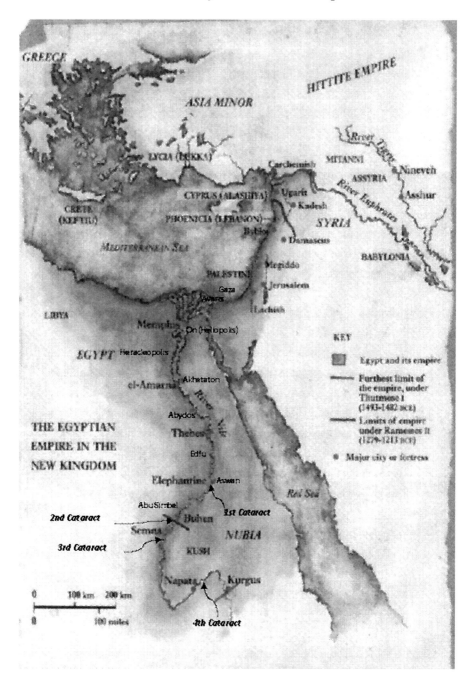

Figure 4-1. The Egyptian Empire in the New Kingdom.

Over the years, Amenhotep IV had to receive the finest education in the arts, sciences, literature, and, of course, religion. Knowledge of the great gods of Egypt must have been part of his early instruction. He also had sufficient time to compare his gods with the gods of the Asiatic vassals introduced through the intermarriage of their daughters. His grandfather, Thutmose IV, initiated the practice of intermarriage by marrying a princess who was the daughter of Shuttarna, King of Mitanni. This Assyrian king reigned in a province that was located between the Tigris and Euphrates Rivers, shown in Figure 4-1.

Amenhotep III also married a daughter of Shuttarna, the princess Gilukhipa. Dushratta (Tushratta), the son of Shuttarna, gave his daughter, princess Tadukhipa, to Amenhotep III and she became his second Mitannian wife. The physical attraction to foreign women was not only exhibited by his grandfather and father, but later, Amenhotep IV himself married the queen Nofretete, believed to be of Asiatic ancestry. He also married the daughter of Dushratta, the Mitannian princess, Tadukhipa. Exposure to the Babylonian gods had to be acquired through the three generations of intermarriage. Such exposure allowed this pharaoh to regard other forms of worship with curiosity, tolerance, and some form of acceptance. The wider worldview of other religious ideas would eventually lead Amenhotep IV to formulate the concept of one god.

Amenhotep's sensitivities as a young boy were nurtured by his mother Tiy and his favorite priest, Eye (Ay), who was Tiy's brother and the husband of his childhood nurse. Eye rose to the position of vizier and royal chancellor. His mother and Eye must have had a powerful influence over him. This influence was complemented later by his wife, Nofretete (Nefertiti), who was bestowed the title, Queen of Egypt. Her parentage is uncertain, but some scholars believe she was an Asian princess from Mitanni. Nofretete had six daughters, two of whom became queens of Egypt. She is best known for her portrait bust, found at Tell el-Amarna (formally Akhetaton). Reliefs found at Tell el-Amarna frequently show her at her husband's side, and the relief in Figure 4-2 shows her worshipping her husband's conception of god, Aton.

It is a wonder how events of the world and personal relationships fall into place to spawn a new stage in a man's beliefs. The following are some of the events and reasons that brought a sensitive pharaoh to dream about all living things being created by one external source; without this life-giving entity, he was convinced life could not possibly exist.

- *Amenhotep IV receives the finest education in all of Egypt.* Amenhotep IV grew up in a period of growth and prosperity whereby the luxury of absorbing a fine education in the arts, sciences, literature, and religion served to formulate the basis of a discerning, questioning, and creative mind.

- *Amenhotep IV grows up with an intimate circle of intelligent people who help to shape his views about the world.* The development of Amenhotep's views about the world was greatly influenced by his mother, Queen Tiy, and her brother, the Priest Eye. Both provided knowledge of the Egyptian gods, which later could be contrasted with the gods he learned from his relationships with foreigners.

Ample opportunity existed for Amenhotep to converse with people who believed in other gods. The Asiatic wives married to his father, and the people he would come to meet as he inspected many of the projects commissioned by his father, offered a source of other beliefs that could be contrasted with his own. Just as the Asiatic wives of his father were educated to a level above the commoners, the worldly views of the craftsmen and builders would also energize his thoughts. Gradually, as he matured, he would assimilate their differences and create a more worldly concept of god.

Figure 4-2. Ikhnaton and Nofretete Worshipping Aton.

- ***The priests of Memphis had begun to expand the creative power of Ptah, patron god of the architect and craftsman.*** Even before the New Kingdom began to flourish with the wealth brought into Egypt and their temples, the priests in Memphis had begun to ascribe some philosophical significance to their gods. As Osiris, god of the dead in the Old Kingdom, became associated with the concept of future accountability whereby the future destiny of the dead depended entirely upon the ethical quality of their earthly lives, so were the powers of their local god Ptah extended. Just as Ptah furnished all designs to the architect and craftsman, he was able to do it for all men, no matter their vocation. The world existed as thought in his mind, and his thoughts only needed to be spoken to bring into reality all matter, life, and humanity. Just as gods and men proceeded from his mind, all that they did was through the mind of Ptah working in them.

The power of Ptah's supreme mind was a breakthrough in Egyptian theology and was a radical change. Amenhotep IV saw that through the course of Egyptian religion, changes were possible, for even Ptah was replaced by the increasingly popular Amon-Re. The idea that Amenhotep IV had been exposed to several religious ideas and perceptions that had advanced within his own culture as he matured into manhood is to be emphasized. Absorbing these ideas, his thoughts advanced to a broader perception of god; a development that allowed him to conceive that all of the Egyptian gods could be replaced with one god.

- ***Egyptians had accepted the idea of a single intelligence.*** Their god, Ptah, provided the intelligent power for the creation of all things, beings and gods. The force by which this intelligence brought reality into being was through the spoken word. The Priesthood of Ptah expressed this in *The Theology of Memphis,*[1] several lines of which are printed below:

---

[1] **James B. Pritchard**, ed. by, *Ancient Near Eastern Texts Relating to the Old Testament,* The Theology of Memphis, **Page 5.**

There came into being as the heart and there came into being as the tongue (something) in the form of Atum. The mighty Great One is Ptah, who transmitted [life to all gods], as well (to) their ka's, through this heart, by which Horus became Ptah, and through this tongue, by which Thoth became Ptah.[2]

(Thus) it happened that the heart and tongue gained control over [every] (other) member of the body, by teaching he [3] is in every body and in every mouth of all gods, all people, all cattle, all creeping things, and (everything) that lives, by thinking and commanding everything that he (Ptah) wishes.

In the local area of Memphis, Egyptians accepted the idea that a controlling intelligence created his designs for this world through the spoken word. But this idea, conceived prior to the New Kingdom, had not spread into the minds of all Egyptians until the pharaohs expanded Egypt's boundaries into Nubia and Syria. The idea that a supreme force in the image of Ptah was responsible for the creation of all things, encouraged the sensitive mind of Amenhotep IV to envision his one god with such power.

- *The Egyptian priests had to eventually replace their local gods for the dominance of a world-god, as Egypt became a world-empire.* The priests had to finally agree on the name of a god that would dominate a more expansive view of their religion. The Memphite priests were in favor of Ptah, while the priests at Thebes would favor Amon, their state god. However, the High Priest of Re at Heliopolis pointed out that since the pharaoh was the son of Re and heir to his kingdom, Re must be

---

[2]   Ptah thought of and created by speech the creator-god Atum, thereby transmitting his divine power to all other gods. The gods Horus and Thoth were associated with the organs of thought and speech. Note: the Egyptian equated the heart as meaning mind and the tongue with speech.

[3]   Ptah controlled the heart and tongue.

the supreme god of the entire empire. Other priests in the local townships with their own obscure gods easily acquiesced and accepted the sun-god, Re. But as faith would have it, the father of Amenhotep IV had also recognized the power of the sun, for which the Egyptian word was Aton. Amenhotep III had named the barge upon which he and his wife Tiy sailed on the beautiful lake excavated for her, "Aton Gleams." Here is another event in Amenhotep's life that impressed upon him a reverence for the sun-god, and helped to form his concept of one god.

• ***Accession to the throne gave Amenhotep IV the power to implement his concept of one god.*** The greatest ideas fail to live in the minds of mankind without the support of a powerful authority. History has documented the spread of religions through the massacre of human beings attributed to the authority of Christian and Islamic leaders via the:

> *Catholic Holy Wars, Reformation, and Inquisitions; and*
> *Islamic Holy Wars (Jihad) and Muslim Extremists.*

Although the Catholic and Islamic religions have claimed the lives of millions of people, of the two faiths, the followers of Islam's Qur'an are still actively spreading their religion through the murder of nonbelievers. Judaism is not an exception to force by a people or zealous leaders to establish their religion. The Hebrew Bible relates that after Moses came down from Mt. Sinai and found his people worshipping the golden calf, Moses announced that those who were on the Lord's side should come to him. All the sons of Levi went to Moses, and he ordered them to kill those who abstained. Moses and the sons of Levi murdered about 3,000 of their own men in one day.[4] The two definite instances where Moses disobeyed God's command, 'Thou shalt not kill,' are presented in Chapter 7. But

---

4   **Holy Bible**, *King James Version*, **Exodus 32:26-28**

worse yet, the Israelite God voided his own command, *'Thou shalt not kill,'* by commanding Moses to invade Palestine. This command by a jealous God resulted in the massacre of innocent men, women and children belonging to the tribes of the Amorites, Canaanites, Hittites, Perizzites, Hivites, and Jebusites.[5]

Amenhotep IV did not resort to the killing of human beings to establish his new conception of god. He had one great advantage, through his position as Pharaoh of Egypt; he had the power to create and implement his vision of one god. This was, however, a great challenge that could not have been accomplished by a mere man; he had to change the religious belief system of his people, and had to replace all the gods of Egypt, except Re. Coalescing his new god with the sun-god, Amenhotep appended an explanatory phrase to the name of Aton: "Heat which is in the Sun (Aton)." Amenhotep was astute to attribute the new faith to Re as its source, and claimed that he was the channel of such a revelation. He deified the vital heat of the sun, acknowledging that without it, life was no longer possible.

- *The simplicity of one god could easily be understood over the traditional set of gods.* Amenhotep IV attributed his new faith to Re as his source of revelation and immediately assumed the office of High Priest of Re at Heliopolis. The older Priesthoods of Memphis and Heliopolis supported the new concept. Although radical, Aton at least presented the image of Re and appeased their jealousy of the rise of Amon who gained in popularity, praise, and wealth due to the conquering pharaohs from Thebes. Also, these priests may have realized that the unification of their gods into the one sun-god could be more easily accepted. Acceptance by their own people would take time because of their embedded beliefs, but people contained within their extended empire could easily understand the one-god concept.

---

[5]   **Holy Bible,** *King James Version,* **Exodus 34:10-14**

- *As Pharaoh of Egypt and High Priest of Heliopolis Amenhotep IV could implement his concept.* By assuming the title of High Priest, Amenhotep IV lessened the powers of the High Priests of Amon who represented the most powerful Priesthood in Egypt. They certainly opposed Amenhotep's new god, but with the support of the older Priesthoods in the north, the pharaoh's personal force of character, and the respect given his royal lineage throughout the land, the implementation of his new god became a reality.

To implement his vision of a monotheistic god, Amenhotep IV broke with the Priesthoods and proceeded with the immediate annihilation of the traditional gods. All the Priesthoods, including the Priesthood of Amon, were dispossessed. Temple worship of the local gods ceased and their names, wherever they could be found at the temples and monuments, were erased. On both sides of the Nile in Thebes, the names of Amon and the traditional gods were hammered out of the statuary monuments and within the temples. Even the royal statues and tombs of his ancestors, including his father's name which contained the prenomen "Amen = Amon" was cut. The huge thirty and ten foot stelas of his father, used to commemorate his accomplishments and included dedications to Amon, were mercilessly hacked out. The word "gods" was obliterated from the walls of temples and monuments. Finally, his own name was changed from Amenhotep, signifying 'Amon rests,' to Ikhnaton, which means 'Spirit of Aton.'

4.1.1 Ikhnaton's Temples and Hymns to Aton

Ikhnaton set his plans for the worship of his god into motion by having temples built for Aton throughout the Egyptian empire. He had the Aton temples strategically located in the three primary sectors of the empire: one was built in Nubia at the 3rd cataract; another along the Nile between Memphis and Thebes; and the third in Syria, where the site of the Aton city remains unknown. By his sixth year, Ikhnaton was living in the pronounced capital city of Aton named Akhetaton, which means 'Horizon of Aton.' The city was dedicated as the domain of his god, and fourteen large stelas, one of which was about 26 feet in height, were used to mark the boundaries of this sacred city. On the west side of the Nile, the city was built adjacent to a beautiful bay bounded by cliffs that started about 160 miles south of the Delta and formed a semicircle around the city. The natural borders of the cliffs and bay encircled the Aton city such that it was about eight miles wide north to south, from twelve to over seventeen miles long from cliff to cliff.

With Ikhnaton, three temples were constructed: one for the king, another for his queen mother Tiy, and the third for his princess Beketaton who bore the title, Maidservant of Aton. Surrounding these temples were the pharaoh's palace and the chateaus of his nobles, whom he rewarded for their loyalty and trust with opulent gifts of gold and silver. By this time, Ikhnaton no longer held the distinction of High Priest and relegated it to one of his more worthy favorites, Merire, which translated means, 'Beloved of Re.'

Ikhnaton's religious movement was extremely revolutionary, for he not only eliminated all the traditional gods replacing them with the sun-god Aton, but he also struck down the emotional concept that tormented people about the hereafter. No longer were the dead to confront the hideous Osiris demon for not living a moral and righteous life. Instead, tombs became monuments to the deceased. The use of magic rites and prayers formerly used by the deceased and portrayed on the temple walls and coffins to appease the monsters and allow humans to join the gods for eternal life were replaced. The tomb, coffin, and walls of the chapel now showed inscriptions and reliefs of fresh and natural pictures of memorable and proud events in the lives of the deceased; especially any events involving discourse with the king.

Although the old mortuary practices were banished, the pharaoh provided the royal favor of having his favorites buried in tombs hewed out by his craftsmen in the eastern cliffs. Many of the tombs show the king and queen standing together under the disk of Aton with one or more of his daughters at their side. In Figure 4-2, Aton is illustrated as the sun with life-giving rays terminating in hands, and in many cases, each holding the symbol of truth. Truth, a prime attribute of the ancient Egyptians, is extolled in Ikhnaton's last lines of *The Hymn to the Aton* (in Revelation to the King).

More impressive is the talent and genius of Ikhnaton reflected in the poems and hymns he wrote for his god. *The Hymn to the Aton* represents beautiful scripture and set the standard by which the Hebrew scriptures were written. It illuminates Ikhnaton's mission to change the direction of mankind's beliefs into the next stage of spiritual development. The subtitles are from Dr. James Breasted's book, *The Dawn of Conscience*. However, to provide a more recent rendition, the passages have been taken from *Ancient Near Eastern Texts* by James B. Pritchard (1955 edition). This hymn is one of two hymns found on the chapel walls of some of the noble's tombs. It is the longer of the two hymns and is presented in its entirety to afford the reader a clear idea of Ikhnaton's beliefs. Where two columns are provided, they illustrate passages of the 104th Psalm that resemble some of the verses to Ikhnaton's hymn. The following hymns give us a very good idea of Ikhnaton's temperament, his love and reverence for life, his belief in one god, and his continued acceptance of an eternal life in heaven.

The Hymn to the Aton [1]
Universal Splendor and Power of Aton

Thou appearest beautifully on the horizon of heaven,
Thou living Aton, the beginning of life!
When thou art risen on the green horizon,
Thou hast filled every land with thy beauty.
Thou art gracious, great, glistening, and high every land;
Thy rays encompass the lands to the limit of
    all that thou hast made:
As thou art Re, thou reachest to the end of them;
(Thou) subduest them (for) thy beloved son (Ikhnaton).
Though thou art far away, thy rays are on earth;
Though thou art in *their* faces, *no one knows thy* going.

Night, Man and Animals

When thou settest in the western horizon,
The land is in darkness, in the Manner of death.
They sleep in a room, with their heads wrapped up,
Nor sees one eye the other.
All their goods which are under their heads might be stolen,
(But) they would not perceive (it).
Every lion is come forth from his den;
All creeping things, they sting.
Darkness is a *shroud*, and the earth is in stillness,
For he who makes them rests in his horizon.

Thou makest darkness and it is night,
Wherein all the beasts of the forest do creep forth.
(Psalm 104:20)

The young lions roar after their prey;
And seek their food from God.
(Psalm 104:21)

---

[1]   **James B. Pritchard,** ed. by, *Ancient Near Eastern Texts*, 1955 second edition, The Hymn to Aton, **Pages 369-371.**

Day and Man

At daybreak, when thou risest in the horizon;

When thou shinest as Aton by day,

Thou drivest away the darkness and givest thy rays.

The Two Lands [Egypt] are in Festivity *every day*.

Awake and standing upon (their) feet,

For thou hast raised them up.

Washing their bodies, taking (their) clothing,

Their arms are (raised) in praise at thy appearance.

All the world they do their work.

The sun ariseth, then get them away,

And lay them down in their dens.

Man goeth forth unto his work,

And to his labor until the evening.

(Psalm 104:22-23)

Day and the Animals and Plants

All beasts are content with their pasturage;

Trees and plants flourishing.

The birds which fly from their nests,

Their wings are (stretched out) in praise to thy *ka*.

All beasts spring upon (their) feet,

Whatever flys and alights,

They live when thou hast risen (for) them. *(Psalm:11-14)*

Day and the Waters

The ships are sailing north and south as well,

For every way is open at thy appearance.

The fish in the river leap up before thy face;

Thy rays are in the midst of the great green sea.

Yonder is the sea, great and wide,

Wherein are things creeping innumerable.

Both small and great beasts.

There go the ships;

There is leviathan, whom thou hast formed to play therein.

(Psalm 104:25-26)

Creation of Man

Creator of seed in woman,
Who makest fluid into man,
Who maintainest the son in the womb of his mother,
Who soothest him with that which stills his weeping,
A nurse [even] in the womb,
Who givest breath to sustain all that he has made!
When he descends from the womb to *breathe*,
On the day when he is born,
Thou openest his mouth completely,
Thou suppliest his necessities.

Creation of Animals

When the chick in the egg speaks within the shell,
Thou giveth him breath within it to maintain him.
When thou hast made him his fulfillment within the egg,
        to break it,
He comes forth from the egg to speak at his completed (time);
He walks upon his legs when he comes forth from it.

Universal Creation

How manifold it is, what thou hast made!
They are hidden from the face (of man).
O sole god, like whom there is no other!
Thou didst create the world according
        to thy heart.
Whilst thou wert alone:
All men, cattle and wild beasts,
Whatever is on earth, going upon (its) feet,
And what is on high, flying with its wings.
The countries of Syria and Nubia, the
        land of Egypt;
Thou settest every man in his place,
Thou suppliest their necessities.
Every one has his food, and his time of
        life is reckoned.

O lord, how manifold are
        thy works!
In wisdom hast thou made
        them all;
The earth is full of thy
        riches.
                (Psalm 104:24)

(Psalm 104:27)

Their tongues are separate in speech,
And their natures as well;
Their skins are distinguished, as thou
distinguishest the foreign peoples.

Watering the Earth in Egypt and Abroad

Thou makest a Nile in the underworld,
Thou bringest it forth at thy desirest,
To maintain the people (of Egypt).[2]
O lord of all of them, wearying (himself) with them,
O lord of every land, rising for them,
The Aton of the day, great of majesty.
All distant foreign countries, thou makest their life (also),
Thou hast set a Nile in heaven,
That it may descend for them and make waves upon the
   mountains,   *(Psalm 104:6, 10)*
Like the great green sea, to water their fields in their towns.
How excellent are, thy designs, O lord of eternity!
The Nile in heaven, it is for the foreign peoples and for the beasts
of every desert that go upon (their) feet;
(While the true) Nile comes from the underworld for Egypt.

The Seasons

Thus thy rays nourish every garden,
When thou risest, they live, they grow by thee.
Thou makest the seasons in order to rear all that thou hast made:
The winter to cool them, and the heat that they may taste thee.

Universal Dominion

Thou hast made the distant sky in order to rise therein,
In order to behold all that thou didst make,
While thou wert alone,
Rising in thy form as the living Aton,

---

[2]   The Egyptians believed that their Nile came from the waters under the
earth, called by them Nun.

Appearing, shinning, *withdrawing or approaching,*
Thou madest millions of forms of thyself alone.
Cities, towns, fields, road and river—
Every eye beholds thee over against them,
For thou art Aton of the day over the *earth . . .*

Revelation to the King

Thou art in my heart,
And there is no other that knows thee
Save thy son Nefer-kheperu-Re Wa-en-Re (Ikhnaton),
For thou hast made him well-versed in thy plans and in
    thy strength.
The world came into being by thy hand, *(Psalm 104:28)*
According as thou hast made them.
When thou hast risen they live, *(Psalm 104:29)*
When thou settest they die.
Thou art lifetime of thy own self,
For one lives (only) through thee.
Their eyes are (fixed) on beauty, until thou settest.
All work is laid aside when thou settest in *(Psalm 104:23)*
    the west.
(But) when (thou) risest (again),
[*Everything is*] made to flourish for the king . . .
Since thou didst establish the earth,
And raised them up for thy son,
Who came forth from thy body:
The king, living in truth,
The lord of the Two Lands, Nefer-khepru-Re Wa-en-Re,
The son of Re, living in truth, lord of diadems,
Ikhnaton, whose life is long;
[And for] the great royal wife, his beloved,
Mistress of the Two Lands, Nefer-nefru-Aton, Nofretete,
Living and youthful forever and ever.

It is fascinating to become acquainted with Ikhnaton's adeptness and sensitivity in writing beautiful poetry expressing the creation of life by his god. Be it a chicken, birds, cattle, mankind, water, plants and trees, he expresses control of the passing day, night, and warmth of the Aton sun-god that instills life into his creations.

Aspects of this hymn are related to scriptural verses of the Bible and therefore demand further inspection. First, the tenor of the hymn is majestic and uplifting. The concept that Aton is associated with the *'Beginning of life!'* in the first two opening lines reminds us of the first line of Genesis,

> In the ***beginning***, God created the heaven and the earth.

It is possible to see how the thoughts of creative minds build upon previous strands of thought to conceive even greater notions of the beginning of life. The key phrase, *"Beginning of life!"* is associated with Aton, and throughout the hymn references are made to his beauty as being embodied in the sky and earth.

The beauty and humane tenor of Ikhnaton's hymn is founded in what is reasonable and true. In Subsection 7.4.1, the authors of Genesis overextended their revelations by incorrectly estimating the creation of the heaven and earth, for their estimate depicts time after the start of the Egyptian civilization. Worse yet, their estimate starts billions of years after the creation of the universe. Both Genesis and Ikhnaton's hymn are majestic and compelling in scope, but in terms of simplicity and truth, the revelation in Ikhnaton's hymn relates to what is real. Ikhnaton does not employ a fabricated revelation used to ignite belief in his all-powerful god.

The poignant lines of his hymn to his sole god Aton are repeated below:

> ***How manifold it is, what thou hast made!***
> ***They are hidden from the face (of man).***
> ***O sole god, like whom there is no other!***

The beauty of this phrase is so captivating that it had indeed inspired the authors of the Hebrew Bible to include it with a minor alteration in Psalm 104:24. Ikhnaton's hymn portrays a god who applies universally to all people. However, because his knowledge of the existence of other countries was limited, he was only able to mention the countries of Syria, Nubia, and his own land of Egypt. With such vision, he may be regarded as the first prophet in history to advocate the concept of one god for all people; a god not only for the creation of mankind, but the beautiful aspects of His designs in nature. Flowers, birds, mountains, seas, the skies, and other wonders are all wonderful gifts given by a beneficent god. For whatever reason, misguided individuals refer to Ikhnaton as a heretic and a criminal. Our world owes a great deal of respect to Ikhnaton for his forward-looking vision of a God who stimulated man's vision to acknowledge *Amon As the Sole God.*

A bit of Ikhnaton's philosophy about himself and man is revealed in his hymn, *Revelation to the King.* In it, he states how the world exists for man as his god rises and sets, controlling the labor that man performs and length of life. He credits himself as personally knowing his god above all others, and becoming wise through his god. But then, Ikhnaton credits his god for establishing the earth for him, raising all life for him, coming forth from Aton's body, and being the Son of Re. It is somewhat disappointing that "The king, living in truth" has expressed the idea that he was the incarnation of Aton and the Son of Re. However, we cannot fault Ikhnaton for this notion; he inherited a tradition in which all pharaohs before him had claimed that they were entitled to the throne because they were the incarnation of a god.

The *'Son of Re'* assertion is disappointing because Ikhnaton truly knew that he was born of human parents, just as he and his wives brought their children into this world. In spite of this fabrication,

Ikhnaton was certainly a man of exceptional ability who lifted mankind to the next level in the belief of God. It could not have been done by a mere man. It took the power of the throne; an exceptional education; and a will to challenge the Priesthood and religious traditions of the past that placed a wonderful idea into the arena of life. It is true that Moses, only 108 years after Ikhnaton's death (1358-1250 BCE), walked out of Egypt with a great number of followers believing in one god. But it was Ikhnaton who laid the groundwork of creating and disseminating, in just 17 years, the concept of one god. The Priesthood desecrated Ikhnaton's tomb and erased his name from many of his monuments, but a powerful idea that embraces mankind and lifts him to a better understanding of his world cannot be erased.

Ikhnaton's hymn does not attribute any of the ethical qualities of a righteous and moral god to Aton. The one attribute honored by Ikhnaton, who believed he was the son of Aton, is *'living in truth.'* He revealed himself and his family as they truly lived their lives. Open to his public, he presented himself and family at ceremonial functions; and allowed artisans to depict his family life in realistic and natural ways on their temple walls and monuments. Under his leadership, freedom of expression in art was seen through a lifelike mirror that reflected feelings and motion. Nowhere else has art risen to the level of capturing life as we see it in the flesh. The artists and craftsmen were able to describe the many positions of animals, be they on the run, sleeping, or in flight. The portrayal of the human figure was so natural that one could easily believe that its sculptor was a Greek master of the Golden Age.[3]

---

[3]   **James H. Breasted,** *A History of Egypt,* **Pages 355-378.**

4.1.2 The Naivety of Ikhnaton

The energy Ikhnaton put into his conception and establishment of the Aton god, blinded him to the practical world. One wonders how an educated man with his proud and masterful ancestors became insensitive to the very real threats rising in Palestine and Syria. The one fault with receiving a fine education, is that it encourages understanding, tolerance, and sensitivity towards the higher nature of mankind so that reason tends to precede action.

But reason may overshadow the need for direct force when it is required. The desire for reason also requires trust to be able to exchange motives and withstand political maneuverings. The more sensitive, trusting person, who prizes reason and the beauty of life is at a disadvantage when confronting an opponent who will not deal with honest intentions and seeks only power and even one's life.

The education Ikhnaton received, at least for this sensitive man, was just one element that prevented his lack of action in the face of rising Asiatic threats. There was also the influence of his mother Tiy; and her brother, Ay, who was close to Ikhnaton not only as family, but as his vizier. Ay, who was associated with the Priesthood, must have influenced Ikhnaton's religious ideas. His mother along with his queen, Nofretete, also shared a very close relationship with Ikhnaton. The love he received from these two women and religious instruction provided by Ay had to give him a great appreciation for the beauty and sacredness of life. Another wife, the princess Tadukhipa, daughter of the king of Mitanni, must also have influenced him in her beliefs. The history of Asiatic women, in the past three generations of pharaohs, had produced many Asiatic relatives, such as: fathers-in-law, brothers and sisters-in-law, uncles, aunts, their children, and close Asiatic friendships. This extension of love for foreigners had to give Ikhnaton an even greater disposition to tolerate, rather than fight, relatives who had vowed allegiance to Egypt.

A fine education enhancing Ikhnaton's ability to express himself eloquently; women being a strong influence in developing his more sensitive nature; and a number of relatives existing in the Asiatic territories, are all very real factors that played into his reluctance to confront the enemy. However, one has to sympathize with the state of mind of the illustrious pharaoh. He was a poet, a dreamer, who had the power to set into motion ideas that would elevate man's concept of god. It is impossible to divert a person from an idea so noble. There are those who would die for an idea; an idea that would further mankind in the quest for a cure or contribute to truth, knowledge and a higher quality of life—and this could have been the case for Ikhnaton.

Prior to Ikhnaton's ascension to the throne, his father Amenhotep III did not carry on the tradition of his ancestors; which was to show continued strength and control by marching, almost on a yearly basis, into the conquered territories of Asia and inspecting the lands for adequate supplies at their garrisons. Disaffection of the Syrian vassals was encouraged as a new power, the Hittites, moved into northern Syria. The Hittites, a non-Semitic people, existed as far south as Palestine and settled on the Orontes River. Before the coming of Israel, they existed as a number of petty tribes. Intermarriages with the Semites was a common event as they extended their people into the Euphrates, which was often referred to as the land of the Hittites. Hebrews sometimes intermarried (Judges 3: 5-6; Genesis 26: 34) and lived in relations both amicable and tyrannical. For example, the Hittites were made tributary bondsmen by Solomon (I Kings 9: 20, 21; 2 Chronicles 8: 7, 8).

Before reviewing the downfall of the Egyptian empire under Ikhnaton, the reader must become a bit familiar with his enemies. The leader, Labarna, founded the Hittite kingdom, and under later kings it was extended to cover all of central Anatolia (Asia Minor), located northeast of the Mediterranean Sea and extending down to its shoreline. The Hittites spoke an Indo-European language. Although they were a warrior people, they had an advanced civilization in terms of writing skills and invented the production of iron used to forge weapons.

The Hittite kingdom became strong enough to conquer the Old Babylonian empire around 1595 BCE and dominated Mesopotamia to 1200 BCE. But the kingdom itself was never stronger than its leader, and there were no clear laws for how a new king should take power. Because of weakness at the top, the Hittite kingdom entered a period of decline. After several leaders emerged, the Hittite king, Suppiluliumas I, became king around 1380 BCE and reigned for about forty years. Upon consolidating the Hittite homeland and improving its defenses, he applied himself to the task of conquering Mitanni, the principal enemy of his immediate predecessors. By a carefully planned attack from the rear by way of the Euphrates valley, he met little resistance and was able to enter and sack the Mitannian Capital. West of the Euphrates, the Hittites took control of most of the northern Syrian cities. The king of Kadesh put up some resistance but was defeated, and the Hittite armies penetrated southward, almost to Damascus. [1]

As shown on Egyptian monuments, the Hittites were beardless, with long hair hanging in prominent locks before their ears and over their shoulders. However, their own native monuments often show them with heavy beards. To appease their climatic demands, their garments were close fitting and made of heavy wool that extended down to the knees, and in some cases, the ankles. For their heads, they wore tall pointed hats that were rounded like the shape of a sugar loaf with a little brim; while their feet were in boots turned up at the toes. They were by no means primitive; though their art in stone appeared a bit crude, they were masters in the art of writing. Scholars have yet to decipher their pictographic records. However, they were adept in corresponding with their neighbors using the Babylonian cuneiform style of writing.

---

[1]   Internet: http://ragz-international.com/hittite_empire_to_c.htm

As formidable opponents, they employed foreign mercenaries in their infantry and they used the sword, bow and arrow, spear and axe. Their chief weapon, however, was the chariot, and they fought in close formation. Unlike the Egyptians, who would employ two men, the driver and bowman, the Hittite's more heavily built chariot used a third man who was a shield-bearer.

Not long after the successful campaigns of Thutmose III, whereby his fame as a military leader reached many of the nations of the north, the Hittites began to actively trade and correspond with the Egyptians. The interaction between them was so frequent that the king of Cyprus feared that Egypt might develop too close a friendship, and that his own position would become tenuous. The Aton god obsession that absorbed Ikhnaton's time and energy became so serious a fault, that he neglected to keep up sorely needed friendships with the Hittite kings. When Ikhnaton moved his new capital to Akhetaton, a Hittite embassy appeared with gifts and greetings including an inquiry from the Hittite king as to why Ikhnaton had ceased correspondence. The message may have been seen as a subterfuge by Ikhnaton in not returning a reply, for by this time, the Hittite empire now stood on the northern threshold of Syria.

From the very moment Ikhnaton became pharaoh, some of the disaffected dynasts were already moving against the faithful vassals of Egypt. Abd-ashita, a Semitic vassal, and his son Aziru, who were at the head of an Amorite kingdom on the upper Orontes, initiated an insurrection against Egypt. They formed a union with the Syrian prince Itakama, who had seized Kadesh, and together with the Hittites they took possession of the Amik plain that lies on the north side of the lower Orontes. Figure 4-3 shows this river cuts through the Amanus Mountains to the sea. Although three faithful vassal-kings fought to recover the lost territory, they were driven back by Itakama, the head of the Hittite troops. The three kings immediately wrote to the pharaoh about the traitor Itakama, but no response came back.

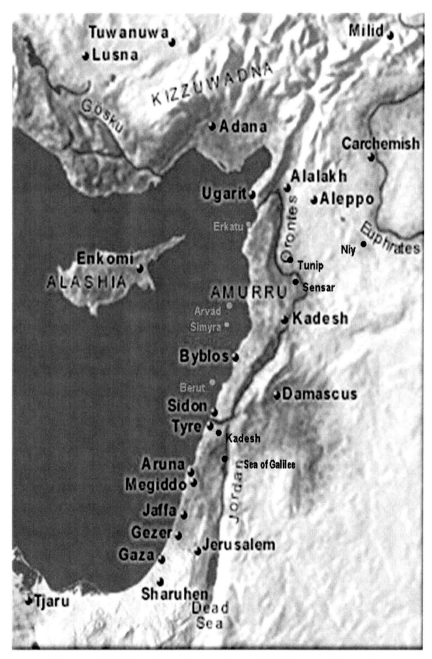

Figure 4-3. The Phoenician Coastal Cities and Orontes

Meanwhile, Aziru had advanced upon the Phoenician and north Syrian coastal cities, which he captured as far as Ugarit. There, he killed their kings, divided their wealth, and repeated this routine as he joined the Hittites to conquer the city of Niy.

Tunip was the next city in line of the Hittite advance and sensing the grave danger, the leaders wrote an urgent request for protection to the pharaoh. The request did not find a reply; for a response could not hold back the immediate takeover of Tunip and the city of Simyra. The request to Ikhnaton is very poignant and appears in Breasted's book. It reads:

To the king of Egypt, my lord—The inhabitants of Tunip thy servant. May it be well with thee, and at the feet of our lord we fall. My lord, Tunip, thy servant speaks, saying: 'Who formerly could have plundered Tunip without being plundered by Manakhbiria [Thutmose III]? The gods . . . of the king of Egypt, my lord, dwell in Tunip. May our lord ask his old men [if it be not so]. Now, however, we belong no more to our lord, the king of Egypt . . . If his soldiers and chariots come too late, Aziru will make us like the city of Niy. If, however, we have to mourn, the king of Egypt will mourn over these things which Aziru has done, for he will turn his hand against our lord. And when Aziru enters Simyra, Aziru will do to us as he pleases, in the territory of our lord, the king, and on account of these things our lord will have to lament. And now, Tunip, thy city weeps, and her tears are flowing, and there is no help for us. For twenty years we have been sending to our lord, the king, the king of Egypt, but there has not come to us a word, no not one.[2]

One by one, the cities along the northern coast fell to the Hittites under the strong and conniving leadership of Aziru. In response to the pharaoh's demand to appear at the Egyptian court to explain his

---

[2]   **James Herny Breasted**, *A History of Egypt*, **Page 382**

aggressive actions and provide retribution by rebuilding Simyra, the conspiring Azriu displayed Machiavellian skills. He used his friends in Egypt to deliver dispatches that explained to Ikhnaton that he was unable to come and give an account of himself at the Egyptian court, as commanded. The Hittites were in Nukhashshi, and he feared that Tunip would not be strong enough to resist them!

To the pharaoh's demand that he rebuild Simyra, Aziru explained that he conquered Simyra to prevent it from falling into the hands of the Hittites; and because he was defending the king's cities in Nukashshi against the Hittites, he would rebuild the city within a year. Aziru also reassured Ikhnaton that he would pay the same tribute as the cities formerly paid before he had taken them. Surprisingly, Ikhnaton responded by granting Aziru the year he had asked to appear in court. Aziru had evaded the pharaoh's response with impunity; for the gained time of a year to account for his actions was used to continue his war successes. What is shocking was Ikhnaton's lenient response, but more regrettably, his shameful naivety.

It is evident that Ikhnaton was averse to the use of force. He accepted another letter from Aziru indicating regret that an expedition against the Hittites in the north had deprived him of the pleasure of meeting the pharaoh's envoy, in spite of the fact that he had made all haste homeward as soon as he had heard of his coming! Added, was Aziru's excuse for not rebuilding Simyra. Ikhnaton accepted the information in the letter because of his trusting nature and: his preoccupation with establishing the worship of his one god Aton. In addition, there is a strong probability that he did not have trustworthy advisors, especially throughout his Egyptian cities where the people were divorced from his leadership. They did not truly understand his new conception of god that was to replace their old traditions of worship, and the Priesthood outside his sphere of loyal followers did not support the Aton god. All these factors were at play, as Iknahton failed to aggressively fight the insurrections by his vassals and the Hittite enemy that loomed as an imminent threat to Egypt.

In the city of Byblos, shown in Figure 4-3, Rib-Addi, a faithful vassal of the pharaoh, had sent dispatch after dispatch to the Egyptian court appealing for aid against Aziru. But the letters sent by the hostile dynasts so confused the court that the Egyptian deputy in Galilee misinterpreted the threat, and in error sent his Bedouin mercenaries into Byblos, overwhelming Rib-Addi's garrison troops. After sustaining the siege for three years, Rib-Addi was now at the mercy of the enemy. He fled to Berut to obtain help from the Egyptian deputy there, and having found no support, returned to Byblos to find his brother had seized control of the government. Adding to his distress, his brother, in his absence, had delivered his children to Aziru. In short time, the Hittites and the Khabiri, or Bedouin mercenaries commanded by Aziru, swarmed the city walls and Byblos fell. Like the kings of the other coastal cities, Rib-Addi was slain and with him, the last vassal of Egypt in the north had perished.

By this time, even the faithful vassals submitted to the enemy, which were the Khabiri; the Aramaean Semites. These Semites were Bedouin mercenaries of Azriu, who prevailed in the south, as did the Hittites in the north. The Khabiri coordinated strikes that took the cities of Kadesh, Damascus, Megiddo, Askalon, Lachish, and Gezer; an important stronghold of southern Palestine. The inhabitants of these cities fled in terror from the Khabiri who burned the towns and laid waste the fields. Many Palestinians left their towns and took to the hills or sought refuge in Egypt. Ikhnaton sent his general, Bikhuru, to restore order and suppress the Khabiri but he was entirely outnumbered. He advanced just north of Galilee, but soon retreated to Jerusalem and finally fell back to Gaza where he was probably slain.

The provinces of Palestine and Syria had now passed entirely out of Egyptian control. The south was in such a state of anarchy that even survivors of Bikhuru's army gave up any attempt to maintain control, and residents who did not perish joined the enemy. Traders' caravans were no longer able to move from city to city to sell their wares without being constant prey of marauding dynasts; for the Egyptian Empire in Asia had ended.

In spite of Ikhnaton's loss of the tribute he once enjoyed from his Asiatic vassals, in the twelfth year of his reign, he continued to be borne in gorgeous state on the shoulders of eighteen soldiers who received tribute from the cities of Egypt. As before, he continued to be steadfast in his propagation of his new faith. In addition to the three temples he had built in Akhetaton, the Gem-Aton temple in Nubia, and the Aton sanctuary in Thebes, he built other Aton temples in Heliopolis, Memphis, Hermopolis, Hermonthis, and in Fayum (Faiyum), a province in Upper Egypt.

Lacking the organizational and leadership skills of his great-great grandfather, Thutmose III, the construction of Aton temples was not matched with the conversion necessary to instruct his people about the virtues of his new god. Understandably, the Priests of Amon and the high priests of the upper Nile did not eagerly offer support. During all of Ikhnaton's reign, the power of the Priesthood both openly and secretly did all in their power to undermine him. The indifference of the priests throughout Egypt to assist Ikhnaton in the spread of his god was compounded by the emotional convulsions felt by the people throughout the land. The new faith deprived them of a deep-rooted belief in Osiris, their god of the hereafter and their solace in going from death to eternal life. They no longer could cling to the magical rituals, symbols, and prayers that had played such a strong role in protecting them from threatening foes and that had provided passage through the gates to heaven. Local gods were a point of reference in their lives and could immediately be associated with the life forms around them. The Egyptians therefore found it difficult, especially without tutoring and instruction from the priests, to understand the elevated concept of the Aton god.

Ikhnaton did not realize that a complex new idea must be slowly assimilated and nurtured with care. Powerful leaders that have introduced new ideas in the belief system of their people have failed to recognize that it may take many generations before they accept them. This axiom of learning was proven 1800 years after Ikhnaton's revolution by the Roman emperor, Flavius Theodosius[3] who banished the old Egyptian gods in favor of Christianity. Nevertheless, centuries after the death of Theodosius the so-called pagan gods continued to be worshipped in Upper Egypt. Changing the customs and traditional faith of a whole people is extremely unlikely in the short span of one lifetime. Despite resistance, the Aton faith remained a cherished dream of the idealist, Ikhnaton. Except for the few nobles and circle of people who were indebted to the throne for their livelihood, the monotheistic god Aton never replaced Amon; whose image was still embedded in the hearts and minds of the Egyptian people and subconsciously lingers on in modern times every time we use the word "*Amen*."

4.2 The Ignoble End of Ikhnaton's Reign

The loss of the Asiatic empire must have aroused indignation among those men whose relatives had served under Thutmose III, Amenhotep II, Thutmose IV, and with those who had seen the glorious and momentous days of Amenhotep III. The memories of many military men must have kindled their desire for a leader who would recover

---

[3]   Flavius Theodosius, Roman Emperor from 379-395 CE. After much debate and many bishop councils, he was the one person who brought Arianism and paganism to their ends in the Roman Empire. He made Christianity the official religion of the Roman Empire.

what had been lost. Fortunately such a man, an officer named Harmhab who enjoyed Ikhnaton's favor, was appointed to command the army. He was successful in winning the support of the military class. More importantly, he gained the favor of the Priests of Amon, who were hoping for someone who could further their goal of returning to the worship of their traditional gods.

As Ikhnaton's seventeenth year approached, he must have sensed the animosity of an offended people whose cherished traditions of worship had been abolished. The realization that the military and priestly classes where formulating plans to remove him from power led him to appoint Sakere to be his successor and coregent. Without a son to ascend the throne, Sakere, a noble who married his eldest daughter Meritation, was a logical choice. Ikhnaton survived on the throne some seventeen years, but by 1358 BCE, he succumbed to the forces around him and was buried in a tomb excavated for him and his family; a tomb where his second daughter Meketaton already rested.

The reign of Sakere at Akhetaton is fairly obscure. How he disappeared from the throne is not clear, for he was soon replaced by another son-in-law named Tutenkhaton (Living Image of Aton) who was married to Ikhnaton's third daughter, Enkhosnepaaton (She lives by the Aton). The Priests of Amon applied their influence in returning people to worship the Amon god. Soon after, Tutenkhaton conceded and compromised his allegiance to Aton by moving into the city of Amon (Thebes) in order to maintain his royal position. Akhetaton soon became a forsaken city, as its craftsmen in colored glass, granite, and metals found their artistry no longer needed. The people gradually left, and the temples fell to the resentful emotions of the Theban people. The once beautiful city of Aton became a desolate ruin and today it is known as Tell el-Amarna. It is here, in a low brick room that some three hundred letters and dispatches were found. These letters reveal the friendly relations initiated through the intermarriages with Asiatic princesses in addition to the pleas of the kings and princes as their cities fell to the Hittites, Khabiri mercenaries, and conniving dynasts who dismantled Egypt's sovereignty.

In Thebes, despite his new found allegiance, Tutenkhaton continued to worship Aton and made some repairs to the Aton temple. However, it did not take long for him to oblige the Priests of Amon and resume the worship of Amon. The new king restored the old festal calendar of Karnak and Luxo and in obtaining favor with the priests, conducted the greatest festival of all; the festival of Amon. Totally relinquishing his worship of the Aton god, he had the name of Amon and prenomen Amen restored on all monuments as far as Soleb, located in Upper Nubia, just south of the third cataract of the Nile river (a monument built by Ikhnaton's father, Amenhotep III). As his final concession to the Amon priests, Tutenkhaton had his name changed to Tutenkhamon (Living Image of Amon).

The length of time Tutenkhamon remained on the throne is not clear, but it could not have been more than a few years. He was able to exist as a puppet for the Amon priests, and Egypt still remained an empire without its Asiatic territories. Egypt was still in control of its lands from the Nile Delta down to the fourth cataract. The Nubians had become Egyptianized; wore Egyptian clothing and paid thier annual dues to the pharaoh's treasury. The reason for replacement of Tutenkhamon by another representative of the dismantled Akhetaton court is not known, but he was succeeded by Ay Itnetjer. It-netjer means, 'Father of God.' His throne name was Kheperkheperu-Re, meaning, 'Everlasting are the Manifestations of Re.'

The Pharaoh Ay was related to the Ikhnaton family as the brother of Tiy, who was married to Ikhnaton's father, Amenhotep III. Consequently, he was quite old, possibly seventy, when he was married to Tutankhamon's widow, Enkhosnepaamon (also spelled Ankhesenamon). Although a queen, she may have married the aged

Ay only to preserve part of her father's legacy since he was a close ally of her father and advocated his ideas. Ay's reign was brief, and it is believed that he died as he approached his fourth year on the throne. We learn from Hittite archives that after Ay's death, Ankhesenamon wrote to Suppiliumas I, the successful Hittite king who was encamped at Carchemish. She proposed to marry one of his sons, which would make him pharaoh. Suppiliumas agreed to her request and sent her his son Zannanza. But he was murdered when he reached Egypt. Ankhesenamon's image was hacked out of several monuments, and it has been suggested that her dealings with the Hittites may have disgraced her, resulting in her death.

It is believed that Ay, who was close to Ikhnaton as his mother's brother and vizier, was an exponent of Ikhnaton's ideas and is credited for leaving us with the two Ikhnaton hymns; one of which was previously presented in Subsection 4.1.1. It seems he had been tolerated by the Amon priests as he built upon the Aton temple in Thebes. Soon after his tomb was excavated in the 'Valley of the Kings,' he died. Upon his death, one or two pretenders to the throne appeared, and anarchy ensued as Thebes became prey to plundering bands of thieves. They forced their way into the royal tombs and robbed the tomb of Thutmose IV. The prestige of the Theban family, which gave Egypt the renowned pharaohs who had cast out the Hyksos and built the greatest empire it has ever known, had lost its highest honor of respect with the loss of the Asiatic territories. The weakness of Ikhnaton's leadership in a time of crisis, and the fact that he did not produce sons to carry on the Theban legacy, gave the Priesthood the opportunity to bring in a new line of pharaohs who would further Egypt's traditional ways of worship.[4]

So much is owed to the men who broke the hieroglyphic code and enabled Egyptologists to interpret the events that occurred in Egyptian

---

[4]   **James H. Breasted,** *A History of Egypt,* **Pages 379-395.**

history from the Predynastic Period to beyond the New Kingdom. Through their efforts, the modern world can appreciate the moral values and beliefs that not only made Egypt's civilization endure over thousands of years, but provided the beginning of Scripture infused in the Judaic, Christian, and Islamic religions.

In this chapter, the reader was given the opportunity to better understand the development of a monotheistic god, which was first introduced by the dreamer, Ikhnaton. Fate exposed him to both Egyptian and Asiatic beliefs and placed him in the position of a pharaoh. As pharaoh, he was capable of widening the scope of man's vision of God. He should be honored as a father who had the courage to change embedded religious beliefs and raise mankind toward a higher conception of god. His creative efforts belong in mankind's attempt to bring reason and truth into the spiritual realm, whereby one may envision an altruistic purpose to life.

5.0 Power of the Priesthood

Before the close of the 19th Dynasty and at the height of Ramses II reign, the Priesthood of Amon had become a vast organization which had acquired a great amount of power and wealth. It was during this dynasty, at the height of Ramses II reign, that much of Egyptian Scripture had advanced to proclaiming *Amon As the Sole God* and creator of all things. However, at the end of the Ramses line, with the reign of Ramses XII, there was a transition of power from the pharaoh to the High Priest of Amon. Wealth and power of the Amon Priesthood led to complete theocratic control of Egypt.

5.1 Wealth and Power of the Amon Priesthood

As a monument to his father, Ramses XII added to the temple of Khonsu a colonnaded hall preceded by a court and pylon to the Holy of Holies and the rear chambers (which were completed by Ramses III). Figures 5-1 and 5-2 illustrate the majestic beauty of the colonnaded court and rear chambers built by Ramses II in Abel Simbel. However, instead of Ramses XII name around the base of the temple walls, there was an inscription never before attempted. The inscription credited somebody other than the pharaoh for the building, and was written by the High Priest, Hrihor.

"High Priest of Amon-Re, king of the gods, commander in chief of the armies of the South and North, the leader, Hrihor, triumphant; he made it as his monument for 'Khonsu in Thebes, Beautiful Rest'; making for him a temple for the first time, in the likeness of the horizon of heaven . . ."

The transition of power from the pharaoh to the High Priest of Amon was complete. On both sides of the central door leading out into the Khonsu court are a pair of reliefs; each showing the procession of the god. But in the place which was occupied by the pharaoh for

Figure 5-1. Eight Columns of Ramses II Lead into the Sanctuary.
From: http://www.galenfrysinger.com/egypt abu simbel interiors.htm

Figure 5-2. The Inner Sanctuary of Ramses II at Abel Simbel.
From: http://www.touregypt.net/featurestories/abusimbel.htm

thousands of years, stands the High Priest Hrihor offering incense, with the pharaoh standing by receiving the conventional blessings of the god. An inscription on the doors also proclaims the High Priest as the "overseer of the double granary." Since grain was always Egypt's chief source of wealth, the position of overseer made him the most important fiscal officer in the state, next to the chief treasurer. The power and authority of the High Priest was complete. He commanded all the armies and was viceroy of Kush. As controller of the treasury, he ordered the refurbishment of old temples and construction of new ones. The newly transfered authority from the pharaoh enabled the Priesthood of Amon to manipulate their people through the pronouncement of oracles from their god.

As a visitor passes through the central door of the Khonsu temple into the inner hall, he will see the names of both Hrihor and Ramses XII. But as the visitor approaches the outer court, built by Hrihor, traces of the Ramses king vanish and only the High Priest's name, with Pharaonic titles, are inscribed on the royal cartouche. As the New Kingdom ended with the 20th Dynasty, the name of Ramses had lost its power and honor.[1]

Upon the pronouncement by Hrihor as the leader and commander in chief of the armies of the South and the North, Thebes became an independent sacerdotal principality. The unity of the kingdom under the sole responsibility of the pharaoh had ended and Egypt entered its 3rd Intermediate Period. During the 21st Dynasty, several High Priests ruled Egypt until the start of the 22nd Dynasty, when Sheshonk I became pharaoh of Egypt in 945 BCE.

5.1.1 The Extensive Wealth of the Priesthood

Beginning with Thutmose III of the 18th Dynasty, the pharaohs showed appreciation to their gods for their successes at war by giving gifts to the Priesthood. These gifts consisted of gold, copper, rare stones, animals, and slaves along with yearly tributes obtained from their conquered vassals of Syria, Palestine, and Nubia. The total worth of the Priesthood's holdings was not known until a long role of papyrus was found in a tomb near Medinet Habu (Thebes). Referred to as the Great Papyrus Harris, it provides an inventory that covered most of the temples in Egypt and enables Egyptologists to determine the total amount of property held by the Priesthood.[2] The Harris Papyrus describes the following holdings:

---

[1] **James H. Breasted,** *A History of Egypt,* **Pages 511-521.**

[2] The Great Harris Papyrus resides in a British Museum. It is a huge role 130 feet long containing 117 columns about one foot high. Found in a tomb near Medinet Habu, across the Nile River from Luxor, it is the longest papyrus to come from Egypt. This role was purchased by collector Anthony Charles Harris in 1855.

- Over 107,000 slaves; approximately one person for every fifty people were temple property. This equates to two percent of the total population in Egypt.
- Lands endowed for the temples amounted to 15 percent of the available land in Egypt, or about one seventh of the total land.
- Over 500,000 head of large and small cattle.
- Sacred fleets numbered 88 vessels and about 53 workshops and shipyards, which consumed a portion of raw materials that added to their income.
- Over 169 towns in Syria, Kush, and Egypt.
- The treasury taxed none of the Priesthood's holdings.
- The estimate does not include: the many statues lined with or formed from gold; the many bracelets, necklaces and amulets made of gold, silver, jewels, and precious stones; or the priceless vases, furniture, dinning utensils, and drinking cups all made from metals with elaborate inlays.
- The estimate does not include gold, silver, and copper stored in their storehouses and dedicated to the gods.
- he estimate does not include the great quantities of grain in their storehouses used to ward off times of poor growth of crops and to sustain the priests, slaves, and craftsmen.

What must be observed is the fact that it was the more popular gods, Amon, Re, and Ptah, that received the greater portion of endowments from the treasury. By far, the share accumulated by the Priesthood of Amon, through the popular worship of Amon, far exceeded those of all the other priesthoods put together. Besides the great group of temples at Thebes, Amon was revered with numerous other temples, sanctuaries, chapels, and statues including endowments for their maintenance throughout the land.

The borders of Egypt did not restrict reverence for the Amon god. This god had a temple in Syria; the one built by Ramses III in Nubia; and those built by Ramses II. This reverence was extended in the lives of Egypt's people by the increasing number of days for the Feast of Opet, the greatest of Amon's feasts, from eleven to twenty-four days; Ramses III extended these feasts to twenty-seven days long. On an annual basis, the observance of the Amon god averaged a feast day for every three days. It's no wonder that workmen in the city of Thebes had almost as many holidays as working days.

The indulgence in food, wine, and song had to decrease the mental abilities of the artists and craftsmen so that their performance, as verified by the art left on the temple walls, exhibited a lower level of creativity when compared to that produced during Ramses II reign. To compound the low regard for excellence, there was also a great influx of foreigners and poor treatment of workmen and slaves by the Priesthood, who made them forfeit pay and food needed for their well being. These factors decreased national pride, which affected their overall homage to and reverence for their gods.

An examination of the wealth attributed specifically to Amon puts in perspective the power gained by the Priesthood of Amon over all other priesthoods. Below is an inventory of Amon's wealth:

- Of all the land held by the Priesthood, the Priesthood of Amon owned over two-thirds.
- The number of slaves allocated to the Amon temples numbered 86,500, exceeding Re's by seven times.
- The herds of cattle for Amon numbered 421,000 out of about 500,000 heads for all the temples.
- Of the temple groves and gardens, Amon's numbered 433 out of a total of 513.
- Of the fleet of temple ships, Amon's numbered 83 out of 88.
- Of the 53 workshops for the temples, Amon owned 46.
- The Priesthood possessed nine towns in Syria for the worship of Amon in temples whereas, Re and Ptah had none.
- In Egypt, however, the number of temples for Amon was exceeded by Re who had 103 against Amon's 56.
- Amon's annual income was 26,000 grains of gold whereas, Re and Ptah received none.

- Amon exceeded all the other gods in silver 17 times; in copper 21 times; in cattle 10 times; in wine 9 times; and in ships 10 times.

From the above figures, we see that Amon's estate and revenues were second to the wealth of the king (this is speculation since the king's wealth is unknown). The Priesthood of Amon had clearly assumed an important economic role in Egypt, and the political power wielded by this community of priests became a force no pharaoh could afford to ignore. An indifferent attitude by a pharaoh who lacked the ability to compromise and work with the Priesthood of Amon could not have ruled for very long. Ikhnaton was a prime example of a fallen pharaoh who had ignored the multiple Priesthoods that were deeply entrenched with the traditions of an extremely long religious past.

5.1.2 Egypt's Ruling Priest, Amenemopet

It is not known how Amenemopet, either a noble or priest from the Delta region, came to be king of Egypt. He appeared in the 21st Dynasty after the rule of Hrihor from Thebes and Nesubenebded, who ruled from Tanis in the Delta region. Amenemopet became pharaoh in 1026 BCE, after Nesubenebded's son, Pesibkhenno I, who ruled for 17 years. From Thebes, Hrihor's grandson, Paynozem I, ruled for 40 years. Table 5-1 is provided to give the reader a clear picture of the pharaohs who ruled Egypt from the 12th Dynasty to the end of the 21st Dynasty.[1]

Documentation has not surfaced to reveal if Amenemopet had any influence with Paynozem I or his son, Menkheperre. After Paynozem's long rule of 40 years and Menkheperre's position of High Priest of Amon for 15 years, it appears his age prevented him from succeeding

---

[1] **James H. Breasted**, *A History of Egypt*, **Pages 598-600**. Internet: http:// members.aol.com/ egypymous1/ chrono, html. Throne names derived from Peter A. Clayton's book, *Chronicle of the Pharaohs: The Reign-by-Reign Record of the Rulers and Dynasties of Ancient Egypt.*

to the throne. It seems that Amenemopet had a strong connection with the Priesthood as he succeeded Paynozem to the throne. He had to have had some affinity with the Priesthood's worship of Amen, for his name contains the prefix Amen.

From Table 5-1 we see that after Amenmeses, who ruled for less than one year, there was a long succession of pharaohs before the prefix Amen appears again in the name, Amenemopet. This observation lends credence to the fact that after the High Priest Hrihor controlled Egypt the worship of Amen was complete.

It is a mystery as to why little is known about the pharaoh, Amenemopet. He ruled all of Egypt from 1026 BCE to 976 BCE; a period of 49 years. With the exception of the 30 Chapters of Instructions, no eventful accomplishments by Amenemopet have been found within Egypt or bordering countries. However, it appears that many chapters of *Instructions by Amenemopet* have been utilized in the Biblical *Book* of Proverbs attributed to Solomon, the son of King David.[2]

---

[2]   Internet Search: Enter "Amenemopet" and select link titled, *Instructions of Amenemopet—Wikipedia, the free encyclopedia.*

Table 5-1. Chronology of Egyptian Kings.

King / Pharaoh	Reign Years BCE	Yrs	Commentary / Remarks *Derived from Throne Name
12th Dynasty, 2000-1788 BCE Part of the Middle Kingdom (11th & 12th Dynasty)			
Amenemhet I	2000-1970	30	20 years alone, 10 years with son.
Sesostris I	1980-1935	45	10 years with his father, 32 years alone, 3 years with his son.
Amenemhet II	1938-1903	35	3 years with his father, 29 years alone, 3 years with his son.
Sesostris II	1906-1887	19	3 yrs with his father, 16 yrs alone.
Sesostris III	1887-1849	38	Uncertain period with his son.
Amenemhet III	1849-1801	48	Uncertain yrs with father and son.
Amenemhet IV	1801-1792	9	Uncertain period with his father.
Sebeknefrure	1792-1788	4	This Pharaoh was a Queen.
Total		228	
Allow for coregencies		15	
Actual Total		213	
13th Dynasty, 1788-1720 BCE 2nd Intermediate Period (13th-17th Dynasty)			
Wegaf Khutawyre	1782-1788	6	* Re Protects the Two Lands
Amenemhet V (Amen Intef IV)	(?)-1770	?	* The Heart of Re Lives
Hor Auyibre	(?)-1760	?	* Re Succors the Heart
Sobekhotep II	(?)-1750	?	* Powerful is Re, Protector of the Two Lands
Khendjer Userkare	(?)-1747	?	* Powerful is the Soul of Re
Sobehhotep III	(?)-1745	?	* Powerful is Re, He makes to Flourish the Two Lands
Neferhotep I	1741-1730	11	* Powerful is the Soul of Re
Sobekhotep IV	1730-1720	10	* The Soul of Re is Beautiful
Ay Merneferre	(?)-1720	?	* Beautiful is the Desire of Re
Neferhotep II	?	?	* Powerful is Re, Giver of Life to the Two Lands
14th Dynasty, 1720-1663 BCE			
Nehesey Aasehre	?	?	* Great in Council is Re

King / Pharaoh	Reign Years BCE	Yrs	Commentary / Remarks *Derived from Throne Name
15th Dynasty, 1663-1580 BCE **Period of Shepherd Kings and Hyksos**			
Sheshi Mayebre	?	?	* Seeing is the Heart of Re
Yakubher Muresurre	?	?	* Strong is the Love of Re
Khyan Seuserenre	?	?	* Powerful Like Re. Encompasser of the Lands. Ruler of Countries.
Apepi (Apophis I)	?	?	* Great and Powerful Like Re
Apepi (Apophis II)	?	?	* Spirit of Re
16th Dynasty, 1663-1580 BCE **Period of Shepherd Kings and Hyksos—Cont.**			
Anather	?	?	* Ruler of the Desert Lands
Yakobaam (Hebrew name is Jacob)	?	?	?
17th Dynasty, 1663-1580 BCE **Period of Shepherd Kings and Hyksos—Cont.**			
Sobekemsaf II	?	?	* Powerful is Re, Rescuer of the Two Lands
Intef VII	?	?	* Golden the Manifestation of Re
Tao Sanakhtenre I	?	?	* Perpetuated Like Re
Tao Seqenenre II	?	?	* Who Strikes Like Re
Kamose Wadj-kheperer	1573-1580	13	* Flourishing is the Manifestation of Re
Total		208	From 13th to 17th Dynasty
18th Dynasty, 1580-1350 BCE **New Kingdom (18th-20th Dynasty)**			
Ahmose I	1580-1557	22(+x)	Son Amenhotep I. * The Lord of Strength is Re
Amenhotep I	1557-1547	10(+x)	* Holy is the Soul of Re
Thutmose I	1547-1517	30(+x)	* Great is the Soul of Re
Thutmose II	1517-1516	1	* Great is the Form of Re
Queen Hatshepsut	1516-1501	15	Father Tuthmose I, husband Thutmose II. *Truth is the Soul of Re
Thutmose III	1501-1447	54	Father Thutmose II, mother Isis. Napoleon of Ancient Egypt * Lasting is the Manifestation of Re
Amenhotep II	1448-1420	26(+x)	Father Thutmose III * Great are the Manifestations of Re

King / Pharaoh	Reign Years BCE	Yrs	Commentary / Remarks *Derived from Throne Name
18th Dynasty, 1580-1350 BCE New Kingdom Cont.			
Thutmose IV	1420-1411	8(+x)	* Everlasting are the Manifestations of Re
Amenhotep III	1411-1375	36	* Lord of Truth of Re
Amenhotep IV Changed his name to Ikhnaton. Known as Akhenaton.	1375-1358	17(+x)	Mother Tiy, wives Nefertiti, Kiya, Merytaten, Ankhesenpaaten, Mekytaten. Son Tutenkhamon by Kiya. * Beautiful are the Manifestations of Re. Servant of the Aton.
Sakere (also Smenkhkare)	1358-1357	1(+x)	* Living are the Manifestations of Re
Tutenkhamon	1357-1353	4(+x)	* Lord of Manifestations of Re
Ay Itnetjer	1353-1350	3(+x)	* Everlasting are the Manifestations of Re
	Total	227(+x)	Minimum, 230 years.
19th Dynasty, 1350-1205 BCE New Kingdom Cont.			
Harmhab (Horemheb)	1350-1315	34(+x)	* Holy are the Manifestations of Re, Chosen of Re. Epithet: Beloved of Amon.
Ramses I	1315-1314	2	* Eternal is the Strength of Re
Seti I	1313-1292	21(+x)	Son of Ramses I. * Eternal is the Justice of Re
Ramses II	1292-1225	67	Son of Seti I. * The Justice of Re is Powerful, Chosen of Re
Merneptah	1225-1215	10(+x)	Father Ramses II. * The Soul of Re, Beloved of the Gods
Amenmeses	1215	x	Father Merneptah. * Eternal Like Re, Chosen of Re
Siptah	1215-1209	6(+x)	* Beautiful for Re, Chosen by Re
Seti II	1209-1205	2(+x)	Father Merneptah. * Powerful are the Manifestations of Re, Chosen of Re
?	1205-1200	5(+x)	Anarchy and reign of Syrian usurper(s).
	Total	142(+6x)	Minimum, 145 years.

King / Pharaoh	Reign Years BCE	Yrs	Commentary / Remarks *Derived from Throne Name
20th Dynasty, 1200-1290 BCE New Kingdom Cont.			
Setnakht	1200-1198	1(+x)	* Powerful are the Manifestations of Re, Chosen of Re
Ramses III	1198-1167	31	Father Setnakht. *Powerful is the Justice of Re, Beloved of Amon
Ramses IV	1167-1161	6	Father Ramses III. *Ruler of Justice is Re
Ramses V	1161-1157	4(+x)	Father Ramses III. *Powerful is the Justice of Re
Ramses VI	1157-1142	}	Father Ramses III. *Lord of Justice is Re, Beloved of Amon
Ramses VII	1157-1142	15	Father Ramses VI. *Powerful is the Justice of Re, Beloved of Amon
Ramses VIII	1157-1142	}	Father Ramses III. *Powerful is the Justice of Re, Helpful to Amon
Ramses IX	1142-1123	19	* Beautiful is the Soul of Re, Chosen of Re. Epithet: Beloved of Amon.
Ramses X	1123-1121	1(+x)	* The Justice of Re Abides
Ramses XI	1121-1118	x	* The Justice of Re Remains, Chosen of Ptah
Ramses XII	1118-1090	27(+x)	* Throne name not found.
	Total	104(+5x)	Minimum, 110 years.
21st Dynasty, 1090-945 BCE 3rd Intermediate Period (21st-25th Dynasty)			
Nesubenebded ** (Smemdes I) ** Ruled together	1090-1085	}x	* Bright is the Manifestation of Re, Chosen of Re. Epithet: Beloved of Amon.
Hrihor **	1090-1085	}x	* The First Prophet of Amon
Pesibkhenno I (Psusennes I)	1085-1067	17(+x)	* Great are the Manifestations of Re, Chosen of Amon
Paynozem I	1067-1026	40(+x)	* The Soul of Re Appears, Chosen of Amon. Epithet:Beloved of Amon
Amenemopet	1026-976	49(+x)	* Powerful is the Justice of Re, Beloved of Amon, Chosen of Amon
Siamon	976-958	16(+x)	* Like a God is the Manifestation of Re, Chosen of Amon
Pesibkhenno II (Psusennes II)	958-945	12(+x)	* Image of the Transformations of Re. Epithet: Beloved of Amon
	Total	134(+6x)	Minimum, 145 years.

Many similarities to Amenemopet's Instructions also exist in the apocryphal book, Ecclesiastes. These observations lend support of historical claims that there was a friendly Israeli-Egyptian relationship during Amenemopet's reign.

The *Instructions by Amenemopet* are but one example of his humanistic qualities. His legacy of 30 instructions is to be admired; however the Egyptians have had wise instructions written as far back as 2200 BCE, by the vizier Ptahhotep. The reader is encouraged to access the footnote link to read, *The Maxims of Good Discourse,* by Ptahhotep. It provides Ptahhotep's Prologue; his written teachings of 37 instructions; and an Epilogue that exemplifies hearing and listening; and concluding remarks. Ptahhotep's writings reveal a depth of moral and fatherly knowledge, and its contents fully competes with, and may surpass, *The Proverbs* by Solomon in the Hebrew Testament.[3]

5.1.2.1 Amenemopet is followed by Siamon

Following his rule, Amenemopet was succeeded by Siamon in 976 BCE. Little is known about this pharaoh; however, his name has the 'Amon' appendage, which may signify that he was related to the Priesthood in some capacity. In his 16-year reign, as with the passing of Ramses III, Egypt continued its steady economic decline. It appears that there were no great monuments built to maintain its people in the occupations of architecture, art, and labor for income, whether they be foreigners or civilians. It would seem that with all the years of experience in use of the Nile to irrigate their lands, the Egyptians would harness their knowledge and energy to at least maintain a strong and vigorous agricultural market. But with priests replacing the image of a pharaoh, the Egyptian spirit may not have been committed to building statues and monuments as in the past. Pharaohs had been regarded as gods. With a priest on the throne, the

---

[3]   Internet: http://www.maati.org/ptahhotep_maxims.htm

perception of the pharaoh as the son of a god had been replaced by a priest who did not have the transitional godly rights to the throne.

The *Son of God* tradition that lasted for thousands of years had been broken. The priests, with all their wisdom, may not have considered that claiming their own kind as the offspring of gods would not play as well with the Egyptian people as it did for the pharaohs. The High Priests made a grave miscalculation in believing that they could attain the same honor and respect as the godly pharaohs they replaced.

As a consequence of the priests' taking control of Egypt, there was a steady decline in the political and economic spheres as the Egyptian people became apprenhensive about their religious faith. It is no wonder that the memories of their royal ancestors were no longer respected. During the reign of Siamon, the bodies of Ramses I, Seti I, and Ramses II had to be taken from the tomb of Seti I and hidden in the tomb of a queen named Inhap to protect them from robbers.

The steady moral and economic decline caused the next pharaoh, Pesibkhenno II, who followed Siamon in 958 BCE, to again remove the royal bodies to a final hiding place in an old tomb of Amenhotep I, near the temple of Der el-Bahri. The officials who assisted in the transfer had their scribes record the details of the relocation alongside similar notes made for previous removals on the coffins. The coffins revealed that such transfers were dated back as far as 150 years before; these transfers attest to the moral and religious breakdown of Egypt that occurred with the first tomb robberies under Ramses IX.

After a reign of twelve years, Pesibkhenno II died in 945 BCE, ending the 21st Dynasty of the Tanite kings. Abroad, this dynasty was judged to be just as feeble as was the 20th Dynasty after the death of Ramses III. Though Egypt coexisted with or maintained control of Nubia, Egypt's power was no longer feared by Syria; in fact, they had not feared Egyptian power since the last victorious campaign of Ramses III. In addition, an internally weakened Egypt ruled by High Priests exerted minimal to no control over the dynasts in Palestine. It is during the 21st Dynasty that the tribes of Israel gained the opportunity to consolidate their national organization under Saul and David, whereby they gained victory over the Philistines [1].

For an illustration of the extent of Israel's conquest of Canaan (Jerusalem) and other cities during the reign of Solomon, refer to Figure 5-3. Note that Figure 5-3 indicates Solomon's kingdom was at its greatest expanse by 990 BCE. This does appear to be a reasonable date, as it lies in the 21st Dynasty under the rule of Amenemopet. More importantly, the coincidence of rule between Solomon and Amenemopet suggest a high probability that the Priesthoods of Egypt, Palestine, and Syria worked closely together in the cause of preserving the developed concept of one god. This suggestion will be explored in the next subsection.

---

[1]   **James H. Breasted**, *A History of Egypt,* **Pages 524-526**.

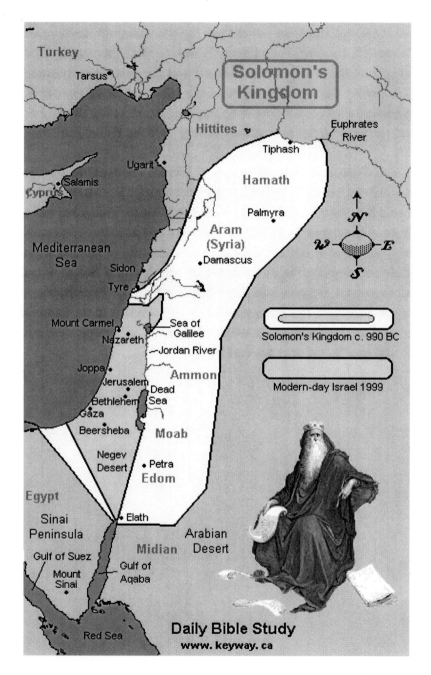

Figure 5-3. Territories of Israel During Solomon's Reign.

5.1.2.2 Did Amenemopet Assist the Israelites?

Below are listed several reasons why the High Priests of Egypt, Palestine, and Syria may have unified their efforts in preserving the belief in one god.

- Amenemopet ruled for 50 years, from 1026 to 976 BCE. He must have had strong organizational and political skills.
- Amenemopet was part of the High Priest establishment, which continued its authority to rule throughtout the 21st Dynasty.
- The prefix "Amen" implies Amenemopet was a religious man. With Egypt undergoing a moral and religious decay, there is a strong possibility that Amenemopet assisted the Israelites by sharing Egyptian Scripture to create the Hebrew Scripture.
- King Solomon, one of four sons of David and Bathsheba and 3rd king of Israel, was on friendly terms with Egypt and from the start of his rule, 992 BCE, he had a close relationship with Pharaoh Amenemopet to the end of his rule in 976 BCE. This relationship lasted for a period of 26 years (992-976 BCE). Early in Solomon's rule he married a daughter of a pharaoh (possibly Amenemopet's daughter) and built a palace for his Egyptian queen. There can be no doubt that the political intermarriage between Egypt and Israel and the close religious connections between their High Priests had formed a common bond to preserve the concept of one god.
- The Israelite priests were aware that through the belief in an all-powerful god could they unite their people. These priests had to have been influenced by the introduction of the Amon god and Egyptian temples in their land erected by several conquering pharaohs. As early as the reign of Thutmose III, Amon temples were in many of the garrison towns in Asia where Egypt maintained strongholds. An Egyptian temple was built as early as 1501 BCE in Byblos, located north of Tyre.
- The Priesthoods of both Israel and Egypt had to have formed a common bond over the years; their beliefs merging into a higher

conception of god, especially after Amon was envisioned the sole and universal god by the Priesthood of Amon throughout Egypt and the Asiatic lands by 1270 BCE.

- Egyptian theology had, during the New Kingdom, the most advanced concepts. Before Egypt, no other civilization developed the concept of a soul, a hereafter, and reverence for one god. Truth and morality, attributes of righteousness, dominated the scales of justice and determined who would be awarded eternal life. During the rule of Ramses II the concept of one god had inspired the Priesthood of Amon to teach the belief of a sole and universal god.

- The first written document that initiated development of the Hebrew Testament was the Yahwist Document created in 950 BCE, 26 years after Amenemopet's reign. It appears that the High Priests of Egypt assisted the Israelites in documenting their one-god belief.

- The universal acceptance of Amon, a variation of Amen '*the hidden one,*' became so ingrained in the mentality and spiritual reverence of the Egyptians that the name Amen would be evoked at the end of every prayer. This practice was emulated by the Israelites and continues to this day in the monotheistic religions of Judaism, Christianity, and Islam.

- It is highly conceivable that Israel and Egypt felt the pressure of a common enemy: the sea peoples and the Philistines, who were also a part of the People of the Sea that originated from Crete. This threat was imminent, as these people possessed Joppa to the Wadi Ghazzeh (West of Gaza), and the cities of Gaza, Ashkelon, Ashdod, Ekron, and Gath. [2] That Egypt assisted the Israelites in their conquest to ward off intruders from other lands is a strong possibility, because they had the resources of an army to suppress common enemies.

---

[2]   **Holy Bible**, *King James Version,* Dictionary of the Bible, Moses, **Page 49.** Regency Publishing House, Nashville, Tennessee, 37202.

After several centuries of Hebrew exposure to Egyptian religious beliefs, beginning with the invasion of Egypt by the Shepherd Kings and Hyksos, it is a remarkable coincidence that the first biblical document, the "J" or Yahweh Scripture, would be created in 950 BCE, 26 years after the reign of Amenemopet. This pharaoh ruled Egypt during Israel's conquest of Asian territory under the command of Joshua. Saul followed to become the first king of Israel and was later succeeded by King David. By 990 BCE, King Solomon controlled the territory illustrated in Figure 5-3. It is a remarkable coincidence that the reign of Solomon and Amenemopet overlapped for 26 years.

5.2 Amenemopet and Hebrew Scripture

Figure 5-4 illustrates that the first Hebrew Scripture, known as the Yahweh or "J (Jehovah)" document, was written in 950 BCE, about seven years after King Solomon's reign. Few people are aware that the Israelites had no written Scriptures before this date. The only known God-given commandments and judgments that were given to Moses were written by him in the *Book of the Covenant*. This may be confirmed by referring to the Hebrew Testament, Exodus, Chapters 20-23 and Chapters 25-30.

Figure 5-4 shows that the 992 BCE date for the start of King Solomon's reign is consistent with the 990 BCE date given in Figure 5-3. It also illustrates that both King Solomon and King David reigned during the 50-year period that Pharaoh Amenemopet ruled Egypt. This date reveals that Amenemopet had friendly relations with King David because they both had to deal with a common enemy, the Sea Peoples, including other Philistine sects. Such friendly relations had to be significant, because if these dates are correct, it is likely that Amenemopet gave his daughter to King Solomon in marriage. Solomon married an Egyptian queen early in his reign, which appears to indicate she was Amenemopet's daughter.

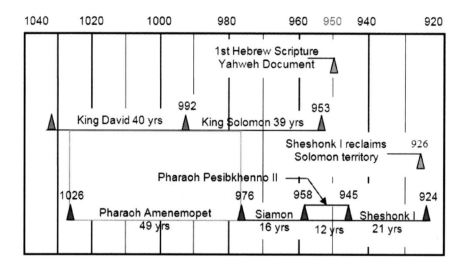

Figure 5-4. Amenemopet Rules During David and Solomon.

It is apparent that the Egyptians and the Israelites were on friendly terms during the reigns of Amenemopet (High Priest of Amon at Tanis) and Siamon (Son of Amon). Both of these Tanite pharaohs had an affinity for the worship of their god because they revered their god in their names: Amenemopet uses the prefix 'Amen' (with the suffix Opet being one of the renowned religious feasts of Egypt) and Siamon uses the suffix 'Amon.' Both men identify and honor the Egyptian god Amen by this use of his name.

5.2.1 The Sharing of Egyptian Scripture

We have learned that the Egyptians had built temples to their gods in the towns and cities of Palestine and Syria as early as the conquests of Thutmose III. These temples were built under Thutmose's command in many of the garrison towns in Palestine and along the Phoenician coast. A temple found at Byblos dates the exposure of the Palestinian and Phoenician people to the Egyptian gods as early as 1450 BCE. This exposure, together with several intermarriages between the Egyptian pharaohs and the daughters of dynasts in Asia, had to influence the religions existing in Palestine and Syria. The Asian people must have found such concepts as the soul, belief in god, and living their lives based upon truth and morality was a way to attain eternal life. Then, too, these foreign people exposed to the magnificence and splendor of Egypt's monuments and temples had to evoke awe and admiration.

After the rule of Ramses III, when Egypt was no longer a threat and the High Priests of Egypt had gained control (a period of 140 years to the reign of Amenemopet), there must have been an alliance between the priests in Asia and Egypt. The Egyptian priests recognized that it was in their interests to preserve their religion, for it had advanced to acknowledging Amon as a universal god. This development of Amon as a universal god by the Egyptian Priesthood had to influence the religions of their Asiatic neighbors. Consequently, the Israelite priests, exposed to Egypt's religion for centuries, had good reason to absorb and utilize the Egyptian Scriptures in their development and acceptance of one god. Both Amenemopet and Siamon, who were closely associated with the Priesthood, would have been more than amenable to complement the Israeli priests' endeavors to produce Scripture that would bring mankind to a higher conception of god.

5.2.2 A Natural Coincidence.

The conjecture given above, that the Egyptian and Israeli priests jointly developed the first Hebrew Scriptures, is based upon circumstances and events rather than suppositions and unrelated facts. It appears that this period of time for the sharing of theological precepts was ripe during the rule of King Solomon and the pharaohs, Amenemopet and/ or Siamon. It is a fascinating coincidence that during the hundreds of years that the Israelites believed in one god, they formulated their beliefs at the same time Amenemopet and Siamon, both strongly religious, were in power. The relative location of both these pharaohs in Tanis (the Delta region) rather than Thebes also highlights a close affinity and friendship with the Hebrews, who predominately inhabited this part of Egypt.

The timing of events whereby the Egyptian priests were in power and the Israeli priests drafted their first written Scripture around 950 BCE leads to a convincing conclusion that these priests jointly contributed to the creation of the Yahweh document. If it was not created on a conscious level by participating priests of both countries, then it would have to have been accomplished through plagiarism. There can be no doubt that the Israeli priests had possession of much of the Egyptian Scriptures and writings that contained the beautiful hymns to their universal god Amon and Ikhnaton's Aton.

We must also recall that, as a matter of policy, the Egyptian pharaohs had many of the children of prominent dynasts in Palestine and Syria educated within Egypt after they were captured. Then, too, there was the exposure by the Israelites within Egypt, Palestine, and Syria to the temples and religious worship of Amon. The extensive intermarriages of the princesses from the ruling pharaohs of Egypt and Asiatic Kings in Syria and Palestine had to cause acceptance of the Egyptian gods and exposure to their Scriptures. Also, by the 19th Dynasty, Amon-Re embodied Atum as the universal god and became the dominant god throughout Palestine, Syria, and Egypt.

The conclusion that the Israeli priests used Egyptian hymns and texts of wisdom to create their first Yahweh Document in 950 BCE is reasonable when one considers past events and becomes aware that the Hebrew Scriptures not only emulate Egyptian beliefs and reverence for one God that created all things, but the similarities between the ideas and word patterns expressed in these Scriptures and Egyptian texts are overwhelming.

6.0 Amen, the Universal God

Today, Amen has survived usage in the Judaic, Christian and Islamic religions. Amen is announced at the end of a prayer, supplication, and expression of praise, thanks, or approval. Although not taught by Christian leaders, Jesus Christ in John's Revelation, 3:14 of the New Testament, clearly states that *Amen* was the beginning of the creation of God:

> *These things saith the Amen, the faithful and true witness, the beginning of the creation of God.*

Many followers of the Judaic, Christian, and Islamic religions have not been informed that Amen was worshipped as the greatest Egyptian God for thousands of years. There has also been confusion as to why the names Amon and Amen are interchangeable. Table 5-1 provides a ready reference of the chronology of Egyptian pharaohs, beginning with the second half of the Middle Kingdom. It is to be noted that Amen began to be used in the throne name of pharaohs as early as 2000 BCE with Amenemhet I. From a vigorous Theban family of royal blood, Amenemhet assumed the throne as first king of the 12th Dynasty. With the unprecedented skill of a great statesman, he succeeded in gaining the support of many of the local nobles and nomarchs who rose to power during the Old Kingdom and 1st Intermediate Period. It was Amenemhet I that reestablished the bureaucratic state of the Old Kingdom and initiated Egypt's second great period of productive development, the Middle Kingdom.

After the expulsion of the Hyksos from Egypt by the successful pharaohs of the 18th Dynasty, the reverence for Amon became more pronounced as temples sprang up both in Egypt and in the conquered lands of Palestine and Syria. The use of Amen as part of a pharaoh's throne name began as early as 2000 BCE, whereas the use of Amon was introduced in the 18th Dynasty with the young

Pharaoh Tutenkh*amon*. By this time, the pharaohs and Priesthood of Amon had promoted their local god in Thebes as their principal god. Amon came to be worshipped as the sole and universal god during the rule of Ramses II. In spite of the popularity of Amon, it cannot be overlooked that the pharaohs used Amen in their throne names before the use of Amon. Table 5-1 reveals that the pharaohs' use of Amen occurred 12 times and Amon only twice. After 958 BCE, the end of Siamon's reign, the use of Amen and Amon within a throne name was no longer used. Causes for this omittance may be due to foreign invasions and an apparent loss of reverence by the Egyptian people who may have lost trust in their Priesthood after the Hebrew priests wrote Scripture in 950 BCE that emulated the Egyptian belief in one God.

6.1 Amen, a God and a Revered Word

Religious leaders of the three monotheistic religions—Judaism, Christianity, and Islam—have not instructed modern man to the true meaning of *Amen*. People announce this holy word at the end of every prayer, supplication, expression of thanks, and act of reverence to the God they worship. Yet, few people know the word's origin. Most people are familiar with the *Amen* definition taught by the monotheistic religions, which is the proverbial 'So be it.' This definition of *Amen* in Webster's Ninth New Collegiate Dictionary (Copyright 1987) falls far short of the three definitions provided in the Britannica World Language Dictionary (Funk and Wagnall's Standard Edition, 1959 Edition):

Webster, *Amen*—Used to express solemn ratification (as of an expression of faith) or hearty approval (as of an assertion).

Britannica, *amen*—*n.* So it is; so be it. **1.** The word amen at the end of a prayer or hymn, meaning *so be it.* **2.** Any expression of hearty consent or conviction. **3.** A concluding act or word; termination.—*vt.*

1. To say amen to; express hearty concurrence in or approval of. **2.**
To say or write the last word of. *Adv. Obs.* Verily; truly. [< Greek,
< Hebrew, verily]

Britannica, *Amen*—*n.* Christ, the true and faithful witness. *Rev 3:14*[1]

Britannica, *Amen*—*n.* In Egyptian mythology, the god of life and
procreation represented as having a ram's head; later identified with
the sun-god, as the supreme deity, and called Amen-Ra. Also spelled
Ammon, Amon (and Amun, Amoun, and Imen).

In addition to "So be it," the Hebrew usage of Amen includes truth,
to trust or believe, firm or faithful, true, verily, etc. In Isaiah 65:16,
emphasis is on truth as, "the God of truth", which is, "the God of
Amen." This usage is consistent with the Ancient Egyptians reverence
for *Truth* and was the most esteemed attribute of their God Amen.
Before we review the origin of Amen it will be instructive to return
to some of the definitions given above.

6.1.1 So be it

The interpretation of Amen as "So be it" is somewhat wanting because
it does not apply in all cases. For example, if we were thanking God
for anything that has transpired that gave us peace, happiness, health,
or a favorable outcome, to then say 'So be it' would be out of place
because the good fortune has already occurred. "So be it" would be
applicable as a supplication for something requested for the future or
a prayer that emphasizes the need for God's help. When one exclaims
Amen as a hearty approval of something, then the connotation *"So be
it"* does not apply. Rather, a thankful acknowledgement to God, by
simply announcing his name Amen, would be more appropriate. "So
be it" does not convey thankfulness to God for your good fortune.

---

[1]   **Holy Bible**, *King James Vers.*, **Revelation 3:14** by St. John.

6.1.2 Amen, a Revered God

In Revelation 1:11, Jesus Christ reveals himself to Saint John the Divine and instructs him to write down what he sees and hears into a book for seven churches he specifically names. Jesus, in Rev 3:13, states, "*He that hath an ear, let him hear what the Spirit saith unto the churches.*" Then, the most profound statement in the New Testament is presented in Rev 3:14; Jesus instructs John to write:

> *And unto the angel of the church of the Laodiceans write;*
> *These things saith the **Amen**, the faithful and true witness,*
> *the beginning of the creation of god;"*

This statement by Jesus Christ clearly reveals a truth about God. For, if Amen was indeed the faithful and true witness at the beginning—he is the God of all creation. Single-minded religious scholars may try to twist and reinterpret the words of Jesus in an effort to deny his acknowledgement of Amen. However, this reference to Amen reveals that the reverence formerly given to Amen by the Egyptians had never lost its impact, even though modern man has reduced its meaning to "So be it."

An Egyptian translation of Amen means "The Hidden One" and was associated with the air we breathe or the God of Air. As such, the Egyptians sensed or felt the air manifesting itself as gusts of wind but the god remains unseen and without form. The true nature of this god is therefore a mystery; he is unknowable and incomprehensible to human beings.

In summary, the definition for Amen as "So be it" is rather weak. It is a disservice to the intended reverence and adoration of God by the Egyptian people and acknowledgment by Jesus Christ.

During the reign of Ramses II, the Priesthood of Amon created a long hymn in praise of their imperial god, Amon-Re. After exposure to the concept of one god by Ikhnaton, the Priesthood wrote the hymn, *Amon As the Sole God*.[1] The following extracts illustrate their perceptions of god and emphasize that Amen was highly revered as the one God of all creation.

Amon As the Sole God, 100ᵗʰ Stanza

The first to come into being in the earliest times. Amon, who came into being at the beginning, so that his mysterious nature is unknown. No god came into being before him; there was no other god with him, so that he might tell his form. He had no mother, after whom his name might have been made. He had no father who had begotten him and who might have said: "This is I!" Building his own egg, a daemon [2] mysterious at birth, who created his (own) beauty, the divine god that came into being by himself. All (other) gods came into being after he began himself.

Amon As the Sole God, 200ᵗʰ Stanza

Mysterious of form, glistening of appearance, the marvelous god of many forms. All (other) gods boast of him, to magnify themselves through his beauty, according as he is divine. Re is united with his body. He is the great one who is in Heliopolis [3] . . .

---

[1] **James B. Pritchard**, ed. by, *Ancient Near Eastern Texts*, **Page 368 and 369**, Amon As the Sole God.

[2] The ancient connotation of daemon is not an evil spirit but rather a spirit of supernatural intelligence, a genius.

[3] **James B. Pritchard**, ed. by, *Ancient Near Eastern Texts*, **Page 3**, 'The Creation By Atum'. Note: the great one is Atum. From the text of the 6ᵗʰ Dynasty, carved inside the pyramids of Pepi II (Nefer-ka-Re) and Mer-ne-Re, it recalls the first creation when Atum of Heliopolis rose out of the waters of chaos and brought the first gods into being.

The procreator of the primeval gods, who brought Re to birth; he completed himself as Atum, a single body with him. He is the All-Lord, the beginning of that which is. His soul, they say, is that which is in heaven . . .

One is Amon, hiding himself from them, concealing himself from the (other) gods, so that his (very) color is unknown. He is far from heaven, he is absent from the underworld, (so that) no gods know his true form. His image is not displayed in writings. No one bears witness to him . . . He is too mysterious that his majesty might be disclosed, he is too great that (men) should ask about him, too powerful that he might be known. Instantly (one) falls in a death of violence at the utterance of his mysterious name, unwittingly or wittingly . . .

To the Egyptian belief that Amon is the sole god, *"the All-Lord, the beginning of that which is."* it is Jesus Christ that confirms Amen is, ***"the beginning of the creation of God."***

Jesus's confirmation that Amen was the faithful and true witness at the beginning of the creation of God acknowledges that Amen is God. Unfortunately, worshippers have been misled to believe Amen is simply a phrase, "So be it." Many of the Egyptian perceptions about God are still relevant for us today, but are ignored by today's religious institutions. They do not acknowledge God's original name Amen, but instead worship Yahweh, Jehovah, and Allah. Worse yet, portions of the Old and New Testament, and the Qur'an (Koran) are not acceptable to our present world. Many portions need to be revised or disposed of as they convey fear of God. We will later review portions of scripture where God authorized and sanctioned the killing of our sisters and brothers. A contradiction of the very first command given by God to Noah regarding murder:

Whoso sheddeth man's blood, by man shall his blood be shed: for in the image of God made He man. [4]

---

[4]   **Holy Bible**, *King James Version,* **Genesis 9:6**.

As clearly stated in Genesis, the taking of a life is not permissible. However, God does state that man shall defend the taking of life by eliminating the person who killed a human being. God, therefore, encourages the righteous to defend truth and justice by equal retribution, but He equally makes clear to us that man was made in His own image; to defile His creation, especially through murder in His name, is an affront to God. In spite of His command, today we have people with minds that have been misled; who kill in the name of God. Such distortion of righteousness has been caused by religious leaders who control the hearts and minds of their worshippers rather than imparting truth and wisdom, which embody the elements of justice and peace.

The above exposition provides another example of the need to revise the present Scriptures: they need to deal with the more loving aspects of God, the creator of all matter, organic and inorganic. The need for fear to induce belief may have been necessary in the early stages of social development, when the priests and pharaohs used it to create a common unity to strengthen their new civil, political, and religious orders. It is to be noted that the Egyptians did not force their religion upon the people; it was a natural outgrowth of thousands of years of humans learning to live together as one nome absorbed or overtook another in an environment isolated from the rest of the world.

It is foolish to ignore and distort the belief in *Amen*; a god that originated within the Egyptian civilization. To do so deprives believers of the complete history of their faith. To understand how the belief in God developed and why they announce Amen today brings respect and greater trust in their religious institutions. There is no shame to inquire about God and to learn about mankind's spiritual nature. The religious leaders of the Judaic, Christian, and Islamic religions have got to acknowledge that Egyptian concepts and beliefs form the core of their present religious beliefs. They have denied what they have learned from their Egyptian brothers simply because they wanted to form unique and separate religions for their own people. While there is nothing wrong with individuality, not acknowledging the contributions by the first formal religion of the world discredits, rather than elevates, a religion and its leaders.

6.1.3 The Origin of Amen

Egypt's first primordial gods of the Ennead presented in Section 3.3 did not refer to Amen, but dealt with other gods that represented physical elements such as the sun, ocean, earth and the heavens. It is not certain when Amen became a conceptualized deity, but the Pyramid Texts, described below, indicate that by the 5th Dynasty, around 2,650 BCE, Amen was venerated by the priests of Heliopolis as, the god of life and procreation. By the 18th Dynasty, Amen came to be worshipped as the principal god of Thebes, the Capital of Egypt. And by the 19th Dynasty, Amen was fused with the most powerful god, Re the sun-god, and became **Amon-Re**.

It is worthwhile to digress and examine the influence of the Egyptian concept of creation in Genesis of the the Hebrew Testament. Texts carved inside the pyramids of Mer-ne-Re and Pepe II of the 6th Dynasty, a period between 2625 and 2475 BCE, depict the beginning of creation by the first god, Atum. He was born out of the primordial waters that was characterized as the other existing god, Nun. There is a strong similarity in the Egyptian and Genesis concepts of creation. Both believed in a great body of water. In Genesis, after God created heaven and earth, light and darkness, He then had land emerge to divide the waters from the waters.[1]

The Egyptian creation concept also speaks of a body of water. The god Atum rose from Nun that existed as a limitless expanse of water. More than an ocean, Nun existed as motionless water around the margins of the world. In Genesis 1:6-10, God divided the waters from the waters to create the firmament, which He called Heaven. These

---

[1]   **Holy Bible,** *King James Version,* **Genesis 1:6-8.**

waters existed both above and below Heaven. God then gathered the waters under Heaven and created dry land to form the Earth and gathered the remaining waters to form the Seas.

Therefore, the Genesis Creation begins with the primordial waters; much like the limitless waters attributed to the Egyptian God, Nun. This similarity is striking and not coincidental. There could have been many other innovative ways for God to create heaven and earth, yet the authors (high priests) of Genesis borrowed the Egyptian concept of primordial waters. Certainly God could have created heaven and earth without starting with water. Then also, what happened to the waters that were left above the firmament? Perhaps this is the water counted upon for rain from the skies. It should also be noted that Nun had the power to destroy the world and begin the cycle again if mankind no longer respected Re. Surely this is reminiscent of the myth of God's Flood (Noah's Flood is a misnomer) whereby sinners who did not obey His commands were destroyed and the cycle of life continued with the survivors from the ark.

Although Amen came into existence as the 'Hidden One' at the end of the 5th Dynasty as verified by the Pyramid Texts below, he was not identified as the first primordial god. It is possible, however, that Atum may be an alternate for the name, Amen. For, by the 19th Dynasty, Amen was the principle god of Thebes and became known as the creator of all gods, matter, and life. He even embodied the great god Atum who, as described above, was the first primordial god. The transformation of Atum to Amen is illustrated by the following excerpts from *Amon As the Sole God* and clearly indicates that Amon is the embodiment of Atum:

*The first to come into being in the earliest times, **Amon**, who came into being at the beginning, so that his mysterious nature is unknown. No god came into being before him; there was no other god with him, so that he might tell his form . . .*

*The procreator of the primeval gods, who brought Re to birth; he completed himself as **Atum**, a single body with him. He is the All-Lord, the beginning of that which is. His **soul**, they say, is that which is in heaven . . .*

The above excerpts show the flexibility of the Egyptians to be able to transform the conception of Atum into a universal God, Amon-Re. By the 19th Dynasty, the concept of *Amon As the Sole God* incorporated the concept of a soul, which was formerly referred to as the ka. This concept by the Priesthood became an accepted belief by the Egyptians. The idea of a soul, a replacement of the *ka* and *ba* (hence, another transformation), made their God demand a greater morality from mankind enabling them to join Him for eternity after leading a righteous life. It remains for today's religious leaders to follow these examples of changing spiritual beliefs. Just as Ikhnaton was innovative in consolidating multiple gods into one universal god, today's religious leaders must also be courageous enough to improve their Holy Scriptures in order to keep pace with an ever changing, more civilized, and educated populace. If they do not do so, their congregants will find their messages increaseingly irrelevant.

6.1.4 The Pyramid Texts

The Pyramid Texts are religious literature which reflect ancient Egyptian beliefs. Thousands of lines of hieroglyphics were written on the walls of the early Egyptian pyramids at Sakkara and date back to the 5th and 6th Dynasties (2750-2475 BCE) of the Old Kingdom. The texts provide evidence that their initial compositions were conceived as early as the Predynastic Period (4500-3400 BCE), making reference as they do to hostilities between the kings of the North (Lower Egypt) and the South (Upper Egypt) occurring before the 1st Dynasty. This body of text includes drama, hymns, litanies, magical texts, offerings, rituals, prayers, the ascension and arrival of pharaoh in heaven, and miscellaneous other writings. The Pyramid

Texts are the oldest sacred texts known and represent the oldest body of theology in the world. Utterances 273-274, Lines 398b-399b, from the Pyramid Texts, reveal that Amen, the 'Hidden One,' was known and worshipped by the Egyptians during the 5th Dynasty. Within the pyramid of the pharaoh, Unis, inscriptions on the walls of his tomb make reference to the hidden god Amen. Note that where an *N* appears, it would be where the pharaoh's name would be inserted.

The Pyramid Texts, Extract from Utterances 273-274

398b. N. dawns as the Great One, lord of those with (ready) hands.

398c. He sits, his side towards Geb (the earth).

399a. It is N. who judges with him whose *name is hidden*,

399b. (On) this day of slaying the eldest (gods).

6.1.5 The Attributes of Amen

One of the many attributes of Amen stated in the following subsections is his development into being the universal god of Egypt. His worship spread into the neighboring Asiatic towns and cities of Palestine and Syria. As early as the 18th Dynasty (1580-1350 BCE), as Amen became the dominant god and was introduced into Egypt's conquered territories, the Egyptian Priesthood began to expand their idea of god. The concept that Amen was the creator of all life preceded the introduction of Aton by the Pharaoh Amenhotep IV (Ikhnaton). However, it was Ikhnaton who conceived his Aton god to be the sole god of Egypt, and more importantly, the universal god of the world. His *Hymn to the Aton* clearly expanded the powers of his god into Syria and Nubia. Ikhnaton's vision would have included other lands, but his knowledge of the existence of other countries was limited.

6.1.5.1 Amen, the Universal God

The following excerpts from a *Hymn to Amon-Re*, from the Boulaq Papyrus residing in the Cairo Museum, are dated sometime in the 18th Dynasty.[1] It indicates acknowledgement and joy in praise of Amon-Re to the height of heaven and the width of the earth. These lines honor the Egyptian god as Lord of all lands after the successful conquests by Thutmose III. This perception by the High Priests of Amon in Thebes recorded this attribute with increasing frequency during the 19th Dynasty in the hymn, *Amon As the Sole God.*

Extract from the Hymn to Amon-Re

> *The chief one, who made the entire earth . . .*
> *Jubilation to thee for every foreign country—*
> *To the height of Heaven, to the width of earth,*
> *To the depth of the Great Green Sea!*

Ikhnaton was more specific in his praise of Aton as the god of other countries and ultimately, the entire earth. The following extraction clearly states Ikhnaton's perception that god is a universal force for all mankind:[2]

Extract from The Hymn to the Aton

> *The countries of Syria and Nubia, the land of Egypt,*
> *Thou settest every man in his place,*
> *Thou suppliest their necessities:*

---

[1] **James B. Pritchard**, edited by, *Ancient Near Eastern Texts,* A Hymn To Amon-Re, **Pages 365-367**

[2] **James B. Pritchard**, edited by, *Ancient Near Eastern Texts*, The Hymn to the Aton, **Pages 370, 371**

6.1.5.2 Amen, the God of Creation

In *The Hymn to Amon-Re,* the god Amen-Re is viewed as the supreme god that creates and sustains life. The following excerpts are provided to emphasize Amen as the "Creator and Maker of all that is:"

Hail to thee, Amon-Re, . . .

Lord of what is, enduring in all things, enduring in all things,.

Lord of eternity, who made everlastingness . . .
Who made what is below and what is above, . . .
The chief one who made the entire earth, . . .

Thou art the sole one, who made all that is,
[The] solitary sole [one], who made what exists . . .
Father of the fathers of all the gods,
Who raised the heavens and laid down the ground,
Who made what is and created what exists; . . .

Maker of all mankind, Creator and Maker of all that is . . .

Revisiting *The Hymn to the Aton,* introduced in Chapter 4.0, the eloquent pharaoh and poet Ikhnaton wrote:

How manifold it is, what thou hast made!
They are hidden from the face (of man).
O sole god, like whom there is no other!
Thou didst create the world according to thy heart.

Ikhnaton's Hymn to the Aton also states:

The world came into being by thy hand,
According as thou hast made them.

When thou hast risen, they live,
When thou settest, they die.
Thou art lifetime of thy own self,
For one lives (only) through thee.

To the above perceptions of Amen from "*A Hymn to Amon-Re*" and Ikhnaton's "*The Hymn to the Aton*," we must recall what Jesus Christ told Saint John the Divine to write some 1,500 years later:

"*write; These things saith the **Amen**, the faithful and true witness,*
***the beginning of the creation of God;*"**

Jesus, and the Egyptian hymns, conclusively confirm *Amen* as the God of creation and the beginning of the creation of God.

The leaders of the Judaic, Christian, and Islamic religions agree that they all pray to the same God. Yet the Hebrews and Muslims have assigned unique names to God: Yahweh (Jehovah), and Allah (which means One God), respectively. Although Christians honor the name of the Judaic God, they avoid saying Jehovah.[3] Christians refer to God as the Father, but also believe that God exists as Three Persons: God the Father, Jesus the Son, and the Holy Spirit.[4] Can these religions be truthful and forthright to acknowledge that they all pray to the same god whose name is *Amen?* This would be a courageous act of unification indeed!! Jesus acknowledged *Amen* as the faithful and true witness, the beginning of the creation of God.

---

[3] To avoid speaking and possibly profaning God's sacred name Jehovah or Yahweh, Hebrews omit the vowels and use the consonants to refer to God, which results in the tetragrammaton JHVH or YHWH. However, the Christian sect, Jehovah Witnesses proclaim His name.

[4] Pope John Paul II promulgated the *Catechism of the Catholic Church*, 2nd Edition, Page 902, where Trinity is defined as, The mystery of one God in three Persons: Father, Son and Holy Spirit.

When will these religions eventually accept *Amen* as the same god in which they believe? How much longer will religious institutions continue to divide people and maintain ignorance of God's original name, *Amen*?

It is a New Age hope that in the future people will actively flow into every house of God, be it Judaic, Christian, or Islamic. In this process, all people will strive to seek the truth by comparing and evaluating these religions. As a result of this effort, religious leaders will succumb to a common worship of their one God, *Amen*. In addition to the acknowledgement of Amen by Jesus Christ, *The Dead Sea Scrolls* reveal that followers of God in the 2nd century BCE were instructed to announce with their Priests, *Amen, Amen*![5] Therefore, *Amen* was accepted by the Hebrews. It is an obvious reality that *Amen* continues to be spoken today by followers of the Judaic, Christian, and Islamic religions.

6.1.5.3 Amen, God of War

Amon earned his reputation as the mighty god of war for the many towns and cities that were captured by Thutmose III. Under his leadership, one of his leading army officers, Thoth (or Thutti), became a hero by executing a successful plan in the capture of Joppa. He killed the enemy's leader and proceeded to have 500 soldiers enter the city by carrying 200 men concealed within 200 baskets said to be tribute—a tactical lie to deceive the enemy. The Papyrus Harris manuscript, said to have come from Thebes and dated around 1300 BCE, tells of Thoth's plan and his heroic efforts. This ingenious plan fired the imagination of the writer of "Ali Baba and the Forty Thieves." It is of interest that Amon is regarded as the Egyptian warriors' strength and the pharaoh's mighty god that assures his victories. The following is an excerpt from the Harris manuscript that captures the military's

---

[5]   **G. Vermes**, *The Dead Sea Scrolls in English*, **Page 73**.

reliance on their god for victory. Thoth brings the *great staff of* King Men-kheper-Re (Thutmose III) for the enemy king to see. Rising, he displays the staff and says before striking a deadly blow: [6]

"Look at me, O Enemy of [Joppa! Behold] the King Men-kepher-Re—life, prosperity, health!—The fierce lion, the son of Sekmet! [7] *Amon gave him his [victory]!" [And he] raised his [hand] and struck the Enemy of Joppa on the forehead. And he fell down . . ."*

6.1.5.4 Amen, God of Perception

Perception connotes omniscience, for it allows Amen to foresee any situation. This attribute is identified in the 600th stanza of the hymn, *Amon As the Sole God* [8] and provides the power to create by command. The following excerpts describe this ability:

Perception is his heart, Command is his lips.
Fate and Fortune are with him for everybody.
. . . The faces of everybody are on him among men and gods.
He is Perception.

6.1.5.5 Amen Heals and Responds to Prayer

Amen is regarded as a divine physician and a magical healer who responds to supplications and prayer. The following excerpt is taken from *A Hymn to Amon-Re:*[9]

Who hears the prayer of him who is in captivity,
Gracious of heart in the face of an appeal to him.

---

[6]   **James B. Pritchard,** edited by, *Ancient Near Eastern Texts*, **Page 22,23**.

[7]   Sekmet is the Egyptian goddess of war.

[8]   **James B. Pritchard**, edited by, *Ancient Near Eastern Texts*, **Page 369**

[9]   **James B. Pritchard**, edited by, *Ancient Near Eastern Texts*, **Page 366**.

From the hymn, *The God Amon as Healer and Magician*, another 19th Dynasty document, the following lines (excerpted from the 17th Stanza) describe Amen's powers to heal and respond to prayer:[10]

> *He who dissolves evils and dispels ailments; a physician who heals the eye without having remedies, (iii 15) opening the eyes and driving away the squint; . . . Amon. Rescuing whom he desires, even though he be in the Underworld; who saves (a man) from Fate as his heart directs. To him belong eyes as well as ears wherever he goes, for the benefit of him whom he loves.*
>
> *Hearing the prayers of him who summons him, coming from afar in the completion of a moment for him who calls him.[11]*

6.1.5.6 Amen, God of Mercy

The attribute of mercy by Amen is given to a grateful father whose son recovered from an illness brought about by some impious act associated with a cow of the temple. A 19th Dynasty document illustrates the deep respect for Amen and the humility of an Egyptian artisan who expresses gratitude for his god's mercy. The inscription was carved on a memorial stela, which illustrates Amon-Re seated on the left, and on the right, the father, Neb-Re who kneels in worship before the god.[12] Significant lines, presented below, have been excerpted from the full text. It begins with praise to Amon-Re:

> *Amon-Re, Lord of the Thrones of the Two Lands, the Great God Presiding over Karnak, the august god, he who hears the prayer,*

---

[10] **James B. Pritchard**, edited by, *Ancient Near Eastern Texts*, **Page 369**.

[11] Although Fate played a powerful role during this period, God can intervene via prayer and supplication.

[12] **James B. Pritchard**, edited by, *Ancient Near Eastern Texts*, **Page 380**, Gratitude for God's Mercy.

*who comes at the voice of the poor and distressed, who gives breath
(to) him who is weak.*

*Giving praise to Amon-Re, Lord of the Thrones of the Two Lands,
Presiding over Karnak; kissing the ground to Amon of the City
(Thebes), the Great God the Lord of the great forecourt, the gracious
one. May he grant to me that my eyes look at his beauty. To the ka
of the Outline Draftsman of Amon, Neb-Re, the justified.*

The Memorial Prayer

*Giving praises to Amon. I make him adorations in his name; I
give him praises to the height of heaven and to the width of earth;
[I] relate his power to him who travels downstream and who travels
upstream. Beware ye of him! Repeat him to son and daughter, to
great and small; relate him to generations of generations who have
not yet come into being; relate him to fishes in the deep, to birds in
the heaven; repeat him to him who knows him not and to him who
knows him! Beware ye of him!*

*Thou art Amon, the Lord of the silent man[2], who comes at the voice
of the poor man. If I call to thee when I am distressed, thou comest
and thou rescuest me. Thou givest breath (to) him who is weak; thou
rescuest him who is in prisoned. Thou art Amon-Re, Lord of Thebes,
who rescues him who is in the Underworld, inasmuch as thou art he who
is . . . when one calls to thee; thou art he who comes from afar.*

*Made by the Outline Draftsman of Amon in the Place of Truth,
Neb-Re, the justified . . . {Several lines of appreciation} . . .*

*He says (Neb-Re): Though it may be that the servant is normal in
doing wrong, still the Lord is normal in being merciful. The Lord
of Thebes does not spend an entire day angry. As for his anger—in
the completion of a moment there is no remnant, and the wind is
turned about in mercy for us, and Amon has turned around with his*

breezes. As thy ka endures, thou wilt be merciful, and we shall not repeat what has been turned away! . . .

Made by the Outline Draftsman Neb-re (and his) son, the Scribe Khay.

6.1.5.7 Amen, the Just of Councils

The expulsion of the Hyksos from Egypt was not accomplished in a single generation, and took a series of campaigns by the Sekenenres and two Theban kings—Kamose and Ahmose I. It was Kamose who rebelled against a truce which divided Egypt between his Theban rule and the rule of the Hyksos in Avaris. Rejecting the advice of his officials, he set out to win back the larger dominion embracing Hermopolis (halfway between the Delta and Thebes) to the Delta and shores of the Mediterranean Sea. An excerpt from Kamose's stela, provided below, emphasizes the authority and trust in the judgment of Amen. Strategically, Kamose uses this attribute of Amen to strengthen his case for capturing Lower Egypt while going against the advice of his officials: [13]

I went north because I was strong (enough) to attack the Asiatics through the command of Amon, the just of councils. My valiant army was in front of me like a blast of fire . . .

6.1.5.8 Amen, the Lord of Truth

One of the greatest attributes of the Egyptian god, Amen, is reverence for truth. Truth has been the underlying foundation that shaped Egypt's morality since Egypt's Predynastic age, over 4000 BCE years ago. This moral precept was represented by Maat, goddess of justice, righteousness, and truth. So venerated is this moral element

---

[13] **James B. Pritchard**, edited by, *Ancient Near Eastern Texts*, The War Against the Hyksos, **Page 232.**

that Maat was conceived as the daughter of Re. Truth became the underpinning of the Egyptians' moral upbringing, and was instilled into the education of their pharaohs. Thutmose III exemplified his deep respect for truth when he detailed the successes of his campaigns. He states: [14]

I have not uttered exaggeration in order to boast of that which I did, saying, "I have done something,' although my majesty had not done it. I have not done anything . . . against which contradiction might be uttered. I have done this for my father, Amon . . . because he knoweth heaven and he knoweth earth, he seeth the whole earth hourly.

6.1.5.9 Amen, God of Righteousness and Justice

Together, Righteousness and her sister Truth are the foundations of Justice; without these two elements of morality there can be no justice. The *Hymn to Amon-Re*, which was written prior to the Amarna Revolution initiated by Ikhnaton, depicts Amen's attribute for righteousness by stating: [15]

> *"The righteous one, Lord of Karnak,*
> *In this thy name of Maker of Righteousness."*

James H. Breasted, in his book, *The Dawn of Conscience,* depicts righteousness as one of the sources of our moral heritage from Ancient Egypt. He comments upon a literary document that was preserved in a stately papyrus role dating to the Middle Kingdom between 2000 and 1800 BCE. The story presents a very able-minded peasant who expresses why he should be dealt with fairly after his donkeys were taken from him by a vassal who witnessed some of his grain being eaten along a very narrow path on his property.

---

[14]   **James H. Breasted**, *A History of Egypt,* **Page 320.**

[15]   **James B. Pritchard**, edited by, *Ancient Near Eastern Texts,* **Page 367**

Finding that the vassal was unresponsive to his pleas to return the donkeys, the peasant made several appeals to the Chief Steward of Herakleopolis. The following is one of his most ingenuous appeals from, *The Protests of the Eloquent Peasant*: [16]

Do justice for the sake of the Lord of justice whose justice has indeed become justice, thou (who art) Pen and Roll and Writing Palette, (even) Thoth,[17] being far removed from doing evil; when right is (really) right, then is it (indeed) right. For justice (Maat) is for eternity. It descendeth with him that doeth it into the grave, when he is placed in the coffin and laid in the earth. His name is not effaced on earth, but he is remembered because of right. Such is the uprightness of the word of God.

The idea of calling Amen the Lord of Karnak in Thebes and the *Maker of Righteousness* implies he is a god who is responsible for man's desire to be fair and just to his fellow beings. Following is a prayer to Amen for justice in an appeal for assistance where it appears that the rich find favor among the poor. This appeal, written around 1230 BCE, comes from the Anastasi Papyrus and in whole reads: [18]

O Amon, give thy ear to one who is alone in the law court, who is poor; he is [not] rich. The court cheats him (of) silver and gold for the scribes of the mat [19] and clothing for the attendants. [20] May it be found that Amon assumes his form as the vizier, in order to permit (the) poor man to get off. May it be found that the poor man is vindicated. May the poor man surpass the rich. The End.

---

[16] **James H. Breasted**, *The Dawn of conscience*, **Page 191**

[17] God of writing and legal procedure.

[18] **James B. Pritchard**, edited by, *Ancient Near Eastern Texts*, **Page 380**, A Prayer for Help in the Law Court.

[19] Reed mats were used by the magistrates and clerks of the court to sit on.

[20] Reed mats were used by the magistrates and clerks of the court to sit on.

The appeal for righteousness, truth, and justice comes from the belief that it is God, a higher presence, who desires these attributes. This is a natural appeal when one feels little hope or trust in the application of justice by fellow human beings. Worshippers of the three major religions who pray to the same God continue the belief that an outside, unknowable presence will respond to their prayers. While it may be a noble belief that the loving nature of human beings and all their attributes come from some outside force called god, it is a misdirected belief. The loving nature of all living creatures is an inherent attribute within them. It is nourished and guided by a loving and moral upbringing without the assistance of any outside force.

Mankind's desire for power, wealth, and control tends to be part of the social makeup of a civilization. To compensate for the aggressive traits associated with power, wealth and control, people need to be taught the attributes of righteousness, truth, and justice. These attributes encourage fairness and charity for those less endowed with physical and mental capabilities. The Priesthood and the pharaohs, who indoctrinated the Egyptians, were cognizant of the benefits of these attributes in bringing order and stability to their growing nomes, towns, and cities. Their civilization aspired to become one of the most advanced in the world until their morality and love of righteousness, truth, and justice became corrupted by the many outside forces that could no longer be controlled and to which they eventually succumbed.

6.1.6 The Attribute of Love

It is noteworthy that the ancient Egyptians did not revere love as an attribute of their god(s); be it Amon-Re, raised to a universal god by the High Priests of Amon, or the Aton god of Ikhnaton. Their very early conceptions dealt with a need to comprehend the beginning of life, the earth and its oceans, the sun, the air they breathed and the heavens beyond. The Egyptians answered their own questions about these elements by conceiving gods as being responsible for them. The beauty of the wonders of nature that existed in organic and inorganic form, be they animals, birds, mountains or trees, were also revered and became associated with their local gods.

Once they assumed form in their minds, certain gods rose to take on personal attributes that needed to be emulated in mankind, such as righteousness, truth, and justice. The basic instinctual need to have a god protect and defend them, and furnish the necessary waters to produce abundant food, eventually led to the higher conceptual need of truth and righteousness. This was a necessary development by the Egyptian Priesthood so that social order could be assured and justice administered for the well-being of their communities. Consequently, these attributes came to be worshipped and praised. But where was the attribute of love? This fundamental attribute takes precedence in many religions today. But unfortunately, love for our brothers and sisters is not fully taught and practiced as religious fanatics do exist and kill innocent people in the name of God.

The dominant attribute of the Judaic, Christian, and Islamic God is fear; fear that impresses a torturous feeling upon the mind with the daunting image of being consumed eternally by the scorching flames of hell for breaching any of God's commands. Only recently, have religious leaders come to emphasize that God loves his children. But if the first four of the Ten Commandments are examined (since the others specifically address honor of parents, killing, adultery, stealing, false witness, and covetousness), shown as Table 6-1, it is revealed that there is no statement of God's love for His creations or that they should love one another.[1]

---

[1] In Exodus 20: 3-26, there are 14 not Ten Commandments that the Hebrew god gave Moses to instruct the children of Israel. Religious leaders have not revealed all the commandments but simplified them for universal use. Simplicity is evident as they rather not reveal the picayunish *Shalls* and *Shall Nots* insisted upon by God to Moses. See Exodus 20: 22-26, and Exodus 25, 26 and 27 which describe the many *"Shall* and *Shall Not"* commandments.

Table 6-1. Is Love in the Ten Commandments? [2]

1. Thou shalt have no other gods before me.
2. Thou shalt not make unto thee any graven image, or any likeness *of any thing* that is in heaven above, or that *is* in the earth beneath, or that *is* in the water under the earth: Thou shall not bow down thyself to them, nor serve them: for I the Lord thy God *am* a jealous God, visiting the iniquity of the fathers upon the children unto the third and forth *generation* of them that hate me; and shewing mercy unto thousands of them that love me, and keep my commandments.
3. Thou shall not take the name of the Lord thy God in vain; for the Lord will not hold him guiltless that taketh his name in vain.
4. Remember the Sabbath day, to keep it holy. Six days shalt thou labor, and do all thy work; But the seventh day *is* the Sabbath of the Lord thy God; *in it* thy shalt not do any work, thou, nor thy son, nor thy daughter, thy manservant, nor thy maidservant, nor thy cattle, nor thy stranger that *is* within thy gates: For *in* six days the Lord made heaven and earth, the sea, and all that in them *is*, and rested the seventh day: wherefore the Lord blessed the Sabbath day and hollowed it.

In all fairness, it is the Son of Man, Jesus Christ, who proclaimed love in his commandments received from God. His words emphasize *Love* and broke with the tradition of fear. The attribute of love rather than fear was introduced by the Judaic religion in the fifth book of Moses, Deuteronomy 6:5. However, this commandment instructs followers to love God and not necessarily each other. The second law expresses love for one's neighbor and is stated in Moses' third book, Leviticus 19:18. These laws were combined by Jesus Christ and restated in Matthew 22:37-40 as:

---

[2]   **Holy Bible**, *King James Version*, **Exodus 20:2-26**.

*Thou shalt love the Lord thy God with all thy heart, and with all thy
soul, and with all thy mind.* (Deuteronomy 6:5)
*This is the first and great commandment.
And the second is like unto it, Thou shalt Love thy neighbor as
thyself.* (Leviticus 19:18)
*On these two commandments hang
All the law and the prophets.*

However, in the last Gospel written by John in 13:34, Jesus Christ
further simplifies God's commandments of Love:

**A new commandment I give unto you, That ye love one another; as
I have loved you, that ye also love one another.**

It must be observed that Jesus Christ took two former commandments
of love by God and simplified the whole of Judaic Holy Law formerly
received by men of God. Was Jesus Christ too presumptuous for
restating the words of God? Of greater significance, did Jesus believe
that the greater commandment was to love one's sisters and brothers?
More poignantly put, would God accept you if you have failed to
love your sisters and brothers of every nation?

No Scripture is that holy that it cannot be improved. Many sins in the
Bible[3] and the Qur'an[4] do exist, and many laws are archaic enough
not to apply to modern man. It is time for our religious leaders to be
as courageous as Jesus and the Egyptian pharaoh, Ikhnaton; both of

---

[3]   **John Shelby Spong**, *Sins of Scripture*, released 2005 by **HarperCollins**
       Publishers, New York, N.Y.

[4]   **Irshad Manji**, *The Trouble With Islam: A Muslim's Call for Reform
       in Her Faith*, first published by Random House in Canada and first
       edition in 2004. Published by St. Martin's Press, New York.

whom changed outdated doctrine by respectively simplifying Judaic law with the new commandment to love one another and, by prohibiting the worship of multiple gods. Nothing is so sacred that it cannot be improved to serve mankind. If mankind can survive as long as the dinosaurs, it may be discovered that there is indeed intelligent life elsewhere in the universe. There can be no question that the Scriptures of today will have to be revised to keep pace with the knowledge accumulated. Someday, man's spiritual nature will evolve so that all of God's creations throughout the universe love one another.

All human beings and lower animals have the capacity to love. Love is the dominating attribute of the animal kingdom that enables it to survive and multiply. It is also true that humans and animals have the aggressive impulse to protect oneself or their kind by killing others. However, to say love, kindness, fairness, truth, righteousness, and justice are derived from a higher being is nonsense. People should take pride in their ability to be tolerant, understanding, kind, and loving towards others. To extend themselves in friendship, embrace people out of love, or desire to help them and show affection is not a sin. These are human qualities that are inherent in all mankind. Those who are able to outwardly extend such qualities to others are truly blessed.

In summary, the brief review of the attributes of Amen indicates a highly developed form of God. The Egyptians' perceptions of their God were highly evolved and formed the basis for their morality and their ability to maintain an orderly civilization. As Egypt expanded and introduced their Amon (Amen) god into neighboring countries, Amen became accepted and worshipped by foreigners. It would be a natural set of circumstances for the Semites to follow Moses and evolve Scriptures based upon what they had learned from Egyptian teachings and writings. The following subsections will reveal that the Egyptian God, as well as many concepts of Egyptian theology, have been adopted by the monotheistic religions of the present world.

Figure 6-1 is provided to share the insights of the English poet, Gerald Massey (1828-1907). This writer and Egyptologist dedicated his life to dispelling falsehoods and revealing truths previously clouded by myth. It is fitting that his hope for a loving people be stated and illustrated with the Egyptian symbol of Truth.

Egyptian Symbol of Truth

Hope on, hope ever! After darkest night,
*   Comes, full of loving life, the laughing morning;*
Hope on, hope ever! Spring-tide flush with light,
*   Aye crowns old Winter with her rich adorning.*
Hope on, hope ever! Yet the time shall come,
*   When man to man shall be a friend and brother*
And this old world shall be a happy home,
*   And all Earth's family loves one another!*
*   Hope on, hope ever.[1]*

Figure 6-1. The Egyptian Symbol of Truth

---

[1]   **Gerald Massey,** *Poems by Gerald Massey,* **page 355.**

7.0 Egyptian Roots of the Jewish Religion

The first formal religion to develop from the religious beliefs of the Egyptian religion and into our present culture is the Jewish, or Judaic, religion. To understand the impact the Egyptians had on the Judaic religion, it would be beneficial to review the period of time between the first foreign intrusions into Egypt and the conquest of Judah by the Romans.

As early as the 1st Dynasty, the Egyptians had frequent encounters with foreign intruders from territories east of the Delta region. The repeated influx of marauding Bedouin[1] tribes were repelled by Egyptian kings during the earlier dynasties. The first invasion into an Asiatic land was led by Sesostris III about halfway through his reign (1887-1849 BCE). The brief summary outlined below describes the many Egyptian encounters with people of Semitic origin that migrated from as Far East as Ur, off the northern tip of the Persian Gulf, and westward to the Mediterranean Sea.

Sesostris III came to power after the death of his father, Sesostris II, in 1887 BCE. He extended his father's conquests into Nubia, and though Egypt did not claim sovereignty in Kush, in his 16th year, he had added two hundred miles of the Nile valley up to the 2nd cataract (Figure 4-1). The gold captured in Kush was so plentiful that it became less valuable than silver. An aggressive pharaoh, Sesostris III led the first invasion that ended with the plundering of Syria. During a reign of 38 years, he vigorously expanded his rule of a kingdom that embraced a thousand miles of Nile territory. During

---

[1] **James H. Breasted,** *A History of Egypt,* **Pages 135, 135.** The Beduin tribes were a Semitic people that settled in Southern Palestine and the Sinai. Many campaigns were conducted by the Egyptian kings since the 1st Dynasty and a decisive victory by Pepe I during the 6th Dynasty went as far north as the highlands of Palestine.

the 2nd Intermediate Period (refer to Figure 2-1), the 13th Dynasty had a short succession of pharaohs who claimed the throne based upon legitimate lineage. However, the fourth succession was interrupted by a 12th Dynasty name that was not of royal form. After this usurper, rapid dissolution followed as the provincial lords rose against each other in their bid for the throne. Without any dynastic division, the ceaseless struggles to gain the throne of the pharaoh culminated into a list of at least 118 names of kings. This unsettled period of warring factions resulted in a lack of administration of the irrigation system; instability in the production of agricultural products; a reduction of the building and craftsmen trades; and oppressive taxation. By the 14th Dynasty, the breakdown of centralized control exposed Egypt as easy prey to foreign aggression.[2]

Before the end of the 13th Dynasty, the Abriu, Apiru, or Habiru, a sect of Semitic tribes, migrated from Mesopotamia. Figure 7-1 illustrates that the migration started as far east as the city of Ur. To the Northeast, the Tigris and Euphrates Rivers, along with the yearly spring rains, attracted people to settle in groups and build towns before 4000 BCE. The people inhabiting these lands were called Sumerians after the city Sumer, and they lived in neighboring cities such as Kish, Babylon, Nippur, Uruk, Lagash, and Ur. In the plains, these people grew such crops as barley and raised sheep and cattle on the area's rich pastures.

Ur is the city where Abraham lived before taking his family to Egypt. The second time families of Abraham entered Egypt was after Isaac and his son Jacob were born. Through a pharaoh's approval of a request by Jacob's son, Joseph, the seed of Abraham, was allowed to enter Egypt.[3]

---

[2]   **James H. Breasted,** *A History of Egypt,* **Pages 187-208.**

[3]   **Holy Bible,** *King James Version,* **Genesis 45:1-7.**

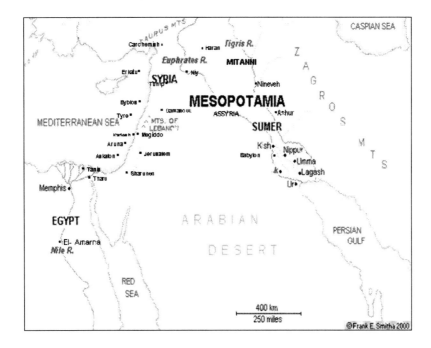

Figure 7-1. Sumerian and Semitic Cities Close to Egypt.

Figure 7-1 illustrates the close proximity of the Assyrian and Sumerian cities along the Tigris and Euphrates Rivers westward to the tributaries of Lower Egypt. It becomes apparent why the events of warfare between cities, famine due to lack of rainfall, neglect of agriculture due to frequent battles by the Babylonians, and the need to feed herds of animals on fertile land would lead to a natural advance of people from Ur into areas around the tributaries of the Nile River.

As early as 1800 BCE, Semitic people from Assyria began to migrate peacefully into the upper regions of the Nile Delta and Lower Egypt. At this time, immigrants were welcomed and the royal palace of the pharaohs was opened to foreign counselors and favorites, while Semitic dancing girls and concubines were highly esteemed. But as Hammurabi expanded the Babylonian empire by subduing the settlements along the Euphrates,[4] lands were not maintained during war campaigns making famine a reality. This climate of war and famine induced whole families and Shepherd Kings with their tribes to migrate into Lower Egypt.

By 1675 BCE, Abraham and his descendents migrated into Egypt. Around this time, the Hyksos,[5] an aggressive people from Assyria, invaded Egypt with the support of Shepherd Kings and their tribes. The Shepherd Kings set themselves up as pharaohs and used Avaris (Tanis) in the Nile Delta as their capital rather than the Egyptian capital of Thebes. This was a strategic move that anticipated the possibility of a hostile Babylonian advance, and allowed them more centralized control over their conquered territories which extended into Palestine and Syria.

Under their influence which lasted over a century, the invaders established a powerful kingdom and maintained peace and prosperity in their territories. They introduced horses drawn by chariots and the composite bow. Their successful conquests were furthered by a type of rectangular mound fortification of beaten earth used as a fortress. Archaeologists have uncovered examples of these mounds at Jericho, Shechem, and Lachish. Their most influential contribution to Egypt was the introduction of Canaanite deities and Asian artifacts. Exposure to these new ideas was instrumental in weakening the autocracies and isolationism of the Old and Middle Kingdoms.[6]

---

[4]   **James B. Pritchard,** edited by, *Ancient Near Eastern Texts,* **Page 165**

[5]   **James H. Breasted**, *A History of Egypt,* **Page 217**. It was the ancient Egyptian historian Manetho who introduced the term Hyksos. The first syllable 'hyk' denotes a king and 'sos' signifies a shepherd. Together, Hyksos means Shepherd Kings.

[6]   Internet: The Columbia Electronic Encyclopedia, Copyright © 2003, Columbia University Press.

Beginning in 1775 BCE, the Semites interbred with the Egyptian people and their pharaohs ruled the Delta for more than a century. Intermarriage continued well into the New Kingdom under the leadership of Thutmose III and other pharaoh conquerors of the 18th Dynasty. They brought many Syrians back to Egypt, and many women became wives or concubines of the officers and nobles. The mix of Semitic and Egyptian blood had caused the physiognomy along the Nile to develop a definite Egyptian-Syrian cast.[7]

The impact of the Hyksos invasion during the 2nd Intermediate Period caused the stability of Egyptian life to vanish so that the occupation of pyramid building came to an end. During the inundation of the Nile, farm workers by the tens of thousands who would otherwise be idle for three or four months were no longer used as an inexpensive labor force. Previously, the mobilization of Egyptian citizens served to keep people productive and reinforced their beliefs in eternal life after death.

The pharaoh projects of pyramid building had a positive influence in terms of strengthening the people's religious and moral beliefs. Such projects required the participation of engineers, artisans, and priests who directed the engraving of magical rites within and outside the pyramid walls. However, the instability of the 2nd Intermediate Period brought an end to pyramid building, with only several small pyramids being completed in Thebes. By the 18th Dynasty, Ahmose I may have had to complete a few pyramids as monuments for his father and brother. Therefore around 1570 BCE, the building of pyramids were designed on a small scale; made of bricks, such monuments ended about ten years into Ahmose I's reign,. The labor and use of resources to transmit quarried stone and build the imposing pyramids of the past were no longer available.

---

[7]   **Homer W. Smith**, *Man and His Gods*, **Pages 89, 90**

The war campaigns required during the 18th Dynasty ended pyramid building.

To summarize the first foreign invasion of Egypt, some important dates are repeated below:

- The Semites were a people that settled from Ur, part of the Sumerian empire, to cities along the Tigris and Euphrates Rivers. The fertile lands along these rivers attracted these people to settle in groups and build towns before 4000 BCE.
- Semitic people migrated into Egypt as early as 1800 BCE.
- Hyksos and tribes led by Shepherd Kings conquered Egypt around 1675 BCE. They maintained control until 1577 BCE, when Ahmose I initially drove them out of Avaris. Their control extended beyond the Nile Delta into Palestine and Syria and as far south as Thebes to the 1st cataract in Nubia.
- One should dispel the movie misconceptions that captured Semitic slaves assisted in building pyramids. The building of small, brick pyramids ended around 1570 BCE. Since the Hebrews were in captivity as slaves about three centuries later for only 144 years before the Moses Exodus in 1250 BCE, they did not contribute to the building of pyramids.

7.1 Did Abraham Support the Hyksos?

The brief history presented above relates that Shepherd Kings and their tribes assisted the Hyksos in the invasion of Egypt's Delta region to the 1st cataract of the Nile. This conclusion was documented by Manetho, an Egyptian priest commissioned by Ptolemy II to record the history of Ancient Egypt. Manetho wrote three books called the Aegyptiaca, which divided Egyptian rule into 30 dynasties and provided a wealth of information on Egyptian myths, rites, and historical events.

Although the Aegyptiaca was summarized, abused, reviewed, and falsified for political and religious motives, a Jewish historian, Flavius Josephus, born in 37 CE, was able to quote from much of Manetho's writings. Below are some of the quotes attributed to Manetho concerning the Hyksos as shepherds:

*"Later Amenophis returned from Kush with a great army, his son Ahampses led another army, and both of them joined battle **with the shepherds** and the polluted people, and conquered them, and killed a great many of them, and pursued them to the borders of Syria."*

*"After this people or **shepherds** had left Egypt to go to Jerusalem, Tethmosis (Ahmose), who drove them out, was king of Egypt and reigned for twenty five years and four months, and then died."*

Finally, one last quote from Manetho (Aegyptiaca. Frag. 42, 1.75-79.2) is provided below to verify that the Hyksos invaded and ruled Egypt. He also points out that the Hyksos fortified themselves in Lower Egypt in anticipation that the Assyrians of the Babylonian empire were likely to challenge them eventually.

"Tutimaeus, in his reign, for what cause I know not, a blast of God smote us; and unexpectedly, from the regions of the East, invaders of obscure race marched in confidence of victory against our land. By main force they easily overpowered the rulers of the land, they then burned our cities ruthlessly, razed to the ground the temples of the gods, and treated all the natives with a cruel hostility, massacring some and leading into slavery the wives and children of others. Finally, they appointed as king one of their number whose name was Salitis. He had his seat at Memphis, levying tribute from Upper and Lower Egypt, and leaving garrisons behind in the most advantageous positions. Above all, he fortified the district to the east (Avaris in Lower Egypt), foreseeing that the Assyrians, as they grew stronger, would one day covet and attack his kingdom."

To illustrate the events that occurred during the 430-year sojourn of the Hebrew people that led to the Exodus conducted by Moses, it is necessary to gather the history of Abraham and his descendants from the Hebrew Testament of the Bible. The sources of data have been listed in Table 7-1. By linking the Moses Exodus with the descendants of Abraham within the 430-year period, it becomes possible to clarify when key events occurred.

Utilizing Table 7-1, the timeline shown as Figure 7-2 was created. It illustrates the events that began with Abraham's first covenant with God at the age of 75, when he was promised the land of Canaan. Soon after this event, Abraham left Haran and entered Egypt (Gen 12:4-10) with his wife Sa'rai and his brother's son, Lot. After a short stay in the pharaoh's house, the trip was terminated when the pharaoh learned that Abraham had lied by saying his wife was his sister. Abraham and his wife then settled in Hebron, a city 25 miles below Jerusalem (Gen 13:1-18). It was not until Joseph, Jacob's son, came to be the pharaoh's favorite that Abraham's seed returned to Egypt. Knowing that the Hebrew sojourn took 430 years, it is possible to derive when he started his journey. Most historians agree that the Moses Exodus occurred about 1250 BCE. By adding the 430-year sojourn to 1250 BCE, it can be noted that Abraham started his journey around 1680 BCE.

The historian John B. Noss places the Hebrew Exodus around 1250 BCE. [1]The respected Jewish scholar, Max I. Dimont in his book, *Jews, God and History,* indicated that Moses led the Hebrews out of Egypt in 1200 BCE.[2] Here, we have a difference of 50 years in the timeline of Figure 7-2. But the 1250 BCE date appears to be valid, since the Hyksos invaded Egypt in 1675 BCE and Abraham, a Shepherd King, entered Egypt at around that time.

---

[1] **John B. Noss**, *Man's Religions,* **Page 359**, Copyright 1974, printed in the U.S., ISBN 0-02-388440-1

[2] **Max I. Dimont**, *Jews, God and History,* **Page 36**

Table 7-1. Source Data of Hebrews 430 Years Sojourn.

1	**Genesis 25:7**	Abraham lived 175 years. For reference only.
2	**Genesis 12:1-7**	Abraham was 75 when the Hebrew God promised him the land of Canaan.
3	**Genesis 17:17**	Abraham was 100 when Isaac was born.
4	**Genesis 35:28**	Isaac lived 180 years. For reference only.
5	**Genesis 25:26**	Isaac was 60 when Jacob was born.
6	**Genesis 47:28**	Jacob lived 147 years.
7	**Genesis 41:46**	Joseph was 30 when appointed 2nd in command by the pharaoh.
8	**Genesis 41:53**	There were seven years of plenty and
9	**Genesis 45:6, 9**	two years of famine when Jacob came to Egypt which makes Joseph 39 years old.
10	**Genesis 47:28**	After being brought to Egypt by Joseph, Jacob died after 17 years. By adding 17 years to 39, we derive Joseph's age = 56 when Jacob died at 147 years.
11	**Genesis 50:26**	Joseph lived 110 years.
12	**Exodus 12:40**	Abraham's seed sojourned 430 years (215 in Egypt).
13	**Acts 7:23**	Moses left the Pharaoh's house at age 40.
14	**Acts 7:30**	40 years later, Moses led God's people out of Egypt.
15	**Deuteronomy 34:7**	Moses lived 120 years. For reference only.
		Above data gives time *from Joseph death to the birth of Moses* by using Hebrew sojourn of 430 years. 430-286 (From Figure 7-2: 25 + 60 + 147 - 56 + 110 - 80 which gives 64 years. After Joseph died, some years later a new pharaoh (that did not know Joseph) enslaved the Hebrews. He had determined that the children of Israel had multiplied exceedingly. Refer to Bible, Exodus 1:1-14. Therefore the *years of Hebrew bondage to the Exodus is **144 years*** maximum. 64 + 80 = 144 years.

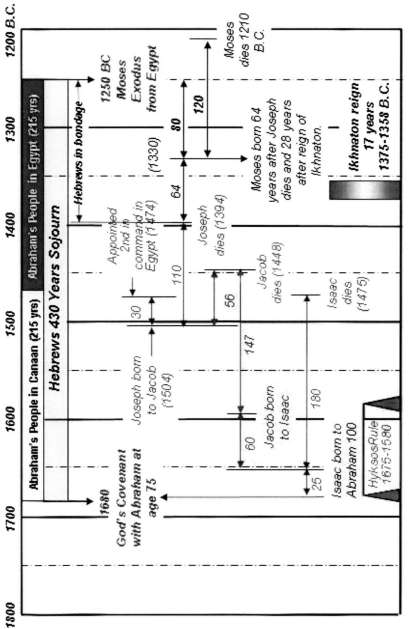

Figure 7-2. Timeline of Israelite 430 Years Sojourn.

Abraham and his family were the first to be called Hebrews. Dimont indicated that the Bible identified Terah, Abraham's father, and his family group as Ivriim. The English translation is Hebrews, which means people "who crossed over," or "from the other side of the river," which happens to be the Euphrates River.[3] It appears the Hebrews avoided associating their Semitic origins with their Hyksos, Babylonian, and Sumerian origins. This suppression is accentuated by Jacob's god naming him Israel (Genesis 32:28 and 35:10). This may be due to a conscious desire by the authors of the Bible to emphasize the birth of a new nation by Israelites and the birth of a new monotheistic faith, Judaism.

The following summarizes some significant points and events:

- Abraham migrated to Canaan around 1680 BCE, about 5 years before the Hyksos invasion of Egypt around 1675 BCE. Abraham was a Shepherd King and may have participated in the Hyksos invasion. According to the Bible, Abraham was a mercenary who joined with other Shepherd Kings in the land of Canaan (Genesis 14:14-19).
- Abraham's family and his seed were Hebrews. After the Exodus they came to be known as Israelites, after the name given to Jacob by his God (Genesis 32:27-28).
- Of the 430 sojourn years, 215 were spent in Canaan and 215 were spent in Egypt. The Hebrews were in bondage some years after Joseph died, which would be *less than 144 years*.

One very important event illustrated in Figure 7-2 is the reign of Ikhnaton. This pharaoh had the courage to defy the religious dogma and livelihood of the Egyptian priests by introducing the concept of one God. His reign from 1375 to 1358 BCE clearly emphasizes that his conception of one god was cast in stone in the

---

[3]   **Max I. Dimont,** *Jews, God and History,* **Page 28**

temples of Egypt. Ikhnaton's god, Aton, was introduced at the start of his reign; 125 years before the Moses Exodus occurred in 1250 BCE (1375-1250).

Prior to examining evidence substantiating that the Jewish religion was influenced by and has its roots in the Egyptian religion, it will be instructive to present the character of two of the most revered men in Jewish history, Abraham and Moses. These two men have respectively earned the recognition as the "Father" and "Founder" of Judaism.

7.2 Father of the Hebrew People

Devout readers of the Old and New Testament were introduced to Abraham in the first book of the Bible, Genesis. Between the 13th Dynasty and the end of the 17th Dynasty, a period of 208 years, Semitic invaders had stamped the Egyptian language with their unmistakable dialect.[4] These people entered the eastern Delta along with Shepherd Kings and their tribes. The Bible reveals that there was a descendant of the Chaldeans,[5] named Terah from the city of Ur. Terah had three sons: Abram, Nahor, and Haran. Before the journey from Ur, Haran had a son named Lot and died. With Abram, his wife Sarai and Lot, Terah journeyed into Haran, a semibarren caravan center north of the Arabian Desert between the Euphrates and Tigris Rivers (Figure 7-1).

Abram's god first spoke to him when Abram was 75, promising him the land of Canaan which included the land between the Jordan River and the Mediterranean Sea (refer to Figure 4-3). From this point in the

---

[4]   **James H. Breasted,** *A History of Egypt,* **Page 214.**

[5]   **Funk & Wagnalls**, *Britannica World Language Dictionary.* Note: A Chaldean is relative to an ancient Semitic people of the Tigris and Euphrates Valley, who conquered and ruled Babylon.

Bible we get to learn a bit about the character of Abram that rabbis, priests, ministers, imams, and mullahs are not proud to share.

7.2.1 What We Know and Don't Know About Abram

In the biblical account of Genesis, Abram gave his allegiance to an El (divinity) whom he called El-Shaddai, a god associated with a mountain. In Abram's first encounter with El-Shaddai he was promised the land of Canaan without any stipulations, a covenant, or set of moral rules by which to live. Although the Bible is not specific about Abram's moral values, one is led to believe that he followed the way of El-Shaddai; to do kindness, practice justice, and live a righteous life. Teachers of the Bible have also proclaimed that Abram was himself generous, hospitable, and forgiving.[1] These are beliefs that caused many worshippers to envision Abram as a humble, wise, and venerable old man. Yet none of these attributes are described in the Genesis account of Abram, who was later renamed Abraham by his god.

The one event in which the Bible gives the reader an appreciation of Abraham's compassion was when he questioned his God's decision to destroy the cities of Sodom and Gomorrah. Abraham asked, "Wilt thou also destroy the righteous with the wicked? Peradventure, there be fifty righteous within the city: wilt thou also destroy and not spare the place for the fifty righteous that are therein?" When his God replied that he would save the cities from destruction if there were to be found fifty righteous within, Abraham entreated his God to again reconsider and finally, after several negotiated requests from 50 to 45, to 40, to 30, then to 20, Abraham got his God to concede to sparing the cities if only ten righteous people could be found within. This is the one event that reveals Abraham's compassionate nature. This show of humanity, however, was exhibited to his God and not to his fellow human beings. The Bible does not portray Abraham as

---

[1] **John B. Noss,** *Man's Religions,* **Page 358.**

possessing an abundance of humanity, compassion, or charity. On the contrary, further examination will show that the Bible portrays a negative picture of Abraham.

7.2.2 What was Abraham's Status among the Semites?

Few people acquainted with the Bible are aware that rather than being a venerable and humble man, Abraham was an aggressive Shepherd King and mercenary who had vast riches and authority. He ruled over thousands of people which included: 318 trained servants that were born in his own house and armed to lead his army of soldiers; and the multiple wives, children and servants that belonged to the tribe. In addition, he owned hundreds of sheep and cattle, herders to tend them, camels, asses, silver, and gold. Indeed, in Hebron, a city of Canaan where he buried his wife Sarah, he was respected as a mighty prince (Genesis 13:2; 14:14; 24:35; 23:1-6).

The extent of Abraham's riches and authority over thousands of people within his tribe was so great that when he returned from his first visit to Egypt, he had to give Lot the choice to take his flocks of sheep and herds of cattle to Jordan or Hebron in Canaan. Lot went to Jordan near the wicked city of Sodom and Abraham dwelled in Hebron (Genesis 13:1-18).

The mercenary endeavor was his coalition with the Semite kings Chedorlaomer, Tidal, Amraphel and Arioch and their success in battle over the kings of Sodom and Gomorrah (Genesis 14:9-11). When Abraham learned that Lot was taken captive in Sodom, he took 318 of his own trained servants and surrounded the enemy at night.[1] His

---

[1]   **Flavius Josephus,** *The Wars of the Jews—Or The History of the Destruction of Jerusalem,* translated by William Whiston, Book V, Chapter 9, Section 4. Josephus states that Abraham had three hundred and eighteen captains under him, and an immense army under each of them.

soldiers successfully overwhelmed the enemy and pursued the rest into Hobah, a city to the left of Damascus (Genesis 14:14-17). In Genesis 23:6, the Hittite leader Ephron addresses Abraham as a mighty prince. Thus, we see Abraham as a powerful and respected Shepherd King.

7.2.3 Abraham Deceives the Pharaoh

After Abraham had been in Hebron several years, the land of Canaan was struck by a grievous famine, and Abraham journeyed with his wife Sarai (later named Sarah by his El) and Lot into the upper Delta of Egypt. The timeline of Figure 7-2 indicates that this trip occurred during or shortly after the invasion by the Hyksos and Shepherd Kings. It would appear that Abraham's visit with his family took place after the Hyksos invasion in 1675 BCE. The preparation for the takeover of Egypt had to require planning, the mobilization of men and horses, the production of armor, swords and battle-axes, and large amounts of water and food. However, Abraham, being a Shepherd King himself, may have participated in such an invasion and returned to Egypt with his family soon after the campaign was a success. Therefore the pharaoh that Abraham had intended to meet may have been a Semite leader who lived on the estate of the vanquished pharaoh, enjoying the splendor and authority of the throne. Since Abraham was 75 years old when his El promised the land of Canaan to his people, it is possible that at least five years elapsed before he returned to Egypt, which would place his age at 80 years and his wife Sarah's at 70. (Genesis 17: 17 reveals Abraham was 10 years older than Sarah).

What unfolds next in Genesis is the following deliberate lie that Abraham had his wife repeat to the pharaoh in order to protect his life. In fairness, his reasoning is provided below:

"Behold now, I know that thou art a fair woman to look upon: Therefore it shall come to pass, when the Egyptians shall see thee,

*that they shall say, This is his wife: and they will kill me, but they
will save thee alive. Say, I pray thee, thou art my sister: that it may
be well for me for thy sake; and my soul shall live because of thee."*
(Genesis 12:11-14)

Abraham wife complied with his request, and it became his insurance
against being killed if the pharaoh desired her. As a sister, she
would be available to any advances on her person. This insurance
would not be necessary if, in fact, the land was controlled by
Semites. But because the Semite coalition consisted of Hyksos and
Shepherd Kings that may not have known Abraham, this precaution
seemed necessary in Abraham's mind. What transpired was that
the pharaoh was pleased with Sarah's beauty and took her into his
house. In return, the pharaoh gave Abraham sheep, oxen, asses,
and male and female servants. As for Sarah, she received asses
and camels. This deception was not approved by Abraham's God,
and the pharaoh's house incurred "great plagues." The pharaoh
called for Abraham and implored him, saying, "What is this that
thou hast done to me? Why didst thou not tell me that she was
thy wife?" It appears that out of respect for the mighty Prince
Abraham, the pharaoh sent him and his wife away with their
possessions, including his gifts, under the protection of his men
(Genesis 12: 14-20).

The deception perpetrated by Abraham may have proved to be
an embarrassment to him, but even more disconcerting is that
he placed his wife in a compromising situation where she was
available to the sexual advances of a stranger. The outcome was
very advantageous, for it appears that Abraham's gifts from the
good pharaoh were not relinquished. This episode shows Abraham
as willing to lie to achieve a practical solution even at the expense
of his wife's virtue. It is apparent that Abraham's God was remiss
in promising him a nation without imposing a moral code, nor
admonishing him for lying.

7.2.4 Again Abraham Perpetuates a Lie

Abraham puts Sarah into a compromising position once again; this time she was ninety. When they journeyed into Gerar, a town between Kadesh and Shur in Canaan, Abraham again tells its ruler, King Abimelech, that Sarah is his sister. Abimelech sent for Sarah and took her into his house. But Abraham's God appeared in the king's dream and threatened that he was a dead man for taking a man's wife. Abimelech rose early in the morning and called all his servants to tell of his dream, which caused fear within his whole household. When the king confronted Abraham and asked the same question as the deceived pharaoh, Abraham said:

"Because I thought, surely the fear of God is not in this place; and they will slay me for my wife's sake. And yet indeed she is my sister; she is the daughter of my father, but not the daughter of my mother; and she became my wife." (Genesis 20:11-12)

With this reasoning Abraham had his wife say that she was his sister wherever they went. But this was a compound lie because earlier in Genesis, 11:26, it is stated that Abraham's father Terah had only sons. Genealogy is quite specific in the Bible; yet there is no mention of any daughters by Terah. The outcome of the king's conversation with Abraham was a show of good will and generosity. The king gave back Abraham's wife along with gifts of sheep, oxen, and male and female servants.

Once again we find that Abraham used his wife, even at the age of ninety, as insurance to save him from the possibility of being killed by somebody more powerful who desired her. It is to be remembered that Abraham himself was a powerful and rich Shepherd King. For him to put his wife in compromising situations when he could have offered many female servants who excelled in youth and beauty is somewhat astonishing. More astonishing is the fact that Abraham's God does not severely scold him for lying and compromising his wife.

7.2.5 Why Does the Covenant Require Circumcision?

At the age of ninety-nine, Abraham is visited by his God who repeats the same promise made when he was 75 years old. This time, however, there is a stipulation with his God's covenant; stated below, it requires that all males be circumcised.

And I will give unto thee, and to thy seed after thee, the land wherein thou art a stranger, all the land of Canaan, for an everlasting possession; and I will be their God (Genesis 17:8) . . .

This is my covenant, which ye shall keep, between me and you and thy seed after thee; Every man child among you shall be circumcised (Genesis 17:10).

Here again, Abraham's God makes a promise without requiring any moral code of conduct; not even the command that Abraham and his seed shall worship him with all their heart, with all their soul, and with all their might. As a descendant of Noah, he received from his God only one requirement besides that of being fruitful, multiplying, and replenishing the earth (Genesis 9:1,7). This requirement is stated in Genesis 9:6. It bears repeating because it is the one requirement many religious leaders have ignored by using their people to shed the blood of their neighbors.

> *Whoso sheddeth man's blood, by man shall his blood be shed: for in the image of God made He man.*

It seems remiss for the God of Abraham to promise him land already inhabited by another people without insisting upon a moral code by which Abraham's people would conduct their lives. It was only after Moses walked out of Egypt with the children of Israel that Scripture, called the *Book of the Covenant* (Genesis 24:7), was written. It included not only the Ten Commandments, but also many judgments and ordinances from his God.[1] It therefore seems strange that the promise of land to Abraham included no such code but rather, only the practice of performing circumcision. In addition, this was not a new and unique requirement. The practice of circumcision had been performed by the Egyptians more than a thousand years before the Hebrew God imposed it in His covenant with Abraham. But then, the reader has learned of the practical solutions to which Abraham resorted; such as lying and compromising his wife to save his life. It is apparent that when the Hyksos and Shepherd Kings invaded Egypt, they not only dressed and lived as the pharaohs did—they also took on their practice of circumcision, as it was thought to assist in cleanliness.

Another practical reason for performing circumcision was due to Semites' taking Egyptian women as wives after their invasion of Egypt. The integration and assimilation of Semites with Egyptians became a common matter, and circumcision was a very practical solution to facilitating the intermarriage of these two peoples. Throughout the centuries that followed, intermarriage between these two groups of people became common and acceptable. Surely, the daughters of pharaohs were princesses who were highly esteemed and were received in marriage by Semitic Kings. A prime example was King Solomon, who built a palace for an Egyptian princess. Would an Egyptian woman lie with a Semite who was uncircumcised? Abraham, the practical man, foresaw the need to require circumcision of males for his people. Certainly the Semites as well as Abraham knew that this was more a practical necessity than a godly command to facilitate intermarriage. Does a loving god need to distinguish his people by cutting off the foreskin of a penis? Since this part of the body is always covered in public anyway, would not a loving, moral God rather distinguish his people by actions of righteousness,

---

[1]   **Holy Bible**, *King James Ver.*, **Ex 24:3-4**. The commandments, laws, and judgments written by Moses are in Exodus, Sections 20-23 and 25-30.

truth, and charity? It appears Abraham's God was again remiss; he imposed circumcision, but again, no moral code.

7.2.6 Use of God for Material Gain

We have learned that Abraham was a practical and self-serving man. The Bible does not reveal any gifts of charity or acts of love by Abraham towards his fellow men. Still, in the Hebrew Testament, God promises Abraham to give unto his seed the land of Canaan from the river of Egypt to the great river Euphrates for an everlasting possession. Is it not somewhat remarkable that Abraham and his seed were promised the land of Canaan without being given any commandments of love, charity, and righteousness? The worship of Semitic gods was prevalent during Abraham's lifetime. The logical answer may be that the Hebrews were not ready to accept the belief in 'One God.' This concept was introduced 305 years later by the Pharaoh Ikhnaton.[1] But even when Moses received the commandments from God, the Israelites were not ready to worship Him alone, for they molded a golden calf to revere their Asiatic God.

Regrettably, it seems that Abraham, Father of the Hebrew people, actually used God to invade Canaan, a land occupied by other people. The invasion may have been justified by the strong possibility that the Hebrews themselves once occupied that same territory; possibly not in total, but at least in part. But would a moral God command the shedding of human blood to ruthlessly acquire the territory of another people who had not been aggressors? How is it that the Hebrews felt free to violate the very first commandment given to Noah in Genesis 9:6? The Bible confirms that God himself kept his promise to Abraham by sanctioning and commanding Moses to invade Canaan.[2] It is a sad reality that aggressive leaders, such as Moses,

---

[1]   The 305 years is based upon Abraham's first encounter with his God and the year Ikhnaton first assumed the throne (1680 -1375 BCE).

[2]   **Holy Bible,** *King James Ver.,* **Deuteronomy 1:5-8, 30; 2:31-35; 3:1-7.**

have used God as justification for killing other human beings. This remains a sickening reality even in our own time. Both religious and world leaders find it profitable to mislead people in the name of God to acquire control, power, and wealth.

7.3 Founder of the Judaic Religion

Surfacing in all of the monotheistic religions is the most popular name, Moses, and rightly so, for his God not only freed his people from bondage, but made him the Founder of the Jewish religion. The first five of the 24 books of the Hebrew Bible, known as the Torah[1] or Pentateuch, are presented as the word of God coming through Moses. It is after the first book, that the Bible describes the events in the life of this extraordinary man. Moses communed with his God on a one-on-one basis, and the impact of their relationship accomplished three objectives. First, it insured that his God was worshipped as the sole God who created heaven and earth. Second, it enabled Moses to specify a house of worship and all its articles with specific dimensions, colors, and materials used to conduct sacrifices for his God and services for his people. The third most important objective was to give his people commandments and rules as to how to worship their God and conduct their lives with a high sense of morality.

Before Moses, there was no Scripture and no commandments given to the Hebrews except for the covenants Noah and Abraham received from their God. Only one covenant stated a moral command by God

---

[1]   The Torah originally referred to the teaching or laws written in the fi rst fi ve books of the Bible. Later, the term Torah came to include the oral law or Talmud, which includes explanations, interpretations, elaborations and extensions provided by rabbis, so that the Torah now means the whole of Jewish teaching of what God commands. One would think that God's words need no interpretation, but elaborations and extensions were found to be necessary to keep an ancient document in concert with advances of a more civilized world.

and it was explicitly given to Noah for His proudest creation: man. Human beings have consistently violated His command, and even today many religions and governments have failed to inoculate man's impulse against killing another human being. This command appears in Section 7.2.5 above and bears repeating:

Whoso sheddeth man's blood, by man shall his blood be shed: for in the image of God made He man.

In the following subsections, information that is rarely disseminated about Moses will be revealed. The reader has already been introduced to the greatest contribution from His God, the Ten Commandments, stated in Table 3-3. They are but a subset of 613 commandments or *mitzvoth* given by Moses's God and listed by Maimonides.[2] However, this list from the Torah does not contain the commandments that God specified as to the items required in the tabernacle to worship Him or the manner in which to conduct animal sacrifices to atone for sins. Such items as the ark of the testimony, the mercy seat above the ark, two angelic cherubims at the two ends of the mercy seat, an alter for burnt offerings, an alter for incense, a candlestick, and a table for vessels, dishes and spoons are specified with precise measurements and commanded to be overlaid or made with pure gold.[3] A review of the commands given in the Hebrew Bible far exceed the 613 commands by Maimonides, but may have been omitted by many rabbis for reasons of economics (gold is not easy to come by) and embarrassment (animal sacrifices for the atonement of sins).

7.3.1 What Do We Know About Moses?

The Hebrews have every right to be proud of Moses for giving them freedom from bondage and development of the Torah through his

---

[2]   Maimonides was a great Spanish rabbi who lived during the 12th century between 1135 and 1204. His birth name is Moses ben Maimon.

intimate communion with God. Yet, the rabbis are careful not to venerate Moses too highly, and as presented below, they may have good reason to give Moses a low profile.

Moses, more than any other prophet, has given the world the *Book of the Covenant*; Scripture that provides the commands of God for the monotheistic religions. Indeed, for his direct communion with God, Moses should be revered as one of the greatest prophets. He far exceeds Abraham as a man of God and yet, it appears that Abraham is revered or esteemed as much, if not more. Could it be that the rabbis prefer to draw little attention to this giant of a man? There may be reasons for this lack of reverence; the possibility that he may have been an Egyptian rather than a Hebrew, and that he committed impulsive acts that are not laudable for a man of God.

There are secularists who believe the story of Moses's infancy is a myth, and reject that he even existed. They do not accept events such as Moses being rescued by the pharaoh's daughter retrieving a basket floating in the reeds of the Nile; the astonishing wonders of the ten plagues; and the parting of the Red Sea. Even if these events never happened, it would not be sufficient to reject his contribution, the *Book of the Covenant*. This document was the first written Scripture of the Judaic religion, and served as the core of the first five books of the Bible.

The fact that a vast body of Israelites left Egypt must also be taken into account. There is question as to whether the Moses Exodus was a religious revolution that included other racial groups of people numbering more than 600,000 men. This number does not include women and children.[1] After Joseph invited his family into Egypt with

---

[1]   **Holy Bible**, *King James Ver.,* **Ex 12:37-38**. Line 37 indicates 600,000 men, besides children and, women were not even mentioned. Line 38 emphasizes that a mixed multitude went with the 600,000 men, which indicates people other than the Israelites were part of the Moses Exodus.

the approval of the pharaoh, the Hebrews spent 215 years in Egypt. Producing a number exceeding 600,000 people, excluding women and children, is a prodigious accomplishment for members of one family multiplying in a foreign land. It is surprising, after so many centuries, that the idea of the Moses Exodus possibly including other ethnic people has not occurred to the rabbis.

Moses, a Hebrew baby, was spared from death by being discovered among the reeds by the daughter of the pharaoh. He was, therefore, raised with children of the pharaoh in a palace with the finest education any man could receive in Egypt. He had to be learned in geometry, measurements and weights, and a skilled craftsman. More importantly, he was taught how to write; an asset he would later employ to record his conversations with his God. The instructtion that had to influence his thinking the most was having been taught the traditions and Scriptures of the Egyptian religion. Born 28 years after the death of Ikhnaton (see Figure 7-2), Moses had to be exposed to the novel concept of one God. Here we encounter another puzzling account of the Bible. How is it that Moses lived in the pharaoh's palace for more than three decades and neglects to indicate that pharaoh's name? Even the name of the princess who saved his life and gave him the love of a mother is omitted.[2] Could it be that the author of this account felt he could not provide these names because, in fact, the story would be revealed as a fabrication?

The omission of a pharaoh's name occurs in two other important periods during the Hebrews' 215-year sojourn in Egypt. This is especially surprising when one notes that Moses or the biblical author could accurately remember the names of family members and even kings

---

[2]   **Flavius Josephus**, *Antiquities of the Jews,* **Book II, Chapters 9 and 10**, the king's daughter was identified as Thermuthis but in both Chapters Flavius did not provide the name of her father, the Pharaoh. Flavius apparently did not know who her father was for lack of documentation.

that formed a coalition with Abraham as a mercenary; yet pharaohs who existed for many years and had a profound and humane impact on the lives of the Hebrews are not identified. The Bible relates that Joseph became second in command under the pharaoh's rule. He and his family enjoyed the graciousness of the same pharaoh for over 70 years.[3] But again, the author of the Bible neglects to name this honorable pharaoh.

Figure 7-3 illustrates significant Hebrew events that occurred during the reign of the pharaohs. This timeline indicates that Joseph's pharaoh may have been Thutmose III. This highly capable pharaoh conducted 17 successful campaigns over a 20-year effort to subdue the Palestinian and Syrian kinglets and warlords. It is ludicrous to believe this extremely strong leader needed the advice or support of a Hebrew named Joseph. Also, the Bible reveals that upon Joseph's death, the pharaoh who came into power revoked the honorable treatment formerly given to the Hebrews and enslaved them instead. According to Figure 7-3, this would have occurred under the rule of Amenhotep III; but he was most amenable in his relationships with the Semites of Palestine and Syria. At this time, all the powerful countries: Syria, Palestine, Babylonia, Assyria, Mitanni and Alasa-Cyprus recognized the practical necessity of being on friendly terms with Egypt. Here again, the biblical author would be in error if Amenhotep III or his son, Ikhnaton, are thought to be the despotic ruler. Of all the pharaohs, this would be an impossibility; for they were peaceful men who had many family ties with their Asiatic neighbors.

---

[3]   **Holy Bible,** *King James Version,* **Genesis 50:22** indicates Joseph died at the age of 110 years and was 39 years old when Jacob and his family came to Egypt.

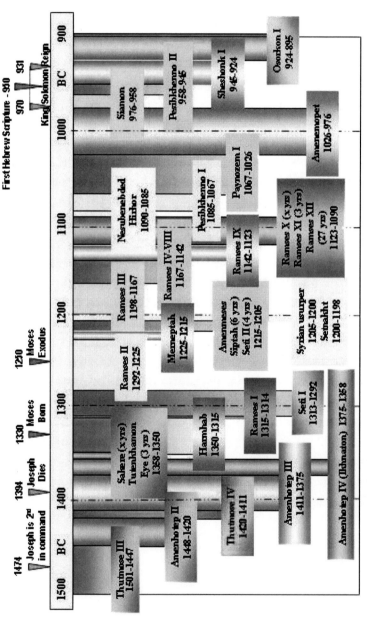

Figure 7-3. Hebrew Events During the Reign of the Pharaohs.

The other important period was the Moses Exodus. It was then that the Hebrews experienced their most memorable events following 144 years of bondage (from Joseph's death to the Exodus). The pharaoh who ordered the death of every male Hebrew born was punished along with his people. Punishments consisted of ten wonders/plagues; the death of all the Egyptian firstborn; and finally, his own death in the Red Sea along with his army. As memorable as those events were for the Israelites, again, the author of the Bible fails to identify the pharaoh's name. Figure 7-3 shows that the 1250 BCE Moses Exodus had occurred mid-reign of the most notable pharaoh, Ramses II. How is it possible for the author of the Bible to not name a ruler that was in power for 67 years? The omission of the pharaoh's name in three distinguishing periods in Jewish history appears to signify an exercise in deception. Could it be that the Israelite priests were so focused on their mission of righteousness that they fabricated a story to illustrate that their god was the sole god who made a covenant with their people?

The possibility that Moses was Egyptian has been discussed by many knowledgeable men. Mose is the Egyptian word for child (and forms Moses with the last letter "s"). The Egyptians use this word to derive a name that infers a proud reference of the father to his child. Some Egyptian kings have named their sons with the attachment 'mose' to mean "child of" such as Ahmose, Thutmose I, Thutmose II, Thutmose III, Thutmose IV, Ptahmose the High Priest of Amon, and the vizier to Amenhotep III, Ramose. This observation does not prove Moses was Egyptian because it would be natural for the pharaoh's daughter to call the baby Mose without attaching the family name; to attach the family name to Moses would be an affront to her father. This was a Hebrew baby, and therefore it would not be acceptable to put the royal throne at risk by the possibility of Moses someday laying claim to become king.

As a young prince in the pharaoh's royal palace, Moses learned the rudiments of warfare and established himself as a strategic military leader. He was appointed General of the Army by the pharaoh to retake the territories lost to the Ethiopians. Moses demonstrated his sagacity by a stratagem that allowed him to safely march his army over land populated by snakes and thereby surprise his enemy. He made use of the ibis, a venerated bird of the Egyptians that is a natural killer of snakes, by placing them in baskets. Upon reaching the habitat of reptiles, he let the birds out to kill and devour them. Invading the enemy unawares, Moses's army beat them in battle and overtook their cities. They then advanced to destroy the city of Saba, the royal city of the Ethiopians. Tharbis, Princess of the Ethiopian King, saw and admired Moses for his great courage and presented him an offer of marriage. Moses accepted the offer with the condition that he save the city from destruction.[4] In this brief history, provided by the historian Josephus, no mention is made as to whether Moses honored this marriage by returning home with his wife, Tharbis.

Moses, in the Bible (Ex 4:10), states to his Lord that he was not eloquent and slow of speech. To compensate for this speech defect, the Lord told Moses that Aaron will be his spokesman for the children of Israel (Ex 4:16, 30). These observations raise the conjecture that Moses may have been Egyptian instead of a Hebrew. Lacking a Hebrew dialect, Moses would not be an effective communicator and required Aaron to speak for him. This leads to the speculation that Moses was an educated Egyptian with an accent that lacked the vernacular of the Semites to be an effective speaker. However, to believe the biblical statement that Moses needed Aaron because he had a speech impediment would be a stretch of the imagination. According to Flavius Josephus, Moses was reputed to have been an articulate,

---

[4]   **Flavius Josephus**, *Antiquities of the Jews*, **Book II, Chapter 10**, How Moses made War With the Ethiopians.

sagacious, and skillful speaker who could readily move the multitude by his discourses.[5] It is very unlikely that a leader and general of the pharaoh's army would have had a speech impediment.

In debating whether Moses was Egyptian, there is the hypothesis that Moses could have been the son of a prosperous nobleman or an Egyptian priest. Being in close contact with nobility and certainly versed in Egyptian religion, Moses had to be exposed to the more advanced concepts of God. As revealed in Figure 7-2, Moses was born about 28 years after the death of the innovative pharaoh, Ikhnaton. As noted in Chapter 4.0, we found that the one-god concept, created by Ikhnaton, was put into practice in the city he established, Akhetaton. Just north of this city lies Memphis and the city On (Heliopolis). There the one god concept of Ikhnaton had survived, along with the more advanced schools of religious thought being taught to aspiring priests. The adage that a good idea cannot die applies here, and it is very possible that Moses was an adherent of this new conception of God.

Coming from a noble family, Moses was a man of great leadership abilities, intelligence, and planning skills. Through the years he had become so committed to the concept of one god that he perceived himself as a leader capable of improving the morality of thousands of people by leading the quest to worship and fear this most powerful god. This conjecture was introduced by Sigmund Freud but may not be compatible with Josephus's historical account that Moses was appointed General of the pharaoh's army. Moses, brought up in the palace of a pharaoh, may have had greater validity as a leader than would a nobleman because his position as a young prince and his

---

[5]   **Flavius Josephus**, *Antiquities of the Jews*, **Book IV,** From the Rejection of that Generation to the Death of Moses, Chapter 2, The Sedition of Corah and of the Multitude Against Moses, and Against His Brother, Concerning the Priesthood. Passage 4 verifies Moses speaking and leadership skills.

close association with the pharaoh would make him the more likely candidate to be appointed General of the Army.[6]

The question of whether Moses was Egyptian or Hebrew does not matter. In either case, Moses was an intelligent man who developed a strong interest in religion and had the motivation to use his abilities to initiate a religious movement towards a new direction, elevating people to a higher conception of god. Using the Bible's account, Moses was astute to realize that he was Hebrew; for as he grew older he had to notice his skin tone, body, and physical features were not Egyptian. He may have secretly resented that his brothers had all the advantages of succeeding to the throne, even though he felt he had more natural intellectual ability. There may have possibly been a need to feel his mother's love. This love may not have been equally given by the princess who would naturally favor her own biological sons and daughters. Consequently, as Moses grew older he associated himself more and more with the Jewish people. These resentments, unconscious or emotionally felt, would eventually cause him to react impulsively to anybody that performed indignant and wrongful acts.

A highly educated man, Moses had the tools of thought and a virile mind that could not waste away. The religious concepts he absorbed through his Egyptian upbringing had to be ulilized. As a natural leader, he was emboldened to lead thousands of people out of Egypt who had also been exposed to the concept of one god. After the death of Ikhnaton, the idea of one god had to germinate in the minds of the elite, the priesthood, craftsmen, artisans and workers who were exposed to the monuments, statues, and temples built in honor of his Aton god. One to two generations elapsed as this fresh concept of god disseminated throughout the land. 108 years after Ikhnaton's death, the people were ripe for a religious revolution led by the impulsive and energetic Moses.

---

[6]   **Sigmund Freud,** *Moses and Monotheism,* **Pages 31 and 32.**

7.3.2 The Impulsive Sins of Moses

The Bible is clear in revealing that Moses, though a great man, was far from perfect. Many men have become great because of their courageous actions and/or years of sacrifice to benefit the human race. Moses was such a man. He had to overcome ignorance and religious traditions practiced by people for many hundreds of years. His frustration and impatience with an undisciplined people who resisted worshipping his god and following a moral code caused him to commit impulsive acts that holy men would cringe at and deem as sinful.

In Exodus 2:11-15, Moses came to the assistance of a Hebrew slave being beaten by an Egyptian taskmaster. The resentments harbored by his status in the royal palace and the mistreatment of one of his people enraged him so intensely that he killed the Egyptian. This killing deserves no justification, but given the consideration that the god he would come to know on a personal level had not yet entered his life allows the sympathetic notion to forgive Moses for his impulsive act of murder.

Another impulsive act by Moses that is not forgivable was when he broke the two tablets of stone written by the finger of God.[1] Before Moses committed this impulsive act, he had a lengthy communion with his God on top of Mount Sinai. Only three months after Moses's people left Egypt, God commanded Moses to cite His many commandments, judgments, and ordinances to the children of Israel.[2] After Moses wrote the words of his Lord into the *Book of the Covenant*, he recited them to his people, whereupon they all

---

[1] **Holy Bible**, *King James Version,* **Exodus 31:18**.

[2] **Holy Bible**, *King James Version*, **Exodus 19:1, 17, 18. Exodus 20:1-17** (Ten Commandments) and Exodus, Chapters 20 - 23 contains many more commandments and ordinances.

agreed to be obedient and do what the Lord said.[3] A week later, the Lord told Moses to go up Mount Sinai to receive tablets of stone on which He had written commandments for Moses to teach his people. Moses communed with his Lord for 40 days and nights.[4]

The Lord told Moses to go down to his people for they had corrupted themselves by turning away from His commandments. Angered, God said, "they have made them a molten calf, and have worshipped it, and sacrificed thereunto, and said, These *be* thy gods, O Israel, which have brought thee out of the land of Egypt." When Moses returned to the camp he heard the people singing and saw them dancing around the calf. The anger waxed hot within him and he cast the tablets on the ground below the mount. It is understandable that such anger should well up within Moses, but to hurl the tablets written by the finger of God to the ground speaks little for his reverence of God. Moses's desecration of God's tablets after he was told by God to teach his people the commandments He had written upon them was not only an affront to God and a violation of God's request—it was a sacrilege. This sinful impulse may imply that it was not God who wrote the commandments but rather, Moses. Moses's mishandling of the holy tablets revealed no fear of God or respect for God's commandments; even with the awareness that they were engraved upon stone by God.

Additional evidence of Moses's impulsive nature is displayed by the order he gave to the children of Levi that caused them to kill about 3,000 men.[5] This sinful act occurred shortly after his Lord announced the Ten Commandments, after Moses wrote the words of his Lord in the *Book of the Covenant* and recited it to his people,

---

3   **Holy Bible**, *King James Version*, **Exodus 24:4-8**.

4   **Holy Bible**, *King James Version,* **Exodus 24:12-18. Exodus, Chapters 25 through 31** contains many more commandments and ordinances.

5   **Holy Bible**, *King James Version*, **Exodus 32:25-28**.

and after he communed with his Lord for forty days and nights. Moses had had the benefit of communing directly with God, writing and reciting His commandments, and yet he violated one of God's prime commands, "Thou shalt not kill." As has been discussed, this was one of the *first* commands his Lord gave when He established his covenant with Noah:

> *Whoso sheddeth man's blood, by man shall his blood be shed: for in the image of God made He man. (Genesis 9:6)*

The act of killing 3,000 men was not committed in response to retribution for their killing other people; the blood of man had not been shed by any of the murdered men. In Exodus 32:27, Moses implicates his God as the source of the bloodletting, stating, "Thus saith the Lord God of Israel, Put every man his sword by his side, and go in and out from gate to gate throughout the camp, and slay every man his brother, and every man his companion, and every man his neighbor." Did Moses or his God order this most grievous act? The statement by Moses that the command came from God must be a lie. Would God defy His own command, *Thou shalt not kill*, when the shedding of another man's blood did not occur? To violate His own command would compromise His integrity and honor as God.

The murder of 3,000 men is not to be taken lightly as an act sanctioned by God. God had made it clear that the taking of a person's life would only be permissible if that person killed another human being. Truly, with this command, Moses seems to have committed another impulsive and sinful act. This is another instance where there is merit to the conjecture that Moses, or an over-zealous priest, wrote the Bible without any direction or revelation from God.

One must pause at this juncture and reflect upon this seemingly sacrilegious conjecture. The impulsive acts by Moses give credence to this conjecture, for he definitely was a man committed to his beliefs, and having written the words formulated within his own mind, he defended his words to the point of violence. The murder of 3,000 people and later, the invasion of Canaan, reveals that all three religions—Judaic, Christian, and Islamic—have and will initiate force to take the lives of *nonbelievers and heretics*. This is shameful behavior exhibited by all three religions which claim to worship the same God. Leaders of these religions have repeatedly ignored and disobeyed God's command: **Thou shalt not kill.** These leaders need to evaluate instruction in their houses of worship to insure that they instill love of brothers and sisters of any nation; this would be consistent with God's command to love one another.

7.4 Judaism has its Roots in the Egyptian Religion

Now that the reader has learned more about the 'Father' and 'Founder' of the Jewish religion, it will be revealed what many people have suspected but kept to themselves for fear of reprisal. The maxim, 'give credit where credit is due' has always been the author's credo because he believes in showing appreciation for outstanding work to those who have contributed to a laudable effort. This book is replete with references to the great minds that have brought the author to the level of awareness that allows him to share some truths he has discovered. He is indebted to them and hopes these truths will serve to enlighten others to act as courageously as the people identified in "Reasons for this Book."

Giving credit where credit is due has lacked in the religious instructtion provided by rabbis, priests, ministers, imams, and mullahs. The adherents of these religions have given no acknowledgment of the influence that the Egyptians have had in the development of their Scriptures and indeed, their God. They have ignored the words of

Jesus Christ who acknowledged the Egyptian God, Amen, as the beginning of the creation of God. [1]

***These things saith the Amen, the faithful and true witness, the
beginning of the creation of God;***

It is healthy for the monotheistic religions to be proud of the thread of history that brings their worshippers to the very beginnings of their beliefs. By being aware that religious concepts were developed by the Egyptian Priesthood over thousands of years, there will be an acceptance that God slowly brings people to a higher conception of Him as they evolve into more sophisticated human beings. God is not a static concept but an integral part of the human spirit. His Holy Spirit must continue to inspire human beings to higher levels of consciousness through the righteous teachers in our world. Ikhnaton, the Priesthood of Amon, and the Israelites learned from and upgraded the scriptures of the Egyptian religion. They reacted to changes needed in their beliefs and so must current religious scriptures be revised and improved to keep pace with the evolution of humans in a changing world.

7.4.1 In the Beginning

It was noted in Subsection 4.1.1 that the hymn written by Ikhnaton, *Universal Splendor and Power of Aton,* contained the line:

Thou Living Aton, the Beginning of Life!

This powerful phrase that associates God to the beginning of life enables the author of Genesis to simply add heaven and earth. Written years later, around 950 BCE:

---

[1]　**Holy Bible**, *King James Version*, **Revelation 3:14**.

In the beginning, God created the heaven and the earth.

This is a fine example of revising a concept or restating an idea. The idea of creating heaven and earth was already cast by the Egyptians in the 6th Dynasty, around 2600 to 2495 BCE, in *The Creation by Atum*. In this hymn, the sole god Atum, who was born out of the waters of chaos, created the fundamental elements of air, moisture, the earth and heaven. Around 1300 BCE, a manuscript known as the *Re-Isis Myth*, contained two wonderful ideas.[1] One idea was already expressed in *The Creation by Atum*, which was that their god was the sole divine god who came into being by himself. But the second idea introduced many of the creations that are stated in Genesis. That is, Atum made heaven, earth, water, air, man, cattle, creeping things, birds, and fish. Let us compare the first line of Genesis with the second line of Ikhnaton's, *The Hymn to the Aton* to the first passage of the *Re-Isis Myth*:

Genesis 1:1—*In the beginning God created the heaven and earth.*

Ikhnaton's Hymn:—*O living Aton, the beginning of Life!*

Re-Isis Myth:—*The SPELL of the divine god, who came into being by himself, who made heaven, earth, water, the breath of life, fire, gods, men, small and large cattle, creeping things, birds, and fishes, the king of men and gods at one time, (for whom) the limits (go) beyond years, abounding in names, unknown to that (god) and unknown to this (god).*

The above comparisons reveal that the first line of Genesis is not original but rather a restatement of what the Egyptians already believed

---

[1]   **James B. Pritchard,** ed. by, *Ancient Near Eastern Texts,* 'The God and His Unknown Name Of Power', **Page 12**. This text, referred to as the Re-Isis Myth is dated to the 19th Dynasty, around 1350-1200 BCE.

in the above Re-Isis Myth. What is of further interest is that Chapter 1 of Genesis identifies heaven, earth, water, and the same life forms attributed to the god in the *Re-Isis Myth*. Though the order may not be the same, notice the use of the same nouns: heaven and earth, water, birds and fishes, cattle and creeping things, and of course—man.

Genesis provides a conceptual advance from the *Re-Isis Myth*; they both identify one *divine god*. However, the Re-Isis Myth is more definitive by also stating that God *"came into being by himself."* Much credit must be given to the author(s) of Genesis for the wonderful ideas that have been borrowed from Egyptian scripture and restated in an eloquent manner.

The *Re-Isis Myth* offers an aspect of time not understood by the authors of the Hebrew Testament in their development of the *Creation* in Genesis. The focus of Genesis in the Bible was the creation of Adam and Eve and a laborious and detailed lineage that leads to the twelve tribes of the Hebrew people. The record of births in the Hebrew Testament has in fact led chronologists and religious scholars to estimate the creation of heaven and earth to have taken place around 4004 BCE. But factual and empirical evidence exists that prove this date to be ludicrous. The Egyptians had a truer understanding that time is not a boundary or parameter in defining when God first existed. Note that the words given in the *Re-Isis Myth* emphasize limits that go beyond years:

. . . the divine god, who came into being by himself, who made heaven, earth, water, the breath of life, . . ., (for whom) the limits (go) beyond years, . . .

The depth of the Egyptian minds in searching for truth is astounding, for they were wise enough to comprehend that time is unbounded and limitless in their conception of God. It is unfortunate that the Hebrews so much wanted to be the chosen people of the one God that they inserted with great efforts a lineage that indicate heaven and earth being created just over 4,000 years BCE.

7.4.2 O Lord, How Manifold Are Thy Works!

The above subtitle appears in the Bible, Psalm 104:24. Note that this powerful phrase was borrowed from Ikhnaton's, *The Hymn to the Aton,* provided in Subsection 4.1.1, which states:

> *How manifold it is, what thou hast made!*
> *They are hidden from the face (of man).*
> *O thou sole god, like whom there is no other!*
> *Thou didst create the world according to thy heart.*

This hymn provides another example that proves that there must have been a joint effort by the Egyptian and Judaic priests to preserve the great body of scripture that was Egypt's greatest contribution in their conception of God. What is also commendable about Ikhnaton's hymn is that his God was for all the people of the earth, not just a chosen people. The hymn states that for all men upon the earth, the countries of Syria and Nubia, and the land of Egypt, his God sets every man in his place and supplies their necessities. Of course, Ikhnaton's world was limited to only the lands he was exposed to, but his God was the God of all people. Is the reader not impressed by the beauty and scope of this pharaoh's conception of God? He has truly left a legacy of which humans should be proud.

7.4.3 How Original Are the Ten Commandments?

There are abundant examples of Egyptian Scripture being emulated in the Hebrew Bible. However, this observation in no way belittles the Hebrew Scriptures, for their authors were righteous men who were indeed inspired to improve lives with a set of moral laws. There is no harm in applying what has been learned from the past. However, every generation owes gratitude for inheriting concepts, theories, inventions, and works of art and literature. The harm exists when plagiarism occurs and in not giving credit where credit is due because it is tantamount to stealing.

In Table 3-3 the reader has been provided with the Ten Commandments and shown that they were not new to Egyptian law. In fact, Tables 3-1 and 3-2 have revealed the numerous noble and righteous laws that exceed the content of the Ten Commandments. The protestations that an Egyptian would utter to his gods in order to be admitted into eternal life were documented as far back as the 18th and 21st Dynasties (1550-950 BCE). However, the observances of their moral and righteous laws were practiced even before being transcribed on papyrus and more than 1400 years before the Moses Exodus. The vizier, Ptahhotep, had written many wise instructions for human conduct that emphasized truth, justice, good sense, and humility under his majesty, King Isesi, as early as the 5th Dynasty.

7.5 Evolution of the Hebrew Testament

Historians estimate the formulation of Moses's first book of the Torah was during the reign of King Solomon. The basis for its initial writing had to be the scripture preserved in the Ark of the Covenant; writings that Moses himself inscribed in the *Book of the Covenant*.[1] This book contains the commands and judgments Moses received from his God at Mount Sinai. They are recorded in Exodus; Chapters 20 through 23 and Chapters 25 through 31.

Biblical scholars believe the Torah (Pentateuch) of the Old Testament was composed of at least five major narratives: the J, E, JE, P, and D documents. The first four narratives are interwoven as one document forming Genesis, and the fifth narrative embodies the Deuteronomic Code. The Book of Deuteronomy became the second book of the Torah, after which followed the last three books of Moses. A brief

---

[1]   **Holy Bible,** *King James Version,* **Exodus 24:4-7.**

summary of the evolution of the Torah is provided as it forms the basis for the word of God as envisioned by Moses. Scripture that reveals what the prophets proclaimed and other religious writings of the Bible will not be critiqued. The admonitions of prophets to their people and the songs, psalms, and Solomon's proverbs are not the subject of this book and may be read in the Bible.

The J narrative is the oldest document, written around the ninth century BCE, placing its origin during the realm of King Solomon, as illustrated in Figure 5-4. The letter J is a mnemonic for the name of Moses's God, Jehovah, also known as Yahweh. The E document is emblematic of those narratives where God is referred to as Elohim and is reputed to have originated during the eighth century BCE in the northern kingdom of Israel. Following are the P or Priestly documents, believed by scholars to have been written by Priests some 200 years after the E documents, around 600 BCE.[2]

Some clarification is in order concerning the J and E narratives. In Karen Armstrong's book, *A History of* God, she indicates that the P document makes Yahweh explain that he really was the same God as the God of Abraham. Abraham's God, known as El, the High God of Canaan, introduced himself as El Shaddai (El of the Mountain), which was one of El's traditional titles. He was a friendly and approachable God; one whom Abraham was comfortable challenging as demonstrated in Genesis 18:22-32. Abraham was able to negotiate with his Lord the reduction from 50 to 10 righteous men; if they were found in Sodom and Gomorrah, He would save these cities from destruction. While El is described as being kind in the J narrative, Yahweh is considered as a God to be feared in the E narrative. On Mount Sinai, for example, Yahweh appeared to Moses and the Israelites in the midst of an awe inspiring volcanic eruption.[3]

---

[2]   **Max I Dimont**, *Jews, God and History,* **Page 40.**

[3]   **Karen Armstrong**, *A History of God,* **Page 15. Exodus 19:16-18.**

The joint mnemonic JE represents those documents that were combined by Jewish priests who added some of their own handiwork (known as a pious fraud) in the fifth century BCE. In these documents, the Moses God was referred to as "Jehovah Elohim," which is translated as 'Lord God.' [4] Finally, the fifth major narrative is the Deuteronomic Code. It is referred to as the D documents, which were written during the interim period between the defeat of Israel in 722 BCE and destruction of the Judean nation in 586 BCE.

7.5.1 The Biblical Contributions by King Josiah

It is a tribute to the Jewish people of Judah to have survived the onslaught that decimated the Ten Tribes of Israel. This survival was due to the good fortune of having inherited the Assyrian ruler King Josiah, who started his reign at eight years of age, in 638 BCE. Josiah was the grandson of Assyrian King Manasseh who profaned the Jewish God by building altars for the sun and star gods of Babylon and Ninevah both in the inner and outer courts of the temple. He set in place a statue of Ishtar, queen of heaven, to which the people would provide libations, burn incense, and bring cakes. Not neglecting some of the Semitic deities, Manasseh also erected altars to various Baals and even sacrificed a son by giving him to the fires of the child-devouring Molech. [5]

Dimont cites the following reasons for King Josiah's actions. During Josiah's early accession, he was aware that Assyria's world empire was weakening and social inequities were corroding the national fabric of the country. He was astute enough to know that he could not institute social legislation without introducing religious reforms. Aware that justice and morality were tied in with the Mosaic code,

---

[4]   **Max I Dimont**, *Jews, God and History,* **Page 40**.

[5]   **John B. Noss**, *Man's Religions,* **Page 378**. Molech, was a god of the Ammonites and Phoenicians to whom human sacrifices were offered.

he decided not only to effect a more just distribution of wealth but to also purge the temples of idols.

In *Jews, God and History*, Dimont writes that Josiah conceived a practical plan to attribute the authority for his social and religious reforms to God. To accomplish his plan, he convened with his High Priests who stood for the same reforms, and they edited and fused parts of the J and E documents into "Holy Scripture." Upon completion, Josiah staged a ruse that this Holy Scripture had been found in a secluded part of the main temple. He immediately announced throughout the land that a book written by Moses at the command of God had been found in the temple and that it would be read aloud to the people. This book came to be known as Deuteronomy, the D document, and the second book of Moses.[6]

Another version of the appearance of Moses's second book is that it had been in the temple since the days of Solomon and was found during the temple's renovation. This version is supported by the *Second Book of Kings* but does not give a chronological account of the find. *The Book of Kings* indicates that Josiah, in the 18th year sent his scribe to the High Priest Hilkiah to have him record the sum of silver collected from the people and use it for the renovation of the temple. The 18th year refers to the number of years Josiah had reigned, not his age. Knowing King Josiah began his reign in 638 BCE, eighteen years later would place renovation of the temple around 620 BCE.

During the renovation effort, the High Priest declared a momentous find: a book of the law. When shown to the king, the king read the book's provisions, tore his garments, and charged his councilors to find out if the book was genuine and a true statement of divine law. Once the prophetess Huldah verified its authenticity, Josiah gathered

---

6   **Max I Dimont**, *Jews, God and History,* **Pages 61 and 62.**

all priests, elders, prophets, and people of Jerusalem into the temple and read the book aloud for all to hear. The king then set upon a campaign to demolish and beat to dust the altars and pillars of all the gods competing against Jehovah in Judah and continued this destruction as far north as the cities of Samaria and as far south as Beersheba.[7] By purging all temples of idols, forbidding the Baal and Astarte cults, and killing the priests of these cults, Josiah initiated a new social idealism throughout the land. The Deuteronomic Code called for greater humanitarianism toward slaves and more consideration for the needs of the poor. Although savage and cruel elements still remained, this primitive era maintained a genuine ethical advance toward justice and righteousness.

The social and religious reforms instituted by King Josiah did have its failures due in large part to their great severity, which resulted in centralized control of religion in Jerusalem. The king brought many of the priests from other city sanctuaries and centralized the performance of sacrifices within Jerusalem. It was held that proper sacrifices could only be offered in the temple. This caused the Jerusalem Priesthood to exercise absolute control over the Mosaic traditions and to maintain vested interest. The rural and village Priesthoods were abolished, causing their people to suffer a diminished sense of their God's divine presence and led many common people to regress to the more satisfying rites outlawed by the D Code.[8] However, II Kings 23:25 recognizes and honors King Josiah with the words: *And like unto him there is no king before him, that turned to the Lord with all his heart, and with all his soul, and with all his might, according to the law of Moses; neither after him arose there any like him.*

In 538 BCE, at the close of Babylonian captivity, the Jews were freed and allowed to return to Jerusalem due to the magnanimity of

---

[7]   **Holy Bible**, *King James Version*, **II Kings 23:8, 19, 20.**

[8]   **John B. Noss**, *Man's Religions,* **Page 379 and 380**.

Cyrus the Great. This founder of the Persian Empire made Babylon its Capital, and the Jews were given the freedom to pursue their faith. By this time, the Jews of Judea and Jerusalem possessed a considerable body of folklore, legends, and genealogies, the Mosaic and Deuteronomic writings, and fragments of history, which the priests now arranged into a composite work that formed the first five books of the Holy Bible. Though it is contended that much of this work was transmitted orally through the ages, the scribes and priestly writers had copied, recopied, reedited, and had given new meanings many times over as their viewpoints changed with the passing centuries. The final edit occurred around 400 BCE by two highborn Jews, Ezra and Nehemiah.[9] Ezra was a scribe at the Persian court, and Nehemiah, a descendant of Zadok.[10]

7.5.2 The Finalized Bible by Ezra and Nehemiah

The success of Nehemiah's leadership is dramatically told in his autobiography. It was through his executive genius and energy that the torn down walls and burnt gates of the temple were repaired at last, having lain in ruin for more than 150 years. Ezra accomplished the spiritual renewal of Jerusalem instituting a new theocratic state with power vested in the priests. They enacted the Mosaic covenant with a self-serving stipulation that caused discrimination against their neighbors; highlighted in bold type below, it has caused hostility toward the Jews for years to come. The following quotation from their new covenant became the center of their allegiance to God, which was adopted under oath by the assembly of Jewish worshippers.[11]

---

[9]   **Homer W. Smith**, *Man and His Gods,* **Page 92**.

[10] **Max I. Dimont**, *Jews, God and History,* **Page 68**. Zadok was the first High Priest appointed by King David. His descendents, known as Zadokites, were highly esteemed and honored by the Jews.

[11] **John B. Noss**, *Man's Religions,* **Page 389**.

"We make and sign a binding covenant . . . and take oath, under penalty of curse, to walk in the law of God which was given by Moses the servant of God, and to be careful to observe all of the commands of the LORD our Lord, and his ordinances and statues; **and that we will not give our daughters to the peoples of the land or take their daughters as wives for our sons; and that, if the peoples of the land bring wares or any grain on the Sabbath day to sell, we will not buy from them on the Sabbath or on a holy day;** *and that in the seventh year we will leave the land fallow and refrain from the extraction of any debt.*

"We also lay upon ourselves the charge to give the third part of a shekel yearly for the service for the house of our God, for the bread that is arranged in layers, and for the regular burnt-offering, for the Sabbaths, the new moons, the fixed festivals, and the holy things, and for the sin-offerings to make atonement for Israel, and for all the work of the house of our God. Moreover, we will cast lots, the priests, the Levites, and the people, concerning the wood-offering, to bring it into the house of our God, . . . to burn upon the altar of the Lord our God . . . ; and to bring the first produce of our ground and the first of all fruit of every kind of tree year by year to the house of the Lord; also the first-born of our sons and of our cattle, as it is written in the law, and the firstlings of our herds and our flocks, . . . and our first batch of baking, our contributions, the fruit of every kind of tree, the wine, and the oil, to the priests in the chambers of the house of our God; and the tithes of our ground to the Levites, since they, the Levites, take the tithes in all the cities dependent on our agriculture. Now the priest, the son of Aaron, shall be with the Levites, when the Levites tithe, and the Levites shall bring up the tithe of the tithes to the house of our God, to the chambers into the treasure house."

The precepts instituted by Nehemiah and Ezra assured the self preservation of their people both ethnically and religiously. The innovation of banning intermarriage between Jews and non-Jews was the first such ban on intermarriage in the world. From the continuous ravages of war over the centuries and years of captivity experienced several times over several generations, it is understandable that this action was strictly a defense against future dilution of their people and their religion. They were the chosen people of God. But their leaders never articulated for what they were chosen. Did their religious leaders clearly express that they were chosen to be the light of the world? This precept was apparently overlooked and never expounded in their houses of worship nor stated in their commandments. Their utmost concern was how they, as a people, would survive in a world that could once again threaten their existence.

The forbidding of intermarriage did not sit well with many Jews, but their high priests were intent on forging a national religious movement that would have a greater chance of success by omitting other ethnic groups who had their own beliefs and gods. Still, the restriction on intermarriage by Ezra and Nehemiah backfired and caused a great deal of discrimination and hostility against the Jewish people. That stigma survived into modern times and has caused them to be ostracized in many parts of the world.

Years ago as a design engineer, the author enjoyed the acquaintance of an extremely capable engineer who worked as a consultant.

He was Jewish and had married a very fine Italian woman. Though their marriage maintained a genuine, loving relationship, this man had been disowned by his parents; as extremely observant Jews will do to children who marry outside their faith. This parental response clearly revealed a reaction due to their instruction within their religion. It appears that the rabbis were more intent in the preservation of their profession than advocating that their people have been chosen to be an instrument of God. If they were chosen to receive the Word of

God, should not their responsibility be to share and bring His Word to all people?

Not to disparage the Jewish people, the reality is that they still continue to renounce intermarriage for fear of dilution of their people and a possible weakening of their religion. Hopefully they will someday recognize that they have been chosen by God to instruct all people with a moral code that promotes respect and love for all people. Admittedly, this responsibility may be overwhelming, but God did not choose them to save only themselves. The exclusion of people who are not of the same religion has also existed among Christians and Muslims. It is amazing that leaders of the three monotheistic religions teach the surrender of oneself to God but fail to teach that God would rather have His children, from all nations, love one another. It is apparent that the whole concept of God is missed when religious leaders encourage separatism, bigotry, and killing instead of loving one another in His name.

Ezra and Nehemiah enacted another innovation that would create national and spiritual unity among the Jews: they decided not only to revise the Book of Deuteronomy but to add four other Books of Moses. They directed their priests and scribes to fuse together the most important Mosaic documents, including the Deuteronomy of Josiah, into what are known as the Five Books of Moses: Genesis, Exodus, Leviticus, Numbers and Deuteronomy. From this point in history, these books were regarded as divine, and no changes would be made.

To commemorate this revered set of books, in 444 BCE Ezra and Nehemiah spread the news that on the Jewish New Year, the Five Books of Moses written by Moses would be read aloud to all the people. Interpreters were on hand since many of the Jews had forgotten Hebrew, and the Aramaic language had become their everyday speech in a land that included dozens of other Semitic nations. The need for interpreters led to the practice of clarifying and explaining obscure parts of the Torah, whereby the word *Midrash* developed, meaning 'exposition.'[12] This practice would eventually lead to the growth of a group of rabbis who came from the ranks of scribes and had a strong grasp of the contents of the Books of Moses.

Another effort by Ezra and Nehemiah was to enforce strict observation of religious duties which the Jews performed with increasing loyalty even if they were lax in their reverence toward God. The observance of the weekly Sabbath day drew them to the temple in Jerusalem or to the outlying towns and villages where the synagogues sprung up as houses of worship. The annual festivals and fasts have become ingrained traditions, including the weeklong Passover or Feast of Unleavened Bread that occurs in the first month of the year (March or April). In addition, there is the Feast of Weeks or First Fruits, occurring in late spring, and the Feast of Trumpets (later called "Rosh Hashanah" or New Year), which is followed ten days later by the fast of the Day of Atonement or Yom Kippur. Five days after Yom Kippur comes the Feast of Booths or Tabernacles, which occurs in the seventh month (September or October). Although the pure religion advocated by the prophets could not hold the allegiance of the common people to their faith, these observances did.[13]

Just over 800 years from the Moses Exodus (1250-444 BCE), the Jewish religion was set in scripture. The Torah, the first Five Books of Moses, was completed as the result of the reforms of Josiah, the innovations of Nehemiah and Ezra, the devotion of High Priests, and the complement of scribes who eventually gained the status of holy men called Rabbis. The impact of these scriptures was the absorption of divine literature that affected the character of the Jews and formed

---

[12]   **Max I. Dimont**, *Jews, God and History*, **Pages 69 and 70**.

[13]   **John B. Noss**, *Man's Religions*, **Page 390**.

an identity that coalesced the Jewish nation. The Jewish people now had a religion packaged in scripture that provided the mobility to carry their God to any country and retain their ethnicity. Their strength against all adversity will later prove to be the Torah.

In concert with the development of the Torah and its supplementary writings of the prophets' warnings, the chronicles and psalms, the High Priest became the supreme authority over the Jewish people. He became not only the ecclesiastical personage but also the civic ruler of Jerusalem. The High Priest was usually a descendant of Zadok, who was said to have descended from Aaron, the brother of Moses. He lived in the temple and under him were the ordained priests who ministered in the temple during religious ceremonies. Also under his authority were the Levites who were in charge of the temple musical services and temple property. Though the High Priest was the chief administrator, his power was held in check by the Sanhedrin whose members were chosen from the leading families, scholars, and intellectuals. This body totaled 71 members when acting in the capacity of a Supreme Court; and for judging capital offenses, as many as 23 judges were present. For civil cases and matters less offensive, a minimum of three judges was required.

This review of religious history has revealed some observations. Just as the Egyptian civilization developed with two major religious and ruling (R&R) authorities, the Priesthood and pharaohs, so did the Jews survive by their reliance on both the political rule by their kings and religious rule through their high priests. In fact, the R&R entities of the Jewish communities were closely fused together to insure their success. This symbiotic relationship between church and state, or R&R organizations, has continued into the present for many countries. Some countries, like Iran, have fused the two components into one while others, like the United States, Italy, and Israel have both bodies existing independent of one another.

The other observation has verified a maxim—that people learn from the building blocks provided by their ancestors. The reader has learned that the first five books of the Bible were not inspired and completed by Moses but that he was the inspiration, through his knowledge of the Egyptian Scriptures, for writing the *Book of the Covenant* that compelled other righteous men to complete the Torah about 850 years later.

7.6 Judaism Conceived the Holy Spirit

The Judaic extension of faith to the gentiles may appear to have been a natural development. However, Chapter 8.0 reveals that the destruction of Jerusalem by the Romans was a critical event that motivated Jewish Holy Men to preserve their God with the birth of a new religion, Christianity. The Jewish people should be honored that one of their sons, Jesus Christ, became a source of worship for followers of Christianity.

In spite of the devastation of Israel's territories and loss of countless Jewish lives during the Jewish-Roman War, history verifies that mankind holds on to those concepts that are powerful and helpful in successfully coping with life's challenges. In addition to the acceptance of Jesus as the Son of God, the Christians have also accepted a belief in a Holy Spirit.

The concept of the Holy Spirit was developed within the Judaic religion before Christian dogma conceived it as being another manifestation of God. In 1961, a manuscript found along with the Dead Sea Scrolls was deciphered by Mr. M. Baillet, who believed it to have been written around the middle of the 2nd century BCE. This document entitled, *The Words of the Heavenly Lights*, contained prayers and hymns intended for various days of the week. Each of the liturgical sections concluded with the pronouncement, *Amen! Amen!* This document may be ascribed to be the earliest, pre-Essene stage of Qumran literature. An excerpt from Part V of this document is provided to verify that use of the *Holy Spirit* was common in Jewish prayer.[1]

> *For Thou hast shed **Thy Holy Spirit** upon us, bringing upon us Thy blessings, that we might seek Thee in our distress [and mur]mer (prayers) in the ordeal of Thy chastisement. We have entered into distress, have been [stri]cken and tried by the fury of the oppressor. For we also have tired God with our iniquity, we have wearied the Rock with [our] sins . . .*

It is comforting to learn that *The Holy Spirit* was an idea embraced by Jewish prophets and priests; holy men who felt a strong affinity for the God they worshipped. Isaiah felt the Spirit of God within him and, in Isaiah 63:10-11, *The Holy Spirit* of God is uniquely identified:

63:10 *But they rebelled, and vexed **His Holy Spirit**: therefore He was turned to be their enemy, and He fought against them.*

63:11 *Then He remembered the days of old, Moses, and His people, saying, "Where is he that brought them out of the sea with the shepherd of his flock? Where is he that put **His Holy Spirit** within him?"*

The concept of the *Holy Spirit* of God gives worshippers a feeling of holiness—a close emotional association with their god. The Holy Spirit pervades space and may be experienced as a subjective feeling. Jesus Christ in John 14:15-17, 26 and 16:13,14 refers to the *Holy Spirit* as the *Comforter*—the *Spirit of Truth*. Because the Catholic Church characterizes the Holy Spirit as the third Person of the Trinity, a theological and philosophical question arises as to

---

[1]   **Geza Vermes**, *The Dead Sea Scrolls In English*, **Page 204**. Derived from Mr. M. Baillet, Revue Biblique, Un recueil liturgique de Qumran, Grotte 4: 'Les paroles des luminaries, Pages 195-250.

whether it is another "Person" or simply the Spirit of God. There is, however, another force that also pervades space and ennobles the human spirit—that is the feeling of love for humanity. To feel holy is a self-seeking desire that promotes closeness to God, but to love is a proactive desire to benefit and improve the lives of others. Whereas the Holy Spirit is received from *without*, the Spirit of Love comes from *within* the human makeup of a person. Human beings are endowed with the ability to love others regardless of any belief in a higher power, such as God. Love given to others with sincerity and respect has been the driving force for man's survival.

8.0   Catholicism Evolves from Judaism

Just as the Torah of the Hebrew Testament evolved from the initial efforts of Moses, the New Testament is based upon the Gospels of Apostles. The apostles brought to light a man named Jesus of Nazareth who ignited the spiritual nature of mankind. Similarly, just as Judaism developed from the Egyptian religion that defined the God Amen, Catholicism developed from the Judaic religion by the efforts of Jewish holy men.

Max I. Dimont has described the events that caused the downfall of Judah as the second kingdom.[1] Within the ruling and priestly families of this kingdom, differences became so overwhelming in reaction to their competing religious teachings and the outside world that three religious sects emerged. The three sects took such divergent views in their religious and political thinking, that increased tensions caused a physical division of devotion to their god. The Sadducees were the party of the aristocrats and priestly class who stood for temple, priest, sacrifice, and a conservative view of religion. The Pharisees were the party of the common man, led by rabbis and scribes who stood for synagogue, prayer, and a liberal view of religion. The third party, the Essenes, were a conservative religious sect which physically withdrew from the political arena altogether and retired to the caves on the western shore of the Dead Sea. The Essenes lived a monastic life, and the fight for religious and political power was of no interest to them.

The outside moral and intellectual influences of the Greeks and Romans led the Sadducees and Pharisees to develop such divergent views of acceptance that a power struggle between these two sects resulted in acts of violence. Both contended for the Kingship and High Priest positions of Judah. Money, always the standard of power,

---

[1]   **Max I. Dimont**, *Jews, God and History*, published by Signet Books.

could be raised by the ruling king through taxation. But the High Priest received a steady and voluntary income from the Jewish people as atonement for their souls.[2] This distinction made the holy office a position often taken by the ruling king in the Judaic kingdom.

The internal strife between the royal families of the Sadducees and Pharisees resulted in the murder of a mother, fathers, brothers, sons and other family relations. Internal conflicts introduced another sect called the Zealots, who strongly desired freedom from the yoke of Roman rule. The differences between these three sects finally caused a collapse of the kingdom as its rule came under a half-Jew, Herod, a commoner without any royal Israeli blood.

The power struggles of the three proactive sects continued well past the death of Jesus's Christ in 30 AD[3] to the destruction of Jerusalem. During Jesus short life of 35 years, his thinking had to be shaped by the views and tensions that existed in the nearby cities and towns. The events he witnessed, his awareness of the appalling internal strife over the past one hundred years, and his religious instruction had to cause

---

[2]   **Holy Bible**, *King James Version*, **Exodus 30:13-16**. The rich or poor shall not give less than half a shekel for an offering to the Lord and atonement for their souls.

[3]   **Holy Bible**, *King James Ver*, Regency Publ House, 1978, **Page 563**. Clarification is necessary regarding what signifies the end of **BC** and the start of **AD**. These mnemonics mean "Before Christ" and "Anno Domini (the year of the Lord)". Confusion arises as to the meaning of **AD**; many people have interpreted it as "After Death" of Jesus Christ.Use of these mnemonics have lost favor for two other reasons: (1) **Common Era** is less offensive to atheists and worshippers of other religions; and (2) according to the Holy Bible, Jesus Christ was born between 5 and 4 BCE. It has become more useful to divide the two eras associated with Jesus Christ with only one common point CE, where **BCE** indicates all years before the birth of Christ and **CE** indicates years following the birth of Christ.

within him a reaction to the discontent felt by the Jewish people. It was almost a generation after his death, that his apostles, Jewish holy men, were responsible for writing the core of the New Testament, namely, the four Gospels of Mark, Matthew, Luke and John. John also wrote, "The Revelation," another inspired work in which he reveals the testimony and prophesy of Jesus Christ. These men, through the advocacy of Paul and the destruction of Israel, provided the foundation of Holy Scripture that gave rise to the Christian religion.

8.1 What Events Initiated Writing of the Gospels?

Why did it take more than a generation before the disciples of Jesus wrote Gospels to advocate their belief in him as the Son of Man, and ultimately, the Son of God? He performed so many miracles: curing many from leprosy; giving sight to the blind; making the cripple and lame whole again; healing great multitudes that followed him; turning water into wine at a marriage in Cana; raising the son of a mother from the dead in the city Nain; raising from death the daughter of a ruler of a synagogue; walking on water to his disciples who were troubled at sea; curing many men of disease in the land of Gennesaret; feeding more than 5,000 men, women and children with only five loaves of bread and two fish; and feeding more than 4,000 men, women and children with only seven loaves of bread and a few fish. Even more unforgettable and never before done by any man, was Jesus' resurrecting a man named Lazarus after Lazarus had been dead for four days. The most marvelous miracle of all was Jesus's own resurrection after three days, and soon after, meeting with his apostles before his ascendance into heaven.

With such a lengthy number of miracles, why did it take so long for Jewish holy men to decide to write Gospels affirming their Lord? A Gospel is defined as good news that is regarded as absolutely true. Yet, it took almost forty years for the Gospels to be written to confirm the miracles of Jesus and his teachings to the multitudes. To raise the dead on three different occasions and then to rise from his own death had to have made an indelible impression not only on his disciples but the thousands of people who witnessed his miracles. Yet, it took close to 40 years before the first Gospel of the New Testament was written by Mark with the Gospels of Matthew, Luke, and John following after 80 CE. It appears that a highly motivating event occurred that compelled several holy men to sit down and write, finally, about Jesus Christ.

The urgency in writing the Gospels occurred to the Jewish Priesthood at the start of the Jewish-Roman war, which started in May of 66 CE. Having seen their temple destroyed and their people almost totally decimated and scattered by 70 CE, it seems plausible that several priests found it necessary to save their religion through the Essene movement. This was the one Jewish sect that, through their strict observance of God's law, 'Thou shalt not kill,' refrained from being involved in the Jewish-Roman war, but also, accepted non-Jews who believed in Jesus Christ as their messiah.

The conjecture that Jewish holy men were concerned with salvaging their religion as they saw the inevitable destruction of their temple and the slaughter of more than a million of their people throughout the many towns and cities in Syria and Palestine is worth pursuing. The conjecture that it was Jewish holy men that: (1) were compelled to advance the Essene movement by using Jesus Christ as its focus; (2) believed it was prudent to open their religion to other nations and peoples of the world; and (3) needed to minimize the death of their religion caused by the utter destruction of their nation will be explored.

In Section 7.5, the reader learned that the Israelites became a people with one identifying feature—the belief in one God taught and recorded by Moses in the *Book of the Covenant* during the 1250 BCE Exodus. This belief was documented during the reign of Solomon by 950 BCE and finally completed as the Five Books of Moses in 444 BCE. It was this belief that unified the Jewish people and strengthened their conviction: being the chosen people of God, they could withstand any adversity by other nations. The short summary below verifies the tenacity of the Jewish people to preserve their way of life and belief in God.

Five years after King Solomon's death, Pharaoh Sheshonk I invaded Palestine in 926 BCE and successfully ransacked the towns on the plain of Jezreel, Rehob on the north, Hapharaim, Megiddo, Taanach, Shunem, and Bethshean on the east side of the Jordan Valley. In the south, Sheshonk plundered Yeraza, Bethoron, Ajalon, Gibeon, Socoh, Beth-Anoth, Sharuhen and Arad. His army entered Judah and in Jerusalem gathered its wealth accumulated during Solomon's rule. Among Sheshonk's records of the Palestinian towns taken was a place called, "Field of Abram." This find raises a speculative assertion that it could be the name of Israel's founder Abraham, related in the Hebrew Bible, Genesis.[1]

After a ten-year war, the Assyrians defeated Israel in 722 BCE. In 597 BCE, Jerusalem fell to the Babylonian king, Nebuchadrezzar. Joining forces with Egypt, Judah strove for independence, but once again Nebuchadrezzar crushed the rebellion in 586 BCE. By 530 BCE, the Jews were under Persian rule, but the Persian king allowed Nehemiah, the governor of Judah and, Ezra, a scribe of the court, to teach Mosaic Law. In 332 BCE, Alexander the Great defeated the Persians and allowed the Jews to practice their religion. Freedom to worship caused internal conflicts within the Jewish nation as the Pharisees and Sadducees resisted Hellenization. After the Romans defeated the Greeks in 64 BCE, the bitter rivalry between these sects continued and worsened as Zealots and Christians emerged in a continuing fight for independence. Strong resistance to Roman culture and religious beliefs led to several Jewish revolts and forced Rome to expend military strength.[2]

---

[1]   **James H. Brested**, *A History of Egypt,* **Pages 526-531**.

[2]   **Max I. Dimont**, *Jews, God and History,* **Pages 56-106**.

By May of 66 CE, at the start of the Jewish-Roman War, religious leaders in Israel realized that the destruction of Israel was evident. By September 8, 70 CE, the Jewish nation was totally decimated and scattered by the Roman armies. During the entire Jewish-Roman War, Flavius Josephus estimated that over 1,100,000 Jews died and 97,000 were captured.[3] Table 8-1 is in close agreement with Josephus's numbers and is provided to emphasize the extent of Jews killed and captured in the cities, towns, and villages of Syria, Palestine, and Egypt. The devastation of the Jewish nation motivated their religious leaders to salvage their belief in God by creating Scripture that is now known as the New Testament. This conclusion is evident because the Gospel of Mark was written just prior to, or at the start of, the Jewish-Roman War and the Gospels of Matthew, Luke, and John were written at least 10 or more years after the war (Section 8.2).

The greatest identifying feature of the Jewish people is their religion; their belief in the one God as received by Moses and embodied in the Torah. The pending outcome of the war posed a pressing need by Jewish religious leaders to preserve their one God belief. By 68 CE, there was no doubt by these leaders that their nation would be torn apart by the war. They also recognized that the Essenes were not only increasing their membership with Jews but also gentiles who believed in the messianic message of Jesus—a Jew grounded in the Torah and their one God belief.

By the end of the war, the Priesthood of the Jews, consisting of Sadducees and Pharisees, was inoperative. It became apparent to perceptive Jewish leaders that the legacy of their one God would continue to live through the Essene movement by incorporating the teachings of Jesus and his apostle, Paul. It should be remembered that

---

[3]   **William Whiston**, translation of Flavius Josephus, *The History of the Destruction of Jerusalem.*

Table 8-1. Jews Slain and Captured in Jewish-Roman War.

Date	Roman or Jewish Leadership	Affected Villages and/or Cities	Jews Slain	Jews Captured
Prior to Jewish-Roman War in 66 CE	Roman procurator, Gessius Florus. Enraged seditious Jews.	Jerusalem (Upper Market Place) Cesarea Syrian villages, Philadelphia, Gerasa, Sebonitis, Pella, Scythopolis, Hippos, Gadara, Kedasa, Ptolemais, Gaba, Cesarea, Sebaste (Samaria), Gaza Askelon and Anthedon.	3,600 20,000 15,000	
	Seditious Jews response to those slain in Cesarea.	Scythopolis (Jews slain) Askelon and Ptolemais Hippos, Gadara and other cities.	13,000 4,500 6,000	
	Alexandria Governor, Tiberius Alexander	Delta in Alexandria, Egypt	50,000	
October, 66 CE Through March, 68 CE.	Syria Governor, Gaius Cestius Gallus.	Joppa Narbatene Sepphoris in Galilee	8,400 5,000 2,000	
	People retaliate after Jews defeat 12th Roman Legion.	Damascus	10,000	
	Roman General, Vespasian and son Titus. Commanders Trajan and Cerealis. Titus came later. Cerealis soldiers. Vespasian Vespasian and Titus.	Jotapata, under the command of Josephus Flavius. Japha Gerizzim in Samaria Joppa Tiberias	40,000 12,000 3,000 11,600 4,200 7,700	1,200 2,130 37,500
	Vespasian and Titus. Titus	Gamala Gischala	9.000 6,000	3,000

Table 8-1 Continued				
Date	*Roman or Jewish Leadership*	*Affected Villages and/or Cities*	*Jews Slain*	*Jews Captured*
March, 68 CE through June, 69 CE.	Zealots under John the Levite. Vespasian commander, Placidus. Vespasian Vespasian commander, Lucios Annius	Cities below Jerusalem (Engaddi). Bethennabris, a village of Gadara. Abila, Julias, Bezemoth and other cities along the Dead Sea. Lydda, Jamnia, Betaris and Caphartobas. Gerasa	700 15,000 2,000 2,000 10,000 1,000	2,200 1,000 2,000
June, 69 CE up to April, 70 CE.	John the Levite aided by 20,000 Idumean soldiers. Zealots again kill Jews. Three seditious parties within the Temple: John the Levite, Simon bar Giora the Idumaean, and Eleazar, son of Simon.	Temple of Jerusalem. Jews not willing to join seditious zealots were killed. Also killed were the high priests Jesus, Ananus and Zacharias, son of Baruch (cited in Mattew 23:35). John fought both Idumaean parties, which not only killed many of their own but also the powerless Jews that were prevented from running away.	8,500 12,000 4,000	
April 14, 70 CE to the destruction of Jerusalem, Sept 8, 70 CE.	Titus supported by several legions commanded by Tiberius Alexander, governor of Egypt and legions from Syria. Together, they attacked the Jewish Temple in Jerusalem.	Deaths by famine in Jerusalem Temple. Deaths due to Jews thrown out the Temple gates and shut up in very large houses. Roman soldiers burn Temple and Jewish-Roman War ends.	115,880 600,000 10,000	20,000
TOTALS	*Estimates are in close Agreement with Flavius Josephus.*		1,012,080	66,830

the Gospels were written by Jewish holy men. They were grounded in the extraordinary restrictions of the Torah. However, Paul's teachings revealed something new: the idea that man could be saved from sin and achieve unity with God through their belief in Jesus.

8.2 The Gospels of Mark, Matthew, Luke, and John

It is held by most religious theologians that the first three Gospels were based upon a source document referred to as "Q", which stands for the German word *Quelle* (meaning source). Matthew and Luke wrote independently of each other but because they contain nearly 200 verses that are nearly identical, the conclusion that they used a third document appears valid. Mark's Gospel has only 30 verses that do not appear in Matthew and Luke, for which reason Mark also must have had the good fortune to make use of the Q document or may have in fact have been the original creator of the document. Existence of the Q document is inferred by theologians since there is no actual surviving copy. But it would seem natural that the followers of Jesus Christ had some unofficial writings that his disciples remembered and recorded up to 20 or more years after his death. Many theologians believe that the Q document was an early "sayings" Gospel. It included many of Jesus's statements with little about his life. These theological analysts believe that it was a pre-Christian document because Jesus's birth, selection of 12 disciples, crucifixion, and resurrection were not mentioned. Their reasoning may or may not be valid, but they agree that this document presents Jesus as a charismatic teacher, healer, and humble man filled with the spirit of God, the wisdom of a sage, and a deep love for mankind.[1]

Due to the widespread impact of Paul's ministry and availability of his epistles, many of his views about how the life of Jesus affects man's relationship to God supplemented the Q document in the creation of the Gospels. More importantly and usually overlooked, is the influence of the Essene sect on the initial establishment of Christian beliefs and

---

[1] Internet: http://www.religioustolerance.org/chr_ntbl1.htm

traditions. One of the greatest finds in archaeology was the discovery of the Dead Sea Scrolls. These scrolls contained old Hebrew manuscripts and provided evidence of the religious beliefs and practices of the Essenes. Among these scrolls were some extremely important documents that date back to about 200 to 100 years BCE. The manuscripts that particularly reveal the Essenes' religious creed and rites are those given the titles: *Manual of Discipline, Habakkuk Commentary, The War of the Sons of Light with the Sons of Darkness,* and the *Zadokite Fragments.* These documents reveal that the Essenes believed in a messiah called the "Teacher of Righteousness" who died a violent death by the Sons of Darkness. The Essenes referred to themselves as the 'Elect of God' and referred to their religious community as the "New Covenant." Their members were initiated through baptism and they had a protocol that closely follows the seating of the Last Supper.

Many similarities exist between Jesus and the Teacher of Righteousness, who met his death around 65-53 BCE. He preached penitence, poverty, humility, love of one's neighbor, chastity, and like Jesus, he observed the Law of Moses. Revered as the divine Messiah of God and Redeemer of the World, he became the object of hostility by the Pharisees and Sadducees and was condemned to death. Like Jesus, this teacher was believed to be the supreme judge at the end of the world. He founded the Essene church, whose worshippers fervently awaited his glorious return. Their essential rite was the sacred meal ministered by other priests. Therefore, the Essenes, a major sect of the Jews, set the stage for accepting Jesus as the messiah and formulated the basic rites of baptism and communion performed by many Christian denominations today. These facts are not acknowledged by either the Jewish or Christian religions; for the former would not want credit for the development of Christianity, and the latter would feel the impact of their New Testament would be lessened if the Christian church were regarded as having its beginnings with the Essenes as far back as 200 BCE. The evidence of the Dead Sea Scrolls also agrees with a handful of scholars and historians, such as Josephus, Philo, the

Roman scholar Pliny, and Christian D. Ginsberg, who published a treatise entitled *The Essenes: Their History and Doctrines.* It would appear that Christianity did not originate with Jesus, but that he was its greatest and noblest spokesman.[2]

In summary, several influences contributed to and sparked creation of the Gospels that form the New Testament. They are:

*   The Hebrew Bible, Tanakh (Hebrew Testament), which embodies: the five Books of Moses (according to tradition) or Torah; Nevi'im, the Prophets; and Kethuvim, the writings.
*   The Essenes refused to join the war efforts of the Pharisees, Sadducees and Zealots. This one sect survived the Roman onslaught and killing of Jews throughout Syria and Palestine.
*   The Essenes strongly believed in the coming of a messiah and performed the rites of baptism and the communion of bread.
*   The sayings of Jesus were captured by Mark and/or the Q documents.
*   The strong influence of Paul's writings that explain the purpose of Jesus by emphasizing that through his intercession with the Father one can be redeemed from sin; that animal sacrifice, circumcision, and the Law are superseded by the overriding command to love one another; and that through belief in Jesus and God's Word, one can attain salvation and everlasting life.
*   The Jewish-Roman War that started in May 66 CE and ended in September 70 CE nearly annihilated the Jews and destroyed their nation. The decimation and captivity of their people initiated an urgency in the Jewish Priesthood to preserve their religion.
*   The urgency of preserving the Jewish belief in one God was fulfilled by the Essenes who accepted Jesus as the messiah.
*   The first Christians were Jews from the Essene sect. They were the Jews who established the first Christian church.

---

[2]   **Max I. Dimon**t, *Jews, God and History,* **Pages 130-133.**

- Jewish holy men created the Gospels of Mark, Matthew, Luke, and John based upon the teachings of Jesus and the religious concepts of Paul. These Gospels provided the groundwork for the birth of Christianity.

It was Paul that interpreted the teachings of Jesus and formulated religious precepts based upon his death. Two precepts he advocated were that circumcision was just as unnecessary as the adherence to Jewish dietary laws in the worship of God. But the most crucial precept was the teachings of Christ; whereby his new command to love one another as he loved us would replace the Torah's abundant sets of commands that included animal sacrifices, the specific requirements for vestments worn by the priests, the requirements for building their house of worship for God, as well as the articles required to worship their God within the temple. To examine the extensive set of commands received by Moses from God, many of which are archaic for worship in the modern world, the reader is referred to Exodus, Chapters 20 through 23, and Chapters 25 through 31. While Jesus's first two precepts as promulgated by Paul caused much consternation among the Sadducees and Pharisees, the final schism between the conservative Jews and emerging Christians was the substitution of the word of God revealed in the Torah by Paul's revelation—that mankind could know God through Jesus Christ.[3]

As the Christian church grew, there came a need to develop a uniform and coherent Scripture. The first attempt to bring order to the chaotic multitude of more than 50 written Gospels was around 170 CE. This initial list was referred to as the Muratorian Canon. It was not until 395 CE that the New Testament was formed with those texts that provided continuity about Jesus and reflected the religious concepts developed by Paul. The other Gospels were banned and possession of them was not only heresy, but heresy punishable by death.[4]

---

[3]   **Max I. Dimont,** *Jews, God and History,* **Page 142.**

[4]   **Max I. Dimont,** *Jews, God and History,* **Pages 148, 149.**

The New Testament consists of four Gospels listed below and includes *The Revelation,* presumed to have been written by Saint John the Divine. Listed in the order of their creation, the dates are given in ranges because scholars and theologians can only agree on estimates.

> The Gospel of Mark 66-70 CE
>
> The Gospel of Matthew 80-90 CE
>
> The Gospel of Luke 80-95 CE
>
> The Gospel of John 90-120 CE
>
> The Revelation 95-120 CE

8.2.1 The Gospel of Mark.

Most theologians and scholars agree that the Gospel of Mark preceded those of Matthew, Luke, and John. Not an apostle of Jesus, Mark assisted Paul on some of his missionary work and is believed to have written the recollections of Saint Peter.[1] It was written in the language of common people at a time when there was great tension between the conservative Jewish Christians centered in Jerusalem and the more liberal Christians who followed the precepts of Paul. Mark's Gospel succinctly states the embodiment of all of Jesus's teachings. His words were not new; he restated Moses's Law presented in Deuteronomy 6:4-5, known as the "Shema," along with the ever popular command given in Leviticus 19:18. What is significant is what has been added to the Torah verses by Mark and is provided below in ***Bold Italics:***

Mark 12:29. Jesus answered; ***The first of all commandments is,***

> *Hear, O Israel: The Lord our God is one Lord (Deut 6:4); And thou shalt love the Lord thy God with all thine heart, and with*

---

[1]   **John B. Noss,** *Man's Religions,* **Page 447.**

all thy soul, and with all thy mind, and with all thy strength (Deut 6:5): **this is the first commandment.**

Mark 12:31. Jesus restates Leviticus 19:18 as:

And the second is like, namely this, *Thou shalt love thy neighbor as thyself (Lev 19:18).* **There is none other commandment greater than these.**

It is the last line spoken by Jesus that simplifies the whole of Moses's Laws given in Exodus, Chapters 20 through 23, and Chapters 25 through 31. It is an astounding concept that love of God and human beings is *"greater than"* all of the laws received by Moses from God. Is it possible that God Himself, through Jesus, was willing to simplify all the law, not only what He provided directly to Moses but also the extensions, explanations, new insights, and interpretations of the scribes and rabbis, which now constitute the Talmud and Midrashim?[2] It will be revealed that the Gospel of Matthew drives the nail deeper to emphasize that the restated commands of Jesus

---

[2]   The Talmud, known as the "Oral Torah" provides the flexibility of Judaic Law to keep pace with changes that take place in each age. As new challenges present themselves, interpretation and reinterpretation may be required based upon new conditions in life. Midrashim is a compilation of Midrash stories, explanations, incidents, and antidotes that illuminates how one may understand a moral truth or law in the Torah. Both the Talmud and Midrashim are provided by esteemed rabbis to supplement the Torah. The benefits of this supplementary scripture are commendable but the Talmud and Midrashim have expanded the written Word of God; consequently, one must be introduced to its intricacies by a competent teacher (Louis Jacobs, *The Book of Jewish Belief,* Page 20). As a reaction to the added rabbinic laws, restrictions and judgments, it was Jesus who simplified and captured the whole of God's Word by the commandments stated in Mark 12:29 and 12:31.

replaces the multitudinous commands, and in many cases, outdated commands of the Torah and laws of the Talmud.

8.2.2 The Gospel of Matthew.

Matthew is identified as a tax collector (publican) and a disciple of Jesus in Matthew 10:3, Mark 2:14, and Luke 5:27. The son of a Levi, he was highly knowledgeable of the Torah, and he made it clear that Jesus was from the line of David by enumerating at the start of his Gospel, a genealogy that starts with Abraham. Created after Mark's, the Gospel of Matthew may have been purposely placed at the beginning of the New Testament by the Church Fathers because it casts Jesus as descending from the revered family of men that have communicated with God.

Much of Matthew's Gospel presents Jesus's teachings in Chapters 5, 6, and 7. Embedded within Chapter 6:9-13 is one of the most holy prayers of Christianity, the *Our Father.* But it is in Chapter 22:37-40 that Matthew takes *"the greatest commandments"* stated in Mark to an even higher level, for he has Jesus state:

> **On these two commandments**
> **hang all the law and the prophets.**

Here, Matthew places the two commands as the greatest of all the laws written in the Torah and causes the greatest break between the conservative and liberal Jews. Matthew follows Chapter 22 with the chastisements Jesus makes against the Scribes, Rabbis and Pharisees (23:1-39). To emphasize the two commandments, Jesus then predicts the destruction of Jerusalem in his generation and cautions them with the following reprimand:

Matt 23:38. *Behold, your house is left unto you desolate.*

Matt 23:39. *For I say unto you, Ye shall not see me henceforth, till ye shall say, Blessed is he that cometh in the name of the Lord.*

The Sadducees, Pharisees, Rabbis, and Scribes that form the set of conservative Jews are admonished by Jesus that God will not bless them until they acknowledge he came in the name of the Lord. This New Testament offers an alternative for all Jews. However, it is a most difficult decision because the Gospel of John no longer emphasized Jesus as the Son of Man; but instead, as the Son of God. The great religious institution of the Jews could not easily extend their belief in one God to include a Son of God. In the first three Gospels, Jesus always claimed that he was the Son of Man. He was from the line of David, a Jew, so that his identity as a child of the chosen people of God would not be compromised. The deeply embedded belief in the worship of only one God has prevented conservative Jews and established Rabbis to extend their vision and accept Jesus as a Son of God. As a people, they cannot be faulted for holding on to their legacy, partly out of pride and partly out of the difficulty of accepting change. Ikhnaton had experienced the same reaction when his greatest religious change was to replace the worship of many gods with one God.

It is to be noted that the destruction of Jerusalem had already taken place, since this Gospel was created between 80 and 90 CE. It may be that Jesus predicted the destruction of Jerusalem as occurring in his generation, but he did not predict the end of the world. During the Jewish-Roman war, the seditious Zealots killed several of their most esteemed high priests; such as Jesus, the son of Gamalas, and Ananus, the son of Ananus. The atrocious act of killing one of the most eminent of their citizens, Zacharias, son of Baruch, is also mentioned in Matthew 23:35. This event agrees with the account given by Flavius Josephus. The event of Zacharias's death, described by Matthew and Josephus, further substantiates that the Gospel was written at the end of, or a few years after, the Jewish-Roman war. Considering that this was an important document for the multitude, it would have required review and approval by Matthew's peers so it would have likely been released several years after the destruction of Jerusalem.

8.2.3 The Gospel of Luke

The Gospel of Luke closely follows that of Matthew. It contains the events whereby Jesus healed the sick, raised the dead, taught his doctrine, and presented parables. They both identify the disciples of Jesus, the Lord's Prayer, the death of Zacharias, and his admonishments to the Sadducees and Pharisees. What is missing is the genealogy of Jesus, showing Jesus as coming from the line of David. But Luke is much more forgiving than Matthew regarding the greatest commandments stated by Jesus. Matthew had Jesus answer the question posed by the Sadducees and Pharisees, "Master, which is the greatest commandment in the law?" Jesus's reply, stated in Matthew 22:37-40, ended with, *"On these two commandments hang all the law and the prophets."* Luke, however, took an approach that was politically correct. First, instead of having the Pharisees and Sadducees ask the question, he had an unidentified lawyer ask, "What shall I do to inherit eternal life?" Jesus requested the lawyer to provide the answer, and his reply combined the two great commandments into one as:[1]

> *Thou shalt love the Lord thy God with all thy heart, and with all thy soul, and with all thy strength, and with all thy mind; and thy neighbor as thyself.*

Jesus reply was, *"Thou hast answered right: this do, and thou shalt live."* Luke carefully omitted Matthew's political statement, *"On these two commandments hang all the law and the prophets".* Apparently much friction had risen since Matthew's version was heard and Luke felt it wise not to further infuriate the conservative Jews.

---

[1] `Holy Bible, *King James Version,* **Luke 10:27**.

Of great significance in Luke's Gospel is the statement made by Jesus when he speaks to his disciples after his resurrection. Here, for the first time, in Luke 24:47, Jesus states:

And that repentance and remission of sins should be preached in His name among all nations, beginning at Jerusalem.

Note that Jesus says *"in His name"* rather than "my name," which means forgiveness of sins by his Father. Jesus made it clear that he did not die for the forgiveness of sins but to follow God's new command—*to love one another*. In John's Gospel the author will clearly show that the mission of Jesus was to spread God's new command - Love one another; not die for our sins.

8.2.4 The Gospel of John

John Zebedee, his father, and younger brother James were fishermen on the Sea of Galilee. Called by Jesus to be one of his disciples, John witnessed the crucifixion and was later charged by Jesus to care for his mother, Mary. John was engaged in missionary work with Peter and founded many churches in Asia Minor. It was much later in life that he wrote the fourth Gospel, three epistles, and 'The Revelation.' Though there is no clear evidence that John wrote The Revelation, most conservative church leaders believe he is the same John who wrote the 4th Gospel. He lived a long lifetime and died about 100 CE.

The Gospel of John takes on a very different approach given in Mark, Matthew, and Luke. He omits the genealogy of Jesus, identification of the twelve apostles, the Lord's Prayer, many parables, the destruction of Jerusalem, and the two great commandments. Instead, John emphasizes the new commandment of Jesus and the greatest break with the first three Gospels—Jesus proclaims that he is lifted up from being the Son of Man to the Son of God.

Throughout John's Gospel, it is the new commandment to love one another that empowered Jesus to state in John 3:14-18 that he is the only begotten Son of God. John further reveals Jesus' empowerment as God's Son by having him state in John 6: 47, 48:

> *Verily, verily, I say unto you, He that believeth on me hath everlasting life. I am the bread of life.*

For the first time, we learn that Jesus brought back to life a man named Lazarus after he had been dead for four days. Such an astounding miracle would not have been forgotten by the writers of the first three Gospels, yet they made no mention of it. It appears that a miracle of this magnitude could not have left the memories of Mark, Matthew, and Luke—unless it never happened. The approach taken by John was to elevate Jesus as the Son of God. Throughout the first three Gospels, Jesus stated that he was the Son of Man. For the first time, in John's Gospel, Jesus refers to himself as the Son of God. This is the most popular Gospel among conservative Christians because, as the reader will see, it initiated many of the doctrines adopted by the Christian Church.

8.3 The Word of God

The beginning of John's Gospel takes on the essence of Genesis, the first chapter of the Torah. In Chapter 1:1, John introduces the "Word" and equates it with God by writing: '*In the beginning was the Word, and the Word was with God, and the Word was God.*' The very first sentence of John's Gospel clearly states that the Word was God. In verse 1:14, John then states: '*And the Word was made flesh, and dwelt among us, (and we beheld his glory, the glory as the only begotten of the Father,) full of grace and truth.*' This verse indicates that the Word became flesh through the birth of Jesus. The parenthesis containing, *"the only begotten of the Father"* had to have been added by the Church to emphasize Jesus was the Son of God. This statement strongly proclaims Jesus as God's son, and John would not have put it in parenthesis.

But what was the Word? The Word, given by Jesus, was the new command received from God. It is stated 3 times:

John 13:34. *A new commandment I give unto you, That ye love one another; as I have loved you, that ye also love one another.*

John 15:12. *This is my commandment. That ye love one another, as I have loved you.*

John 15:17. *These things I command you, that ye love one another.*

It is to be noted that John equates the Word with God but Jesus did not represent the Word until he was born of the Virgin Mary and made flesh as the offspring of David. Many religious teachers misconstrue John's inspirational and poetical lines and advocate that Jesus was with God from the very beginning. This interpretation may have surfaced in the Catholic Priesthood to support the Trinity concept, which defines God as three Persons in One. However, this interpretation is in conflict with Saint Matthew's Gospel (1:1-16) that ties the generations of Jesus Christ to being the son of David and Abraham through his father, Joseph. If the Holy Ghost, the spirit of God, conceived Jesus there is no reason for Matthew to tie the generations of Joseph to David and Abraham. But also, Jesus clearly proclaims that he is the root and offspring of David, which is in conflict with being conceived by the Holy Spirit. Jesus makes this statement in *The Revelation* 22:16:

I Jesus have sent mine angel to testify unto you these things in the churches. I am the root and the offspring of David, and the bright and morning star.

The opening of John's Gospel sets the framework to present some doctrines promulgated by the Church. The experience gained by John's exceptional missionary work, and efforts to establish many churches throughout Asia Minor, allowed him to express new concepts not previously developed by Mark, Matthew, and Luke. What are these new concepts of God?

8.4 Son of God and His Message

The idea of Jesus as the *"true light, which lighted every man that cometh into the world"* was initially expressed in John 1:7-12; this is a beautiful view of Jesus. John proceeds to elevate Jesus from being the Son of Man to being the Son of God. In John 1:34 and 49, John the Baptist and Nathanael (a friend of Philip, a disciple of Jesus) respectively state: "this is the Son of God" and, "thou art the Son of God." Later, John writes what was never written in the first three Gospels; he has Jesus explicitly state he is the Son of God. For the first time, in John 3:18, 5:25, 9:35, 10:36 and 11:4, Jesus states he is the 'Son of God.'

John therefore deviates from the Gospels of Mark, Matthew, and Luke by having Jesus announce that he is the Son of God. This is contrary to Jesus's humble nature, as he always stated he was the Son of Man. Jesus knew he was a man of God whose mission it was to reveal his Father's Word. An advocate of truth, he could not promote a lie by stating he was the Son of God. His purpose was to simplify the Law and spread God's Word to all people so that they would love one another. But it must be remembered that the Church, by this time, was advocating that Jesus was the incarnation of God—*the only begotten of the Father*. Here, in John's Gospel, the Son of God concept introduced by the Egyptian Priesthood for their pharaohs has resurfaced to influence the minds of Church leaders.

During Jesus's lifetime, the idea of men being worshipped as Gods was very popular. During the Roman Empire, the entire line of Caesars were regarded as Gods. As with the Egyptian pharaohs, leaders of nations have found that people are motivated to obey and act through the authority of a God. John's mission was to raise a humble teacher to that of a God so that greater authority is given to the Word. There appears to be greater emphasis given by the Church that Jesus died so that sins may be forgiven. This is far from the truth, for it is the Word of God that Jesus wanted us to follow. Instead of Jesus voluntarily dying for our sins, it was the Council of Pharisees and their chief priests that condemned Jesus to death. They feared that the miracle of Jesus raising Lazarus from the dead after four days would cause the people to follow Jesus in great numbers (John 11:52). This fear was expressed by the Council of Pharisees in John 11:47, 48:

What do we? For this man doeth many miracles. If we let him thus alone, all men will believe him: and the Romans shall come and take away both our place and nation."

The High Priest of the Council, Caiaphas stated in John 11:49, 50:

Ye know nothing at all, nor consider it is expedient for us, that one man should die for the people, and that the whole nation (Israel) perish not."

Caiaphas then prophesied that Jesus should die for their nation. From that day forward, the council was determined to put Jesus to death (John 11:51, 53).

John's Gospel therefore clearly indicates it was the High Priest and members of the Council that were intent on killing Jesus as opposed to Jesus giving up his life so that the sins of mankind may be forgiven. He died so that he would be remembered for proclaiming

God's Word to love one another. Jesus emphasizes his message was to deliver God's words to 'love one another':

John 14:23. *If a man love me, he will keep my words: and my Father will love him, and we will come unto him, and make our abode with him.*

John 17:13. *And now come I to thee; and these things I speak to the world, that they might have my joy fulfilled in themselves."*

John's Gospel makes clear that Jesus's doctrine was that we must love one another as God had loved him. The doctrine advocated by the Church that Jesus died for our sins was not taught by Jesus. Rather, this teacher of righteousness was betrayed and crucified because he claimed he was the light of the world and the Pharisees saw Jesus as a threat. They foresaw that God's new command, the Word, could gain precedence over the Torah and its multiple commands.

8.5 Concept of Salvation

John's Gospel emphasizes that Jesus taught God's Word to love one another. The four Gospels describes Jesus's crucifixion and resurrection but does not express the doctrine, advocated by the Church, that he gave his life for the forgiveness of sins. Jesus made it very clear that those who believe in him and hear his words will not abide in darkness, for he came to save the world. In John, below, Jesus indicates that he came not to judge the world and offer a life of eternity; more importantly, he came to save the world by disseminating God's new command.

John 12:44-47. *He that believeth on me, believeth not on me, but on Him that sent me. And he that seeth me seeth Him that sent me. I am come a light into the world, that whosoever believeth on me should not abide in the darkness. And if any man hear my words, and believe not, I judge him not: for I came not to judge the world, but to save the world.*

The statement by Jesus is most beautiful and thought provoking. In John 17:26, Jesus speaks to his Father, saying that he has declared his Father's name and that his and God's love may be in them—our sisters and brothers throughout the world.

John 17:26. *And I have declared unto them thy name, and will declare it: that the love wherewith thou hast loved me may be in them, and I in them.*

Clearly, Jesus did not give his life so that sins may be forgiven; he gave his life to promulgate the Word of God to love one another.

8.6 Other Sons of God

A most beautiful concept is introduced in John 1:12. It is the idea that those who receive Jesus and believe in his name will be given the power to become '*Sons of God.*'

John 1:12. *But as many as received him, to them gave he power to become the sons of God, even to them that believe on his name.*

This powerful revelation is further confirmed by Jesus in John 14:12. It is provided below with the hope that someday the gender "he" will be revised to "they."

John 14:12. *Verily, verily, I say unto you, He (They) that believeth on me, the works that I do shall he (they) do also; and **greater works** than these shall he (they) do; because I go unto my Father.*

These are marvelous words coming from Jesus. They substantiate that he was a Son of Man and that those who believe in him will do even **greater works** than he. Jesus exhibits his greatness as a teacher of righteousness, for he makes it clear that other 'Sons of God' can come forth and do the works that he did. Many religious leaders will not acknowledge or expound these words by Jesus because these leaders are focused on one doctrine: that God has only one begotten son, Jesus. If these leaders love and believe in Jesus, should they not also believe in his words?

When Jesus states that any man who believes in him can do the works that he did, *"and greater works than these shall he do"*, he is clearly saying that there will be other 'Sons of God.' What he infers is that there is the promise of change through those who are compelled to teach others how to truly love Him and his creations—our sisters and brothers throughout the world.

In the Scriptures of the three monotheistic religions, the male gender is always used. Even in a house of worship, the female has been (or is still) separated as if she were not coequal with men. Education of females in today's world has shown that they are as intelligent and competent as men. It would be wonderful to see Church leaders revise John 1:12 so that both daughters and sons can be embraced by God:

John 1:12 Revised. *But as many as received him, to them gave he power to become the **daughters and sons** of God, even to them that believe on his name.*

Perhaps John's Revelation foretells of a future whereby daughters and sons of God will assist religious leaders who are perceptive and courageous to recognize and implement needed revisions to the Scriptures of the Judaic, Christian, and Islamic religions. The last subsection of this book issues a call to our daughters and sons of God.

8.7 Concept of the Trinity

Since a young man, the author has often thought of the Trinity, a doctrine of the Catholic Church.[1] This doctrine conceives "three

---

[1]   Promulgated by **Pope John Paul II**, *Catechism of the Catholic Church,* 2nd Ed., **Page 902**. Trinity defined as: The mystery of one God in three Persons: Father, Son, and the Holy Spirit.

Persons" that define God. It includes: God, the creator of all there is; Jesus Christ, a man who Christians are taught is the Son of God; and the Holy Spirit, the Spirit of God that embodies Truth—a fundamental attribute of the Egyptian religion.

For many people, the Trinity is a difficult concept to comprehend. For God to have a Holy Spirit since He Himself is holy and omnipresent seems somewhat redundant. However, the concept that instead of God, His Holy Spirit may enter into one's being appears easier for people to assimilate and understand. As an extension of God, the Holy Spirit is believed to pervade the universe and sublimely imparts truth to bring worshippers closer to God.

John reintroduced the Holy Spirit, a beautiful concept that originated within the Judaic religion in the 4th Gospel. This conception appears to extend the omnipotence of God by envisioning His Spirit as present in the entire universe. The Catholic Church, has fused the Holy Spirit and Jesus Christ as "Persons" that are one with God and thereby form the Trinity. This initially may have been a noble attempt by the Church to raise Jesus, the Son of Man, to the level of a God. In the passage below, Jesus states that the Holy Spirit can enlighten and teach those who follow his commandments.

John 14:15-17. *If ye love me, keep my commandments. And I will pray the Father, and He shall give you another Comforter, that He may abide with you forever: even the Spirit of Truth; whom the world cannot receive, because it seeth him not, neither knoweth him: but ye know him; for he dwelleth with you, and shall be in you.*

Jesus goes on to say that the Comforter shall teach us all things and bring into remembrance the Word of God:

John 14:24-26. *He that loveth me not keepeth not my sayings: and the Word which ye hear is not mine, but the Father's which sent me.*

These things have I spoken unto you, being yet present with you. But the Comforter, which is the Holy Spirit, whom the Father will send in my name, he shall teach you all things, and bring all things to your remembrance, whatsoever I have said unto you.

Then in John 14:28, Jesus makes a statement that clearly indicates he is a Son of God spiritually and not one with, or coequal with God by stating—his Father is greater than he.

John 14:28. *I go unto my Father: for my Father is greater than I.*

The Holy Spirit is the Comforter Jesus refers to as the *Spirit of Truth*. The Holy Spirit can be none other than the Spirit of God. It is God's spirit that pervades the universe and is not another Person as taught by the Catholic Church. The Church teaches that the Father, Son, and Holy Spirit are three Persons, called the Trinity. This interpretation has caused much confusion among people around the world. First, this definition shows an inability of the Church to properly describe God. God may be acknowledged as the Father of all creation, but to characterize Him as a *Person* presents a limited view. God is mysterious, unknowable, and incomprehensible to mankind—He is revealed only through the Spirit of Truth, the Holy Spirit. Secondly, only Jesus existed as a *Person*. Lastly, the Holy Spirit is the Spirit of God and therefore should not be defined as a *Person*. With limited knowledge of God, it may be unfair to criticize the Catholic Church for conceiving God as three Persons in One. The Trinity concept is extremely complex and diminishes the concept of God as the creator of all things within and beyond the universe. With the present knowledge that God has not only created the galaxy, but billions of other galaxies with their billions of stars and, most certainly, other life forms that may not be fashioned in His image—it is unlikely that Jesus consists as a third element in a concept of God called the Trinity. In time, mankind may come to know God, but only through the Holy Spirit—the Spirit of Truth.

The concept of the Trinity is nebulous and mysterious, combining three entities that are both physical and transcendent. The Church has embodied as the Trinity: the unknowable, incomprehensible, omnipotent God; a physical man, who became a Son of God; and the Spirit of Truth, that emanates from God. The concept of the Trinity was developed by the Church to establish the godliness of Jesus. However, John's Gospel, and indeed all four Gospels, do not fuse the three entities into One God.

8.8 Born in Sin is a Blasphemous Doctrine

In the Genesis creation story, Adam and Eve are the parents of all the races of mankind. However, it is here that the Church has introduced the doctrine of original sin. It is important to clarify the doctrine of original sin as defined by the Catholic Church. The sin committed by Adam and Eve was disobeying God's command not to eat the fruit from the Tree of Knowledge of Good and Evil. Many Christian sects have misconstrued this act as the reason why all God's children are born in sin. Because Adam and Eve disobeyed God, the Catholic Church has defined Original Sin and claims this: [1]

Sin became universally present in the world. Besides the personal sin of Adam and Eve, original sin describes the fallen state of human nature which affects every person born into the world, and from which Christ, the "new Adam" came to redeem us.

In the Bible, Genesis 3:22-23, after Eve and Adam disobeyed God by eating the forbidden fruit, they were sent out of the Garden of Eden and admonished:

---

[1]   Promulgated by **Pope John Paul II**, *Catechism of the Catholic Church, 2nd Ed.,* **Page 890.**

And the Lord God said, Behold, the man is become as one of us, to know good and evil: and now, lest he put forth his hand, and take also of the tree of life, and eat, and live forever: Therefore the Lord God sent him forth from the Garden of Eden, to till the ground from whence he was taken.

The reader will note there is no condemnation by God that Adam and Eve will henceforth bear children that will be tainted with what the Church calls "original sin". God made it clear that because man now has the ability to know good and evil, that he has been endowed with the ability to make choices, and that because he is capable of becoming like God—he was to lose immortality. God therefore forbids Adam and Eve to live in the Garden of Eden and sends them to labor for the rest of their lives. However, he does not burden Adam and Eve with the punishment of passing on their sinful act to all their children.

Only a foolish God would create mankind in His own image and then have their children born in sin. It is demeaning to God's creation to teach that, *"original sin describes the fallen state of human nature which affects every person born into the world."* As a father, the author taught his children to have self-esteem; not to be so proud as to think they are better than others; to accept all people whether they are more or less gifted than they; to be the best they can be; and to lead their lives discerning truth, while admiring and practicing integrity. More importantly, the author taught them that their mother and father loves them and will assist them as much as is humanly possible with fairness towards others. This means that as a father, nepotism is not to be favored. By example, it is the mother and father who set the moral standards for their children so that they, in turn, will repeat those standards for their children. To accomplish these objectives, they were not taught that they were born in sin. Whether they accept the religion they were raised with, another religion, or are agnostics and simply believe "It's nice to be nice," it is their decision—a decision not founded in guilt and sin, but in God's Word—love one another.

8.9 Jesus refers to Himself as Son of God in John

The life of Jesus is documented in the Gospels of Mark, Matthew, Luke, and John. Everything that is known about Jesus has been revealed through these Gospels. Several other Gospels have been written to glorify Jesus and establish that he was destined to be the Son of God. One Gospel, attributed to Saint Matthew, describes the birth and upbringing of Mary, Jesus's mother.[1] This Gospel relates that Mary came from a royal family, the line of David. Her father, Joachim, was from Nazareth, a city in Galilee, and her mother, Anna, was in Bethlehem. Joachim was visited by an angel of the Lord who told him that his wife Anna would bear a daughter who would be filled with the Holy Ghost, and that her name was to be called Mary. This Gospel foretells the birth of Mary and then the birth of Jesus, which occurs about 15 years later. This is an attempt by Matthew to communicate to worshippers the purity and religious upbringing of Mary, her conception of Jesus as a virgin by the Holy Spirit, and that Jesus descended from the house of David by both parents, Mary and Joseph.

Matthew's Gospel of the Birth of Mary was an effort to support the idea of the virgin birth and the idea that a Son of God from the house of David was to be born through an immaculate conception. The story also relates that Mary was brought up in the Temple from the age of three. By establishing that Jesus's parents came from the line of David, and that Mary had religious instruction in the Temple from the age of three, it becomes obvious that Jesus came from a very religious background. Since Mary had religious instruction in the Temple from the age of three, it is very likely that Jesus also had

---

[1]　Crown Publishers, BELL 1979 Edition, *The Lost Books of the Bible,* "The Gospel of the Birth of Mary", by Saint Matthew, Chapter I. This translation was made from the works of Jerome, a Father of the Church of the fourth century.

formal instruction in the Temple. He had to have been taught the Torah and doctrines within the Essene community where he lived.

Jewish holy men, writers of the Gospels, established the birth of Jesus as a Son of God through the intercession of the Holy Spirit. Yet contained within these Gospels has been the lasting legacy of Jesus's truthfulness. In the first three Gospels of Mark, Matthew, and Luke, Jesus always referred to himself as the Son of Man. Not until John's Gospel does Jesus say he is the Son of God. About 30 years after Mark's Gospel, the Church grew stronger and John became emboldened to make Jesus a God. In Figure 8-1, the four Gospels are identified, as well as the number of times Jesus referred to himself as the Son of Man and the Son of God.

The Son of Man, as stated by Jesus, occurs 13, 31, 23, and 9 times in Mark, Matthew, Luke, and John, respectively (top curve). However, Jesus never refers to himself as the Son of God until the last Gospel (bottom curve). Certainly, since Jesus stated that he was the Son of God in John 5 times, there should have been no reason for Jesus's modesty in the other three Gospels. All four Gospels do confirm Jesus's commitment to Truth. When Pilate asked Jesus, "Art thou the King of the Jews?" his reply was, "Thou sayest it." Note that Jesus is very clear that Pilate said it and not him. Jesus was wise not to answer with a firm "Yes" because such an answer would not have changed the outcome. But it should be further noted that Pilate did not pose the question as, "Art thou the Son of God?" The concept that Jesus had global authority for all mankind did not develop until John wrote the 4th Gospel. It is to be noted that Jesus's use of *'Son of Man'* was not new. The Egyptian vizier, Ptahhotep used this expression around 2200 BCE in his *Maxims of Good Discourse.*[2]

---

[2]   Internet @ http://www.maati.org/ptahhotep_maxims.htm. *The Maxims of Good Discourse.* Pages 13 (Maxim 35) and 15 (III The Epilogue).

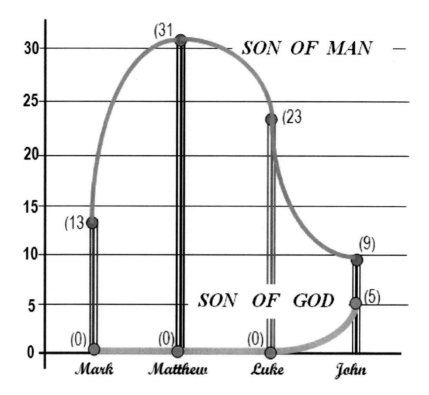

Figure 8-1. Jesus uses Son of God only in John.

The more remarkable differences in John's Gospel from the others is what occurred after Jesus was resurrected. Though there are differences among all of them, the most obvious differences occur in John's Gospel because they are totally new. The well known story where Jesus had Thomas touch his hands and the wound in his side stating, "blessed are they that have not seen, and yet have believed" was never mentioned in Mark, Matthew, and Luke. This was an event that validated the physical resurrection of Jesus and yet the first three Gospel writers fail to mention it.

John also introduces another new encounter where Jesus shows himself to his disciples at the Sea of Tiberias (West shore of the Sea of Galilee) after his resurrection. His disciples had had no luck in catching fish, but after Jesus told them to cast the net on the right side of the ship, they were rewarded with 153 fish (John 21:11). This event serves to burn itself into one's memory because it involved not just talk, sight, smell, touch, and hearing, but physical activity. Psychologists know that memory is greatly enhanced when an event includes motion or activity. Yet, in spite of the disciples dining with Jesus after the great catch of fish, only John remembers this event. Certainly, the other Gospel writers would want to relate these memorable events to confirm the authenticity of Jesus's resurrection. Unfortunately, they are not consistent. Did they forget or, did these events, after the resurrection of Jesus, never occur?

One of Jesus's greatest miracles was the resurrection of Lazarus from the dead after four days. This miracle was known by Lazarus's sisters, Mary and Martha, his disciples, many of the Jews (John 11:45) and the High Priest, Joseph Caiaphas (John 11:49). The miracle of Lazarus's resurrection caused the Jewish Priesthood to fear that Jesus would attain a great following, so their council of high priests determined that Jesus should die (Sect. 8.4). Yet here again, this event is not recorded in any of the first three Gospels.

It becomes evident that John's stories, not mentioned in the first three Gospels, were an effort to establish Jesus as a Son of God. In spite of the fact that fictional events may have been added in John's work, his Gospel is the most inspiring and looks towards the future. In John 1:12, revised to include daughters of God, he presents a hope for the world that is rarely taught by the Catholic Church. The Scriptures of the Judaic, Christian, and Islamic religions sorely neglect to include daughters of God, a foolish oversight. This profound statement is shown below:

John 1:12 Revised. *But as many as received him, to them gave he power to become the (Daughters and) Sons of God, even to them that believe on his name.*

This statement indicates that Jesus will give the power to become Daughters and Sons of God to those that receive him or believe in his name. In Chapter 10, this book issues a call to Daughters and Sons of God to assist religious leaders to revise and unify the Scriptures so that sisters and brothers throughout the world will love and assist one another.

The Gospels of the New Testament does reveal and confirm that Jesus was the greatest prophet and teacher. He was a humble yet spiritually wise man that made it clear that he represented his Father by revealing His Word—*That ye love one another.* Unlike other prophets of God, he never killed in the name of, or the cause of, God. Reflect upon the words of Jesus below; they confirm he was a humble and spiritual teacher—a man who gave his life to spread God's Word to the entire world.

John 8:28-29. *When ye have lifted up the Son of Man, then shall ye know that I am he, and that I do nothing of myself; but as my Father has taught me, I speak these things. And He that sent me is with me: the Father hath not left me alone; for I do always those things that please Him.*

Truly, if you were God, would you not embrace Jesus as your son?

9.0 Islam Evolves from Judaic and Christian Beliefs

In the early part of the 7th century, the religious beliefs of Judaism and Christianity gave birth to another religion for a people that needed to be unified both nationally and spiritually. In the Arab peninsula that lies between the Persian Gulf and the Red Sea, many Bedouin tribes grimly struggled for survival in the arid land now known as Saudi Arabia. However, at the southern end of this large land mass lies Yemen, a rain-bathed area that became famed among the Greeks and Romans for its frankincense and spices. The north Arabians were long-haired, wiry nomads, who spoke pure Arabic. Thousands of years in this hostile land had caused them to protect themselves in tribes where they formed strong bonds against other predatory tribes. Their law was simple: in retaliation for the murder of any one of their tribe members they would kill a member of the opposing tribe, whether or not that member actually committed the crime. Their more fortunate neighbors to the south were characterized as round-headed, hook-nosed people, farmers and horticulturists who spoke with a Semitic dialect with Ethiopic words that sounded strange to northern ears.

The northern Arabians had many contacts with their neighbors above them and never knew a conqueror. They constantly raided their brethren to the south who lived in Yemen. These southerners were blessed with fertilizing rain and sun which allowed them to grow prosperous through trade of their marketable spices. The increased wealth of individuals encouraged the growth of towns and cities that were garnished with gardens and green fields. Along the coast of the Red Sea, two major cities, Medina and Mecca, began to flourish as their trade routes became the connecting link between the southern spicelands and the markets of the Mediterranean world. Foreign ideas began to penetrate the Arabian Peninsula from the more advanced cities in Judea and Syria. Merchants from these countries and other lands that gained access from the Red Sea had exposed them to the wonders of advanced civilizations, other religions, and moral values. The foreign influence of their trading partners slowly changed the harsh, nomadic life the Arabians had known for so many centuries. Their world became stimulated by different interests, ideas, and values. Born into this era was Muhammad ibn Abdallah, a member of the Quraysh tribe in Mecca, who was destined to establish Islam.[1]

9.1 The Religious Arabian Culture prior to Islam

In those regions where commercial centers materialized, such as in Mecca and Medina, Jewish and Christian beliefs secured a foot-hold. Slowly, native converts to these faiths abandoned their primitive beliefs and accepted monotheism. However, a great majority of Arabs throughout the Arabian Peninsula still worshipped many ancient gods and goddesses. Some of the older tribal gods were venerated within natural objects, such as pillar-like stones, noteworthy rocks, caves, springs and wells. There was also widespread veneration of astral deities. In particular, the Moon-god was worshipped during ancient times in Ur and Harran, even before Abraham. Assyrians, Babylonians, and the Akkadians took the word Suen and transformed it into the word Sin as their favorite name for the Moon-god. Sin is a name essentially Sumerian in origin, which had been borrowed from the Semites. In ancient Syria, this god was also known as Hubal and was represented by the moon in its crescent phase. The sun-goddess was the wife of Sin and the stars were their daughters. The Moon-god and/or his symbol have been depicted in Persia and Egypt on wall murals and on the heads of statues.

For the Arabs, the Moon-god was the greatest of all gods and while they worshipped 360 gods at the Ka'ba in Mecca, the Moon-god was

---

[1]   **John B. Noss**, *Man's Religions,* **Pages 508-509.**

their chief deity. The Ka'ba (literally 'the cube') is a meteorite that is worshipped as the "black stone that fell from heaven during the days of Abraham." It is the holiest Arabian site where Muslims from far and near go on a pilgrimage to offer sacrifices of sheep and camels. As part of their ritual, they run around the Ka'ba seven times and kiss it in the hope of obtaining God's blessing. One Meccan belief was that the great patriarch Abraham, while on a visit to his outcast son Ishmael, had built the Ka'ba and imbedded the Black Stone in it.

Mecca was built as a shrine for the Moon-god and his three daughters: al-Lat (a mother goddess), al-Manat (the goddess of fate), and al-Uzza (the morning star). These goddesses were originally adored as the daughters of Allah, which means God or "the diety" venerated by Muhammad's tribe, the Quraysh. Eventually, Mecca became the most sacred site of Arabian paganism. The Moon-god had become so ingrained in Arabian culture that the symbol of Islam is the crescent moon. It sits on top of their mosques and minarets; is found on the flags of Islamic nations; and the month which begins and ends with the appearance of the crescent moon is the occasion of fasting.[1] In addition to the Daughters of God, there were lesser spirits, namely angels and various sorts of jinn. Some were friendly, while others hostile and demonic. The angels were morally irreproachable and of a beneficent nature. The jinn, according to fable, were created from fire two thousand years before Adam and could appear at will to human eyes or remain invisible. They could assume animal or human forms and have sexual relations and progeny. The friendly jinn were beautiful in form and kind in disposition. In contrast, the desert-ranging jinn struck terror in the hearts of Arabs and were active agents of evil.[2]

---

[1]   Internet: http://www.pakistanchristianpost.com/sdetails.php?id=52 by Yeshua Network Communication, Allah-the Mood God, The Archeology of the Middle East. Also, http://yeshua.co.uk

[2]   **John B. Noss**, *Man's Religions,* **Pages 509-510**.

9.2 Who was Muhammad?

Muhammad was born in 570 CE to a noble Arab tribe of the Quraish called the Banu Hashim or Hashimite clan. According to tradition, his father died before his birth and his mother died when he was six years old. He then became the ward first of his grandfather, Abd al Muttalib. Two years passed and after his grand-father died, his uncle, Abu Talib became Muhammad's guardian and new patriach of the Hashimite clan. The Hashimite tribe and Muhammad's family were responsible for the hospitality and welfare of the pilgrims who came to Mecca. Their responsibility included sharing with the rest of the Quraish tribes the honor of being trustees of the Ka'ba, its idols, its Black Stone, and the nearby sacred well. As such, Muhammad's religious beliefs were that of his community, which were the worship of the Moon-god Hubal and his three daughters, al-Lat, al-Uzza, and al-Manat.

Their beliefs incorporated tolerance for the multitude of tribal gods and goddesses, the mysterious jinn, angels and Satan. But also, Muhammad had to be influenced by the religious concepts introduced by the Jews and Christians. It had now been 500 years since the death of Jesus, and the basic concepts of reward in heaven, punishment in hell, and the coming of a Messiah at a day of judgment had found their way into Mecca through religious converts. Exposure to these ideas was inevitable, given the numbers of Jews and Christians in caravans passing through Mecca, the foreign merchants that traded in Mecca, and Jews and Christians attending the commercial fairs where representatives of these faiths addressed the crowds.

The beliefs regarding heaven and hell held by Jews and Christians require further discussion before the fears these beliefs developed within Muhammad's mind can be explored. Jews do not have a conception of a physical hell or heaven. Author Louis Jacobs, describes the Rabbis idea of heaven as follows:

> "We speak of eternal bliss in the nearness of God in the Hereafter, but the truth is that this experience is bound to be unintelligible to us, since we believe in this world of matter. The Rabbis say that we can only have a 'foretaste' of it, say, when we observe the Sabbath and experience the Sabbath delight that is 'out of this world' literally. Maimonides (a most revered Jewish Rabbi, theologian and philosopher, who lived between 1135 and 1204) observes that to try to grasp the nature of eternal bliss in the Hereafter while we are still in this world is like a person born blind trying to grasp the nature of color. God alone knows what is in store for the righteous."[1]

The Jewish idea of hell is also articulated by Maimonides as something other than a literal place where the wicked are punished in fire. According to many Jewish thinkers, hell is the state of a person who rejects the good, and finds upon dying that God is still remote. Maimonides seems to suggest that "Hell" does not suggest torment but rather that a thoroughly wicked soul is annihilated, feels no pain, and simply passes out of existence so that it cannot enjoy the bliss reserved for the good. For the Rabbis, heaven and hell seem to be states of being unlike anything that can be experienced in this life, and that which people have tried to describe as best they can with the language they have. The Rabbis also believe it is the Torah that gives the greatest joy, so it follows that they conceive heaven as the place or state in which God himself teaches the Torah to the righteous. This seems illogical for once they are in heaven as pure souls, they need not be continually instructed upon attaining the grace of God.

It must be remembered that Maimonides gave his interpretations of heaven and hell about 600 years after the life of Muhammad. The physical concepts of the pleasures of heaven and the pains of hell as envisioned by Muhammad were well established and believed as being very real.

---

[1]   **Louis Jacobs,** *The Book of Jewish Belief,* **Pages 234-236.**

Intelligent, sensitive, and a man of reflection, Muhammad had the advantage of being grounded in the many religious beliefs that were practiced by the worshippers who lived and visited Mecca. He also had a cousin, Waraqa, and a poet, Umaiya (born Abi'l-Salt), who were well versed in the traditions of the Jews and Christians. After his marriage to Khadija, fifteen years his senior, Muhammad had the leisure to reflect upon the multitude of religious beliefs. These became more and more difficult to adhere to as they were challenged by his growing awareness of new Jewish and Christian beliefs. His wife, who was a rich Qurayshite widow, mothered him and her love encouraged him to explore the perplexities and incompatibilities of the mix of religious beliefs to which he was exposed. During his marriage, she bore him two sons that died at birth and of their four daughters, only Fatima survived him.

Muhammed's moments of private reflection were energized by those who were brought close to him by marriage. Khadija's cousin, the blind Waraqa, may have been a Christian and a useful source of knowledge concerning matters of Christian faith and conduct. His adopted son, a slave-boy called Zaid, was a Christian and he had also adopted his cousin 'Ali, the son of his uncle Abu Talib. Muhammad thought that the last day and last judgment might be near. This onerous thought began to preoccupy his mind with Christian fears conjuring up visions of the torments of hell, which caused him to wander off into the hills about Mecca and privately reflect on the future. Since his marriage to Khadija in his mid-to-late twenties, he had spent many years in reflection and solitude searching for a Creator who would guide him to a meaningful and contented life. At the age of 40, he began to devote longer periods of thinking and meditation to this subject. It was then that he received the first revelation that became part of the Qur'an. Constant reflection had to have brought about his revelation as he endured a period of spiritual stress. This stress affected Muhammad's psyche as he contemplated the common belief of both Jews and Christians that there would be a last judgment and punishment of idolaters in everlasting fire.

9.3 The Qur'an was Imparted by an Angel of God

Near the cave of Hira, a few miles north of Mecca, Muhammad was visited by the angel Gabriel and received his first revelation, which was cited in the Qur'an as Sura (Chapter) 96. Muhammad was fearful that his vision of Gabriel was not real, and he hurried home to his wife to relate what had been said to him. Khadija consoled him, assuring him that he was honest and that Allah would never put him to shame. It is clear from his wife's response that Muhammad had already believed in the concept of one God. He must have been further reassured about his initial vision when he was revisited by Gabriel in Sura 53. Here, Gabriel defends the authenticity of Muhammed's first vision to his followers. Note however, that Gabriel's reference to We implies an entity other than Gabriel, that finds it necessary to defend Muhammad's sanity by stating:[1]

Sura 53: We cite the Pleidas (a conspicuous cluster of six stars in the constellation Taurus visible to the average eye) as evidence, when it will draw close, that your companion, Muhammad, has neither erred, nor has he gone astray. He does not speak out of his own desire; the Qur'an is pure revelation sent to him; taught him by the Lord of mighty powers, whose powers are manifested repeatedly and Who has established Himself firmly on the Throne.

Muhammad is the only prophet who received the words of God by an angel to form Holy Scripture. In the past, God himself always imparted wisdom directly, as was the case with Moses and Jesus. This does not dilute the authenticity of God's words, but the angel Gabriel neglects to state, "My Lord says" but uses instead *'We,'* which implies a multiple entity, or group, authorized to speak for God. Throughout the Qur'an, God is constantly referred to in

---

[1]   Suras of the Qur'an are arranged in the order of their length rather than when they were received. An arbitrary decision not intended by Allah.

pluralistic form, associating him with entities other than Himself; this observation will be discussed below.

9.3.1 What the Qur'an Reveals

It is incumbent upon truth-seeking people that they read the Qur'an themselves to gain a full understanding of its content. This chapter serves to give only a brief summary, but readers owe it to themselves to judge the sanctity and substance of this Holy Scripture. However, the author insists readers obtain one of the earliest translations by a well-respected Muslim. Many English translations that have been published have included numerous changes in an effort to be politically correct and dilute the negative impact of many of its suras (chapters). The author has deliberately obtained a version of *The Qur'an* that was translated in 1893 by Muhammad Zafrulla Khan.[1]It was published by:

Olive Branch Press
(An imprint of Interlink Publishing Group)
99 Seventh Avenue
Brooklyn New York 11215
ISBN 1-56656-255-4

A truly honorable Muslim, Mr. Khan offers a deep understanding of Arabic scholarship, Islamic learning, and a capable command of the English language. His English translation appeared in 1970 and was reprinted in 1981, 1991, and 1997. His text renders a strictly faithful translation of the Qur'an, includes the Arabic text, and offers clarity and precision for the reader.

---

[1]   Muhammad Zafrulla Khan was the foreign minister of Pakistan in 1947. He became the president of the 17th Session of the UN General Assembly and later served as Judge of the International Court of Justice at the Hague, of which court he became President.

The review of the Qur'an below is based upon a one-for-one wording of the Suras so that an honest and truthful critique may be given for devoted Islam followers. The first revelation, Sura 96, given to Muhammad by the angel Gabriel,[2] sets the tone for the rest of his revelations. Presented below are several observations that this Sura reveals.

- *The Qur'an Begins with Intimidation and Fear.* After many years of reflection, the Christian fears of a last judgment and the punishment of idolaters in hell surfaced in Muhammad's first revelation. Such revelations have occurred to men who have had a deep conviction of God through community exposure, intensive study, and inward reflection. This was true for Muhammad, as it had been for Ikhnaton, Moses, and Jesus. It was the tenor of their bodily and mental makeup, a sounding board so to speak, that compelled their god to reveal morality and righteousness for his creations. But note, in Sura 96, instead of propounding love of one's brothers and sisters throughout the world, Allah only reflects the fear that stressed Muhammad's mind, and advocates dragging sinners by their forelocks into hell:

Sura 96: *In the name of Allah, Most Gracious, Ever Merciful.*

Recite in the name of thy Lord who created everything. He created man from a clot of blood. Recite, for thy Lord is Most Beneficent, Who has taught by the pen, taught man that which he knew not.

*Man does indeed transgress, because he considers himself self-sufficient. Surely, unto thy Lord is the return. Knowest thou him who obstructs a servant of **Ours** when he stands in Prayer?*

Tell me, if he who prays follows the guidance and enjoins righteousness, and he who obstructs rejects the truth and turns his back on it, what will be the end of this

---

[2]   **Muhammad Zafrulla Khan**, *The Qur'an*, Introduction, **Page xii.**

last one? **We** *will surely drag him by the forelock, the forelock of a lying, sinful one. Then let him call his associates,* **We** *too will call* **Our** *guardians of hell.*

Then follow not him, but prostrate thyself and draw nearer to **Us.**

This first revelation is concerned with righteousness that is not defined and is preoccupied with the fear of punishment rather than the reward of heaven. But it also introduces the "We Group."

- *Sura 96 Introduces the "We, Our, and Us" Group.*

The devout reader is quickly introduced to the idea that man considers himself self-sufficient and will transgress from belief in God. But instead of acknowledging the retribution coming from God, the Qur'an introduces the entity *We*; a *Group* that speaks for Allah; instead of one God, a plural form is introduced. This multiple entity becomes evident with the admonition, "*We* will surely drag him by the forelock, the forelock of a lying, sinful one." This cannot be the Most Gracious and Ever Merciful God because He does not need *We* partners or associates. If God is the most powerful entity in the universe, there is no need for any assistance by some *We Group*.

Most importantly, God would never reduce Himself to that of an animal by dragging one of His creations by the forelock of his hair. This statement brings to light that there is a *Group* of Muslims that are making decisions and acting for God without His authority. The *We Group* announces themselves again by stating, "Then let him call his associates, *We* too will call *Our* guardians of hell." It is the *We Group* that challenges the offender's associates with their guardians (angels) of hell. The last line of the Sura states: "Then follow not him, but prostrate thyself and draw nearer to *Us*."

Draw nearer to God would be more accurate, for God needs no *Us* accomplices. Another translation of *The Quran* by Dr. Syed Vickar

Ahamed, published in 2006 by the Book of Signs Foundation, changed the ending from, '*and draw nearer to Us.*' to, '*and bring yourself closer (to Allah)!*' This is an obvious effort to replace the *We Group* reference "to *Us*" with "(to *Allah*)*!* Note: the translator also put Allah in parenthesis. This observation verifies the liberties taken by translators, over the past three decades, to make *The Qur'an* politically correct and acceptable for worshippers of Islam and other religions.

Does this Sura beckon people to follow God or the *We Group*? There is no reason to be drawn to *Us* but only to *God*. To convince the reader that the *We Group* is an entity other than God, let us examine a few verses in Sura 22; it will not be necessary to belabor this observation, for the Qur'an is replete with statements by the *We Group*.

Sura 22:35-38: We *have appointed the sacrificial camels also as the Signs of Allah, for you. In them there is much good for you. So pronounce the name of Allah over them when they are tied up in lines; and when they fall down on their sides slaughtered, eat thereof yourselves and feed the needy, those who are content and those who are distressed. Thus have* **We** *subjected them to you that you may be grateful.*

Note that it is the *We Group* that appoints what animals are to be sacrificed—not Allah. Nowhere in the Qur'an does God command that camels be sacrificed to him as a way to glorify Him. After 500 years since the revelations espoused by Jesus and the Gospels, whereby the sacrifice of animals is not a requirement to honor and pray to God, the Muslims have taken a step backward by reestablishing this practice. It is apparent that the tribal religions still observed strong ritual practices of the past, and that Muhammad continued some of them. Note that the *We Group* is actively engaged in continuing animal sacrifice; but really to serve a practical need, which is to provide meat for the needy so that they may be grateful. This was an expedient way of accommodating the thousands of pilgrims that came to Mecca to worship God. It appears that the *We Group* has a very strong influence on directing the Muslims in many aggressive activities. It will become evident in Section 9.4 that the powerful *We Group* are *religious leaders* who aggressively converted people to Islam. At first, the Qur'an served the noble purpose of unifying the Arab tribes in Saudi Arabia, but soon greed and power led the *We Group* to force Islam throughout the civilized world by the sword—believe in Islam or die as a nonbeliever.

- *The Qur'an Advocates a Party to Forbid Evil.* In Sura 3 the *We Group* advocates a party whose business it is to invite goodness, enjoin equity, and forbid evil. This pronouncement, extracted from verse 105 reads:

Sura 3:105. *Let there be from among you a party whose business it should be to invite goodness, to enjoin equity and to forbid evil. It is they who shall prosper.*

This Sura provides a clear statement and confirms that a **party of religious leaders**, the *We Group*, is empowered to enforce their will in the name of God. They authorize the killing of human beings who will not convert to Islam, or who are disbelievers.

- *The Book of Warnings, Chastisements and Retribution.* The Qur'an contains warnings, chastisements, admonitions and threats of punishment in hell for disbelievers. Instead of building upon and fulfilling the Holy Scriptures of the Torah and Gospels, the Qur'an takes issue with the Jews and Christians as unworthy worshippers and even goes as far as to abrogate or cause to be forgotten the previous commandments of God. This view is stated below and is contrasted with the translation provided by Dr. Syed Vickar Ahamed in *The Quran,* cited above and published in 2006:

Sura 2:106-108. *Whatever previous commandment **We** abrogate or cause to be forgotten, **We** reveal in this Qur'an one better or the like thereof: Knowest thou not that Allah has full power to do all that He wills?*

Note that, "Whatever previous commandment *We* abrogate" was changed in 2006 to, "None of *Our* revelations do *We* change".

The Quran 2006 translation. *None of Our revelations do We change or cause to be forgotten, but We substitute something better or similar; Do you not know that Allah has power over all things?*

Both statements belittles God's all-knowing capability by challenging His previous commandments as being candidates to be abrogated, forgotten, or substituted for something better. This is an affront to God's wisdom and infallibility as revealed to Moses, Jesus, and the prophets of God. If God's commands are subject to being abrogated, forgotten, or changed, then He has failed in His wisdom to direct humanity on its moral and righteous path. Both Suras identifies the *We Group* that arrogantly believes that they have the authority to speak for God. Whenever God delivers his revelations in other Scriptures, they have always been prefaced by "The Lord has commanded" or a direct statement as, "Thou shalt" without the involvement of *We, Our or Us* entities—nebulous substitutes for the One God in plural form.

- *The Qur'an Sanctions Fighting and Killing.* In Sura 2:217-219, there is a defense for fighting and killing people who incite disorder by denying God or profaning the sanctity of the Sacred Mosque. This view is sanctioned in the following verse:

Sura 2:217-219. *Fighting is ordained for you, while it is repugnant to you. It may be that you dislike a thing which is good for you, and it may also be that you prefer a thing and it may be the worse for you. Allah knows all and you know not. They enquire from thee about fighting in the sacred month, Say to them: Fighting in it is a great evil; but to hinder people from the way of Allah and to deny Him and to profane the sanctity of the Sacred Mosque, and to turn out its people therefrom is a much greater evil in the sight of Allah; and disorder is a worse evil than killing.*

Who states disorder is worse than killing? The *We Group* or God? In Sura 7:5-7, the *We Group* reveal themselves as responsible for the destruction of many towns in the name of Allah who is Most Gracious and Ever Merciful—a contradiction of a loving God.

*Sura 7:5-7. Little is it that you heed. How many a town have **We** destroyed! **Our** punishment came upon their dwellers by night or while they slept at noon. When **Our** punishment came upon them all they could utter was: We are indeed wrongdoers.*

This and the following Sura again emphasize the killing of disbelievers, people who did not spill blood but simply believed in their own god. Note the planned strategy of killing innocent people while they are asleep at night, noon, or at play. Also note below that the *We Group* attributes this atrocity to the "design of Allah."

*Sura 7:97-100. **We** afflicted them suddenly with chastisement, while they perceived not the cause thereof. If the people of those towns had believed and been righteous, **We** would surely have bestowed blessings upon them from heaven and earth, but they rejected the Prophets, so **We** seized them because of that which they did. Do the people of these towns now feel secure against the coming of **Our** punishment upon them by night while they are asleep? Or, do they feel secure against the coming of **Our** punishment upon them in the forenoon while they are at play? Do they feel secure against the **design of Allah**? None feels secure against the **design of Allah**, except those that are losers.*

The above Suras violates one of the Ten Commandments given to Moses, "Thou shalt not kill." Under no circumstances should a Book of God convey the killing of our sisters and brothers in the name of, or by the design of, God. The excuses given in the above Sura to rationalize such killing presents a ruthlessness and disregard for God's creations. It is another example of the *We Group* speaking for God; this cannot be God speaking because God cannot be inconsistent with His commands. If God is found to be inconsistent, He can no longer be a God. In fact, the very first commandment given by God regarding killing was stated to Noah even before Abraham and Moses (Bible, KJV, Genesis, 9:6):

Whoso sheddeth man's blood, by man shall his blood be shed: for in the image of God made he man.

God makes it clear that the sanctity of his creation, human beings, is to have utmost reverence for He made man in His own image. Killing another human being is an abomination that God does not ordain or sanction. God would be inconsistent by allowing killing in His name. It can only be the *We Group*, not God, who is responsible for reflecting this diversion from God's command, *Thou shalt not kill.* (Bible, KJV, Exodus 20:13 and Deuteronomy 5:17).

Sura 5:34-35. *The appropriate penalty for those who wage war against Allah and His Messenger and run about in the land creating disorder is that they be slain or crucified or their hands and feet be cut off on alternate sides, or they be expelled from the land. That would be a disgrace for them in this world, and in the Hereafter they shall have a great punishment; except in the case of those who repent before you obtain power over them. Take note that Allah is Most Forgiving, Ever Merciful.*

The above Sura is an edict by the *We Group* to disgrace those who create disorder by cutting off their hands and feet on alternate sides or kill them, unless they repent. Note that the level of disorder is war against Allah; but does this refer to any people who believe in another religion, all disbelievers, or just Arabs who do not believe in the Islamic God? The retribution of the *We Group* is arbitrary and harsh. Nowhere in this Sura is it stated that *God has commanded* this barbarous practice to protect His sanctity. There is ample reason to believe that the indiscriminate maiming and killing of human beings in God's name is the prescription of madmen who comprise the *We Group* and not the Most Forgiving and Ever Merciful God. The Qur'an has many such Suras that do not indicate the *command* is from God.

- *The Qur'an Promotes Suspicion and Animosity.* A plea to Muslims to avoid people who are not of the Muslim faith is provided in the Sura below.

*Sura 3:119. O ye who believe, do not take outsiders as your intimate friends, they will not fail to cause you injury. They love to see you in trouble. Their hatred has been expressed in words, and that which they design is even more virulent. **We** have made **Our** commandments clear to you, if you will understand.*

Here again, the *We Group* speaks for God and does so to cause suspicion and animosity towards non-Muslims. This is a way to insulate Muslims from receiving new ideas that will challenge the will of the *We Group*. The objective of the *We Group* is to sanitize any information that will empower their people to think for themselves. This is an agenda practiced by the Taliban, who tailor education of their children by advocating only fundamentalist Islamic views; additionally, education is restricted to men; women may not be educated, and news from the outside world via internet, television, phones, and books is prohibited.

It is to be noted that the *We Group*, throughout the Qur'an, has neglected to clearly state God's commandments in a body of verses like the commandments given to Moses and embodied in *The Book of the Covenant* (Exodus 24:4-7). It would have been gracious and honorable for Muhammad to have at least referred to God's commandments given in the Torah. Could this have been an unfortunate oversight? Surely, God would have wanted His commandments to be passed down to the rest of His children.

- *The Qur'an Advocates Terror Against Unbelievers.* Sura 3: 150-152 is a call by the *We Group* to strike terror against unbelievers in the name of God. This is another abrogation of God's command to love one another. This Sura states:

Sura 3:150-152. *O ye who believe, if you obey those who have disbelieved, they will cause you to revert to disbelief and you will become losers. Indeed, Allah is your Protector and He is the Best of helpers.* **We** *shall strike terror into the hearts of those who have disbelieved because they associate partners with Allah, for which He has sent down no authority. Their abode is Fire, and evil is the habitation of the wrongdoers.*

The above statement is directed at Christians who associate Jesus with God as His beloved Son ("partners with Allah") as expressed in Mark 1:11, Matthew 3:17, Luke 3:22, and John 1:32-34. Jesus is a proclaimed prophet of God; yet, this Sura claims that God's authority does not support Jesus. The Qur'an therefore undermines Jesus's status as a prophet of God. The Qur'an further dishonors the wisdom of God in using Jesus as his surrogate to simplify the Law (Torah) and bring people from all nations together through belief in His Word—to love one another.

The Muslims fail to recognize that Jesus was the Son of Man who, through his actions of righteousness, became a Son of God. That is, Jesus was embraced by God as a son. He became God's son spiritually and was loved by God. Section 8.9 presents the enigma as to whether Jesus was the Son of Man or the Son of God. It is beholden for Muslims to read the Gospel of John and reflect upon an important revelation that stresses there will be other 'Sons of God' through belief in Jesus. If there will be other 'Sons of God,' John's statement infers that there will be other men, like Jesus, who will be embraced by God as His sons. Jesus therefore, should not to be thought as being the only *Son of God* but rather, a *Man of God*.

John 1:11-12. *He came unto his own, and his own received him not. But as many as received him, to them gave he power to become the Sons of God, even to them that believe on his name.*

- ***The We Group Incites Violence and Hatred Towards Jews and Christians.*** The following passages from Sura 4:47-48 and Sura 5:52-54 are not consistent with a God who is Most Gracious and Ever Merciful. These are inflammatory passages, embedded in a Book of Holy Scripture, advocating violence and murder of human beings from other nations with different beliefs. The religious teachers of the Qur'an have failed to acknowledge that God has revealed Himself to various people of different lands at different times, and the content of those revelations depended upon each people's needs to develop a higher sense of morality, righteousness, and truth. The Suras below condemn Jews and Christians as a whole, and fail to acknowledge that many of these people are extremely devoted to God—the same God of the Muslim people. Below, the Qur'an fails to give credence to the Old and New Testaments by stating *"their works are vain"* and advocates, in Sura 9:29, that Islam is *"the true religion."*

Sura 4:47-48. O ye who have been given the Book, believe in that which **We** have now sent down, fulfilling that which is with you, before **We** destroy your leaders and turn them on their backs or cast them aside as **We** cast aside the people of the Sabbath. The decree of Allah is bound to be carried out.

Sura 5:52-54. O ye who believe, take not the Jews and the Christians as your helpers, for they are helpers of one another. Whoso from among you takes them as helpers will indeed be one of them. Verily, Allah guides not the unjust people. Thou wilt see those whose minds are diseased hastening towards them, saying to themselves in justification: **We** fear lest a misfortune befall us. Maybe, Allah will soon bring about your victory or some other event from Himself favorable to you. Then will they become remorseful of that which they keep hidden in their minds. Those who believe will say concerning them: Are these they who swore the most solemn oaths by Allah that they are entirely with you? **Their works are vain** and they have become the losers.

Sura 9:29. Fight those from among the People of the Book who believe not in Allah, nor in the Last day, nor hold as unlawful that which Allah and His Messenger have *declared to be unlawful nor follow* **the true religion**, *and who have not yet made peace with you, until they pay the tax (tribute) willingly and make their submission.*

Can *The Qur'an* be a Book of God if it advocates violence and death to Jews, Christians and anyone who does not believe in Islam? Again, it is the *We Group* who is responsible for this outrageous declaration against God's children. God alone will exact punishment for those who murder, hurt, deceive, and cheat others—not a *We Group*. What needs to be understood by many Muslims is that one who does not believe in God may still love and assist all children of God. Those who claim to believe in God may be hypocrites if they are incapable of loving and assisting those in need. It is wrong to fight and kill disbelievers and atheists. They, in spite of their disbelief, may love their fellow man; in so doing, they are still carrying out God's Word—to love one another.

The statement that Islam is *the true religion* is an egregious error. It should be obvious to intelligent men that God has revealed Himself to different peoples at different times, depending upon their level of perception and need to follow the precepts of righteousness, truth, and justice. The development of religion started with the Egyptians, continued with the Hebrews, and became available to all people via Christianity. The Muslims found God through the teachings of these religions. It is therefore a truth that there are many paths along which to follow the Word of God. The statement that *Islam is the true religion* is a sign of arrogance that had to have been advocated by the *We Group*—not by God.

- ***The We Group Commands Muslims to Kill for God.*** In Sura 5:67-69, the *We Group* takes it upon themselves to command their people to kill themselves and others for the cause of Allah. The Qur'an speaks for itself below:

Sura 4:67-69: If *We* had commanded them: Kill yourselves in striving for the cause of Allah or go forth from your homes for the same purpose: they would not have done it except a few of them; yet if they had done what they are exhorted to do, it surely have been the better for them and conducive to greater firmness and strength. **We** would then bestow upon them a great reward from **Ourself**, and **We** would surely guide them along the straight path.

Once again the **We Group** acts over the authority of God and sanctions the killing of human beings in his name. They even provide an inducement by bestowing a great reward for those who kill themselves in order to kill others. Spiritual people believe it is God who will punish those who mistreat the brothers and sisters of any nation. The Qur'an is replete with verses that allude to a religious party of fanatical men; men who believe they represent God's cause and will go to extremes to convert disbelievers even if it involves disobeying God's command—*Thou shalt not kill.* It is unfortunate that the message to love and support brothers and sisters of any nation is missing in this Holy Scripture.

- *The Qur'an Incites Anger and Creates Enemies.* Sura 63 incites mistrust and hate of those who are of another religion. In particular, the Jewish and Christian faiths are treated with animosity because first, these religions were the progenitors of Islam and secondly, they appear to compete with Islam over whose God is the truest or mightiest. The result is an effort to malign the worshippers of other religions. A few lines from this Sura read:

*Sura 63:4-5. When thou seest them (Jews being accused of being disbelievers) their persons please thee; and when they speak thou dost lend ear to what they say. They appear as if they were blocks of wood propped up. They imagine that every warning of chastisement relates to them. They are the enemy, so beware! Ruin seize them! . . . It is the same for them whether thou ask for forgiveness for them or not, **Allah will never forgive them**. Surely, Allah guides not a rebellious people.*

Again, the Qur'an speaks for itself in terms that are neither endearing nor respectful of others who are not Muslims or of another religion.

The Qur'an portrays a resentful God who will *"never forgive them;"* a contradiction to the first line of every Sura, which states:

In the name of Allah, Most Gracious, Ever Merciful.

This introductory verse in Sura 63, and indeed in every Sura, presents an inconsistency of a benevolent, forgiving God by stating, "Allah will never forgive them." Only when people have read the Qur'an in its entirety will they realize that this Scripture does not advocate love, peace, and charity for the brothers and sisters of all nations. Rather, it is replete with what God loves, including God loves the benevolent; God loves those who are clean and pure; God loves those who turn to him often; God loves not confirmed disbelievers and archsinners. An Internet search of the Qur'an on the key word "Love" will confirm that nowhere in the Qur'an does it state the command that God revealed in the Hebrew Bible, *thou shalt **love** thy neighbor as thyself.* This command was expanded by Jesus for all people in the New Testament, *These things I command you, that ye **love** one another* (John 15:17).

- **The Qur'an Does Not Clearly Cite the Ten Commandments.** The Qur'an's Ten Commandments are not equivalent to those revealed to Moses and written by the finger of God (Exodus 31:18). Additionally, the Ten Commandments are presented disjointedly in Suras dispersed throughout the Qur'an. The revelations received by Muhammad from the angel Gabriel had introduced modified versions of the Ten Commandments. The variations in the Qur'an's Ten Commandments provide a disservice to the followers of Islam because they do not provide a consistent understanding of what God expects from his children. As an extension of God's Word, no mention is even made in the Qur'an to read the Holy Bible or the New Testament as supplementary Scripture. It would seem that Muhammad's ultimate concern, when he later joined together all of his revelations into a body of Scripture, was to unify the

Arab tribes into a nation. Table 9-1 provides a comparison of the Ten Commandments given in the Qur'an with those received by Moses from God. The comparisons reveal that indeed, some of the commands are statements rather than explicitly stated by God; and, in some cases, appear to have been stated by the *We Group.*

- *Missing is the Message of Love Given in the Holy Scriptures.* The Qur'an mentions Jesus as a prophet of God. Yet, missing from this Holy Scripture is the new commandment of love given by Jesus to love one another. Without this new commandment, many believers in God are easily led astray to hatred and violence towards their sisters and brothers throughout the world. In the Gospel of John 13:34, Jesus states:

A new commandment I give unto you, That ye love one another; as I have loved you, that ye also love one another.

In John 15:12-13, Jesus repeats this commandment:

This is my commandment, That ye love one another as I have loved you. Greater love hath no man than this, that a man lay down his life for his friends.

Did Muhammad love the sisters and brothers of the world and ultimately give his life for mankind? The greatest prophet of all was Jesus, a man of peace. He never advocated violence and murder in the name of God. Can this be said of Moses and Muhammad? The Muslims are our brothers and sisters and must not be deprived of a command given by this wonderful prophet. Jesus was indeed a man of God. The Muslims should understand that God embraced Jesus, a man, as a loving son because he spread His Word—to love one another. As indicated in John's Gospel, other men can do even greater works than Jesus, which implies they also may become Sons of God. Again, Jesus himself states this wonderful revelation in John 14:12:

Table 9-1. The Ten Commandments in the Qur'an.

Internet @: http://www.submission.org.quran/ten.html *C = Command and S = Statement*

1. **Exodus 20: 3** Thou shalt have no other gods before me.	*C*
Sura 47: 19 Know, then, that there is no god other than Allah, and beseech for the . . .	*S*
2. **Exodus 20: 4** Thou shalt not make unto thee any graven image, or any likeness of any thing that is in heaven above, or that is in the earth beneath, . . .	*C*
Sura 42: 11 There is nothing whatever like unto Him.	*S*
3. **Exodus 20: 7** Thou shalt not take the name of the Lord thy God in vain;	*C*
Sura 2: 224 Use not Allah's name for your vain oaths, making them an excuse for refraining from doing good and working righteousness and promoting public welfare.	*S*
4. **Exodus 20: 8** Remember the Sabbath day, to keep it holy. Six days thou shalt labor, and do all thy work: But the seventh day is the Sabbath of the Lord thy God: . . .	*C*
Sura 16: 124 The penalty for profaning the Sabbath was imposed only on those who had differed about it, and thy Lord will surely judge between them on the day of Judgment concerning that wherein they differed. **Note:** The Qur'an does not abrogate the Sabbath and endorses	*S*
God's penalty if it is profaned. It was on the seventh day that God rested from creating the heaven, earth, sea, and all that is within them. On this day He blessed the Sabbath, and hollowed it.	
5. **Exodus 20: 12** Honor thy father and thy mother.	*C*
Sura 17: 24 Thy Lord has commanded that ye worship none but Him and has enjoined benevolence towards parents. Should either of them attain old age in thy lifetime, never say: Ugh; to them nor chide them, but always speak gently to them.	*C*
6. **Exodus 20: 13** Thou shalt not kill.	*C*
Sura 5:33 On account for this *We* prescribed for the children of Israel that who so kills a person, except for killing another or for creating disorder in the land, it shall be as if he had killed all mankind; **Note:** This command by the *We Group* specifically identifies the children of Israel.	
Sura 17: 33 Do not destroy the life that Allah has declared sacred save for just cause.	*C*
7. **Exodus 20: 14** Thou shalt not commit adultery.	*C*
Sura 17: 32 Do not even approach adultery; surely, it is a foul thing and an evil way	*C*
8. **Exodus 20: 15** Thou shalt not steal.	*C*
Sura 5: 39 Cut off the hands of the man who steals and of the woman who steals in retribution of their offence as an exemplary punishment from Allah.	*C*
Note: This command is given by the *We* Group. Would God inflict such cruel punishment?	
9. **Exodus 20: 16** Thou shalt not bear false witness against thy neighbor.	*C*
Sura 2: 284 Conceal not testimony; whoever conceals it is one whose heart is certainly sinful.	*S*
Sura 4: 136 O ye who believe, be strict in observing justice and bear witness only for the sake of Allah, even if it be against your own selves or against parents or kindred.	*S*
Note: Both statements are given by the *We Group* since God does not command them.	
10. **Exodus 20: 17** Thou shalt not covet thy neighbor's house, thou shalt not covet thy neighbor's wife, nor his manservant, nor his maidservant, nor his ox, nor any thing that is thy neighbor's.	*C*
Sura 4: 37 Worship Allah and associate naught with Him, and be benevolent towards parents, and kindred, and orphans, and the needy, and the neighbor who is a kinsman, and the neighbor who is not related to you, and your associates and the wayfarer, and those who are under your control. **Note:** This statement appears to be by the *We Group* and does not address the sin	*S*
of coveting another's possessions; instead it expresses kindness towards others.	
Sura 4:33 Covet not that whereby Allah has made some of you excel others.	*S*

Verily, verily, I say unto you, he that believeth on me, the works that I do shall he do also; and greater works than these shall he do; because I go unto my Father.

These words provide a wonderful insight about Jesus and verify he was a teacher of love and a man of God. The misunderstandings about Jesus as a third person in the Trinity conception of God have been the fault of religious leaders. They have not truly taught the words of Jesus stating there will be other sons of God who will do greater works than him because they have been insistent on making him a God. But also, they have overlooked the words of Jesus because if there will be others who believe in him that can do greater works—the assertion that he, Jesus, is the only Son of God is no longer true. These religious leaders believe that moral beliefs can be promulgated only when the messenger has had a revelation from, or is, a God. This belief is false. One need only believe in God's Word repeatedly spoken by Jesus—to love one another.

- ***The Qur'an Uniquely Describes Heaven.*** Of the Scriptures provided within the Old and New Testament, it is only the Qur'an that gives its worshippers a clear idea of Heaven. One would think that Scripture written after the Torah and the New Testament would follow their example of not describing God's domain in Heaven. Since God is not completely knowable and is thus ultimately impossible to describe, how is it possible for the Qur'an to describe Heaven? The Suras cited below appeal to the senses of men with little mention of rewards for the opposite sex. Surely, Scripture revealed by God would provide equal glorification of both men and women, but the verses below substantiate that the Qur'an focuses only on the appetites and fantasies of men.

Sura 55: 47-62. But for him who fears to stand before his Lord there are two Gardens (which, then, of the favors of your Lord will you twain deny?) having many varieties of trees (which, then, of the favors of your Lord will you twain deny?) and two springs flowing full (which, then, of the favors of your Lord will you twain deny?) and of every type of fruit two kinds. Which, then, of the favors of your Lord will you twain deny? They will recline on couches above carpets the linings of which will be of thick brocade; and the fruits of the two Gardens will be hanging low within easy reach. Which, then, of the favors of your Lord will you twain deny? Therein will be chaste maidens of modest gaze, untouched by man or jinn (which, then, of the favors of your Lord will you twain deny?) as if they were rubies and small pearls. Which, then, of the favors of your Lord will you twain deny? Can the reward of goodness be anything but goodness? Which, then, of the favors of your Lord will you twain deny?

Sura 55: 71-79. Therein will be good and beautiful women (which, then, of the favors of your Lord will you twain deny?) blackeyed, guarded in pavilions (which, then, of the favors of your Lord will you twain deny?) untouched by man or jinn (which, then, of the favors of your Lord will you twain deny?) reclining on green cushions and beautiful carpets. Which, then, of the favors of your Lord will you twain deny? Blessed is the name of thy Lord, Master of Glory and Honor.

Sura 56: 2-41. When the Event comes to pass, the coming of which no one can avert, some it will bring low and others it will exalt.

When the earth is shaken violently, and the mountains are crumbled into dust . . . you will be divided into three groups: those on the right . . . and those on the left . . . and those who are foremost—they verily are the foremost. They will be honored ones, dwelling in the Gardens of Bliss; a large party from the early believers, and a few from the late-comers, reclining on couches inwrought with gold and jewels, facing one another. They will be waited on by ageless youths, carrying goblets and ewers and cups filled out of a flowing spring, neither causing headache nor inebriating, and such fruits as they choose, and the flesh of birds as they may desire.

They will have as companions maidens with lovely black eyes, pure as pearls well guarded; a recompense for what they did. They will not hear therein any vain or sinful talk, but only salutation: Peace, peace.

*Those of the right; how fortunate will those on the right be! They will be amidst thornless lote-trees, and clustered bananas, and extensive shades, and falling water, and varieties of fruit, endless and unforbidden. They will have noble spouses, whom **We** specially created, and made virgins, loving and matching in age, for those in the right. They will be a large party from the early believers and a large party from the late comers.*

Those on the left; how unfortunate will those on the left be! They will be in the midst of scorching wind and scalding water, and in the shadow of black smoke, neither cool nor agreeable . . .

The above Suras have been provided so that the reader can appreciate what the Qur'an contains regarding Muslim beliefs of reward in the Islam hereafter. These Suras exhibit a strong contrast to the hereafter envisioned by the ancient Egyptians. Their hereafter was an extension of their lives on the banks of the Nile where they continued to live in constructive and industrious ways. The Qur'an, on the other hand, elucidates a hereafter that portrays an idle and sensual life that caters to the selfish desires of men whereby they: enjoy the affection of beautiful virgins, blackeyed beautiful women untouched by man or jinn; have as companions maidens with lovely black eyes, pure as pearls; have noble spouses, whom the *We Group* specially created and made virgins, loving and matching in age; drink out of goblets filled from a flowing spring that does not cause inebriation; wear green robes of fine and heavy silk; recline on couches inwrought with gold and jewels; lie on green cushions above carpets the linings of which will be of thick brocade; are given bracelets of gold and pearls to wear; drink from rivers of wine and rivers of pure honey; and are waited on by ageless youths, carrying goblets and ewers and cups filled out of a flowing spring.

The contrasts in the perceptions of Heaven by the ancient Egyptians and Muslims are striking. One view is noble and has mankind continuing a resourceful life utilizing their minds and bodies; whereas, the other has men seeking only to satisfy their physical and sensual desires.

From reading the previous Suras, it is apparent that the Qur'an is repetitive for a great work of literary art. However, worshippers of any religion will defend their faith and regard their Scripture on an extremely high level of competence because they believe it was received as a revelation from God. Many people do not know what Islam Scripture contains, and it would be a worthy and commendable effort for them to read the Qur'an. Likewise, there are truth-seeking Muslims who are tolerant of other religions and seek to gain a better understanding of Judaism and Christianity, which may be achieved by reading the Torah and the Holy Gospels.

9.3.2 Muhammad Uses the Qur'an to Spread Islam

The perceptive and intelligent Muhammad grew up amidst a diversity of religious traditions and tribal customs. Many years after he received revelations from Allah's angel Gabriel, it became clear that in order to accomplish his objective of unifying the Arab tribes, he had to put in writing the moral messages and social laws he had received into a book called, *The Qur'an*. In the beginning, Muhammad met with resistance as he appeared on the streets of Mecca and the courtyard of the Ka'ba. His warnings to the Meccans of a divine judgment day, the predictions of the resurrection of the body, and an everlasting fire in hell were understandably poorly received. The Meccans had already accepted the concept of one god and the concept of the final judgment had been slowly absorbed as the prerogative of a powerful god. What greatly disturbed the Meccans was Muhammad's claim to be a prophet. Such a claim implies a position of leadership and authority whereby he could assert dominance over the whole community. As a result, Muhammad's following during the first four years of his mission was small and consisted of only 40 people; it included the male believers, their wives, and slaves.

As the persistent Muhammad continued to recite his revelations, the hostile members of the Qurayah tribe tried to break up crowds who listened with interest to such ominous news. The Ummayads, a hostile sect of the Quraysh, issued a ban against the Hashimites, the tribal branch to which Muhammad belonged. Such resistance caused Muhammad to reside with his powerful uncle, Abu Talib, in the hills of Mecca for over two years. After the death of his wife, Khadija, and his uncle, he moved to Taif, located about sixty miles southeast of Mecca. While there, he was in a hopeless state until 620 CE when he met with several men from Yathrib. After a lengthy conference, all agreed that Muhammad could help resolve a blood feud between two of the Arab tribes, the Aws and the Khazraj. This secret agreement was well kept until 622, when it was supposed to go into effect. But when the hostile Ummayads learned of the agreement, they attacked Taif with the intent to capture Muhammad. To their dismay, he had already fled and reached Yathrib, a 300-mile trip north, normally an eleven-day journey, in eight days.

After several years in Yathrib, Muhammad was finally able to establish himself as a prophet of Allah and was given such unrestricted power over the town that its name was changed in his honor to Medina (*Madinat an nabi*, the City of the Prophet). There he had the first mosque built, instituted weekly then daily services, instituted taking of alms for the poor, and advocated his objective—the spread of Islam. Muslims in prayer at these services assumed the prostrate position, which at first was directed towards Jerusalem. After the Jews in Medina conspired against him, the direction was changed to face Mecca. Muhammad's objective became more of a reality, and to acquire arms and increase the treasury, he led a small force to surprise and slaughter a Meccan caravan. Only a decade after his first revelation, Muhammad initiated his first engagement for conquest by warring with Mecca. He was successful in his attempt, but the Meccans later prepared for a grand assault against Medina with 10,000 men. With the advice of a Persian follower, Muhammad executed a brilliant strategy of digging trenches at key points, causing the Meccans to give up the battle to capture Muhammad. In January of 630 CE, Muhammad, with a force of 10,000 men, severely cut Meccan trade routes and forced Mecca to surrender.

Muhammad's objective in unifying the Arab tribes with a consistent morality, social code of conduct, and a new spiritual message that prepared Muslims for Allah's judgment, had materialized. He established himself as the 'Prophet of Allah' and reached the stature of being the greatest chief in Arabia. One of his first acts was to reverently honor the Black Stone. After riding seven times around the Ka'ba shrine, he ordered the destruction of the idols within it and the scraping of the paintings of Abraham and angels from the walls. He allowed use of the Zamzam well and restored the boundary pillars that defined the sacred territory around Mecca. Nearby enemy tribes were conquered in battle and tribes far off were sternly invited to send delegations to offer their allegiance. In 632 CE, Muhammad died a sudden death (whether by assassination or poor health at age 62 is not known) but had achieved the start of a theocracy that governed and united the Arab tribes.[3]

It is to be noted that the Qur'an was not revealed to Muhammad in a short period of time as it was to Moses, who quickly transcribed what he heard from God in the *Book of the Covenant* (Exodus 24:4-8). Rather, Muhammad, who had not learned to read or write, had committed his revelations from the angel Gabriel to memory. It was some twenty years after Muhammad's death that a religious group of leaders compiled the first official document of his revelations. This religious group put the longest Suras at the beginning and the shortest at the end. The Qur'an contained Suras that had been accumulated over many years. It also included a Sura to protect the honor of Muhammad by sanctioning his marriage to his son's divorced wife. In Sura 33:37-40, a decree by Allah is announced, "that there should be no constraint in the minds of believers in the matter of marrying

---

[3]   **John B. Noss,** *Man's Religions,* **Pages 513-516.**

the wives of their adopted sons after they had divorced them." What is surprising in this Sura is its first line that states:

*Sura 33: 37-40. It is not open to a believing man or a believing woman, when Allah and His messenger (Muhammad) have decided a matter, to exercise their own choice in deciding it. Whoso disobeys Allah and his messenger, falls into error . . . Then, when Zaid had carried into effect his decision concerning her, **We** joined her in marriage with thee, so that there should be no constraint in the minds of the believers in the matter of marrying the wives of their adopted sons after they had divorced them. Allah's decreed is bound to be fulfilled . . .*

The above passage gives Muhammad equal status with God in the determination of a decree rather than having the decree stated by God alone. Also making the decree questionable is the fact that it is usually the angel Gabriel that speaks to Muhammad, not God. It appears that this decree was added to the Qur'an not only to sanction this particular case for marriage, but also to protect the respectability of Muhammad. Simply stating this decree for all men who wish to marry the divorced wife of an adopted son (or any son) would be sufficient but it also cites Muhammad's adopted son's name, Zaid. This decree is another example where the religious *We Group* is cited in an effort to protect Muhammad's name and arbitrarily act on Allah's behalf.

It is clear that when Scripture contains specifics on behalf of individuals rather than a whole people, such as Muhammad marrying the divorced wife of his adopted son, Zaid, it had to have been written by men without the guidance of or revelation from God. But this Scripture should not be criticized too harshly, for the Tanakh (Hebrew Bible) also contains specific laws and ordinances that deal with nonreligious but practical matters such as how to conduct monetary transactions; the manner in which to slaughter animals for consumption; and what kinds of food believers are allowed to eat. Likewise, followers of the Qur'an are provided specific commands that are not given by God, especially this Sura; designed to retain the honor of their prophet, Muhammad.

9.4 Islam Spreads by Conquering Other Countries

No other religion has grown as rapidly as Islam. Through the conquest of other countries and offering the people a choice they cannot refuse, conversion or death—Islam has grown to claim over 1.79 billion Muslims worldwide.[1] Many sects have emerged, but all adhere to the Qur'an. Two dominant sects have become readily identified as the Shia and Sunni, with smaller extreme fundamentalist sects appearing that aggressively fight for Islamic dominance, such as the Taliban, Hizballah, Hamas, and the Palestinian Islamic Jihad (PIJ) Movement. The key difference between the Sunnis and Shiites is that the former believe in a democratic choice of their leaders, called Caliphs, not by birth but by their capability to teach Islam; the latter, on the other hand, believe that their leaders, called Imams, should be descendants of Muhammad's family.

The Shiites number around 10-15% of all Muslims and the Sunnis are the largest sect; but the Taliban and other extremist groups are not easily quantified because they operate on a terrorist level. The Taliban is a relatively new sect that first appeared on the political scene of Afghanistan in September 1994 and controls 90% of its people. They are harsh fundamentalists who employ strict theocratic rule over their people by searching homes to destroy any television sets, radios, cassettes, photographs, and books; education for their women is limited as is exposure of foreign ideas to their men.

Hizballah, the Party of God,[2] is a militant terrorist organization that operates on a political level to extend and protect the Islamic faith. To keep Lebanon destabilized, they have provoked Israel into a terrorist war with the aim of converting Lebanon into a theocratic Islamic state.

---

[1]   Internet: http:/www.islamicpopulation.com/ Data derived in 2006.

[2]   A Statement of Purpose by Hizballah may be obtained via Internet @ http://almashriq.hiof.no/lebanon/300/320/324/324.2/ hizballah

This Party of God has forced Israel into war because Israel's democratic government, coupled with a successful Lebanese non-theocratic government, would weaken Islamic power and wealth. Syria and Iran support the Hizballah movement with weapons and money. They financially reward the parents of those who commit suicide with the sole purpose of killing innocent people. Countries controlled by Islamic religious leaders feel threatened by any culture or political system that encourages education and the free exchange of ideas.

Over the past two decades, the Hizballah and Taliban desire for total Islamic rule have been supplemented by other militant fundamentalist Islamic organizations known as Hamas and the PIJ Movement.[3] The goal of the PIJ is the liberation of all of Palestine, destruction of the state of Israel, and its replacement with an Islamic state for Palestinians. All of these organizations are united by their desire to destroy the democratic state of Israel. Hamas has clearly stated in their Preamble of the Hamas Covenant in 1988 that,

Israel exists and will continue to exist only until Islam will obliterate it, as it obliterated others before it.

As in the past, when the Arab tribes unified to establish an Islamic Empire, they expanded their Islamic religion based upon the Qur'an. Reclaiming the land Israel acquired from Palestine is a main objective of Hamas, as stated in Chapter III of their Covenant. It states:

Palestine is an Islamic Waqf (sacred possession) consecrated for future Muslim generations until Judgment Day. It, or any part of it, cannot be renounced; it, or any part of it, cannot be abandoned . . . This is

---

[3]   The mnemonic PIJ contains the word Jihad which stands for a struggle in the cause of God or good against evil. Jihad has become mostly associated with armed fighting in the name of God, or Holy War.

*the law governing the land in Islamic Sharia (Holy Law) and this
holds true for all lands that Muslims have conquered by force.*[4]

The last sentence of the above statement is reminiscent of the '*We
Group*' mentality and authority that surfaces in the Qur'an. Palestine
did become an Islamic possession after the Muslims conquered
Jerusalem in 638 CE and Caesarea in 640 CE. But the Jews had
already built their Jewish Temple in Jerusalem after Moses led the
Israelites out of Egypt around 1250 BCE. It was rebuilt during
Solomon's reign and remodeled by Herod the Great to become a
marbled beauty more magnificent than it had been before. To say
the city of Jerusalem is a sacred possession of Islam, rather than
Israel, diminishes the fact that the sacred land of the Muslims is in
Mecca—the birthplace and heart of Islam. It is Mecca, not Palestine,
where every Muslim, man and woman, at least once in a lifetime, is
expected to make a pilgrimage (a hajj). Following a tradition instituted
by Muhammad, thousands of pilgrims enter Mecca annually during
the sacred month of Dhu-al-Hijja to circle the Ka'ba seven times
and kiss or touch the Black Stone.[5]

It is towards Mecca that religious Muslims reserve time each day
for five acts of devotion and prayer. The first comes at dawn, the
second at midday, the others at mid-afternoon, sunset, and after the
fall of darkness or at bedtime. The devotee typically rolls out his
prayer rug, stands reverentially and offers certain prayers; he then
bows down towards Mecca with hands on knees to praise Allah and
declare submission to His holy will. The worshipper straightens up,
still praising Allah, then falls prostrate, placing his head to the ground
while still glorifying God. Then he sits down, reverently offering a
petition and finally prostrates himself once more.

---

[4]   Internet @: http://www.fas.org/irp/world/para/docs/930400.htm. Link
to: The Threat of Islamic Fundamentalism—Background Material.

[5]   **John B. Noss**, *Man's Religions*, **Pages 523-525.**

Throughout, the sacred words *'Allah akbar' (God is the Greatest)* are repeated again and again.[6]

It is obvious that because ritual prayer is aimed toward Mecca, it is further evidence that the sacred land of the Muslims is Mecca; a city within Saudi Arabia, and not Palestine. The above *Sharia (Holy Law)* by Hamas does not show honor and reverence for the birthplace of Islam by claiming *"all lands that Muslims have conquered by force"* are their sacred possessions. Words speaking of such force show disrespect for God's covenant with the Hebrews. God promised the Hebrews in Genesis 15:18, the land from the river of Egypt to the Euphrates river. Genesis 33:1,2 records God's support of the Hebrews whereby they conquered Canaan (Palestine) and built their holy temple in Jerusalem long before the Muslims—a span of about 1,570 years.

The above terrorist organizations and Islamic countries that support them foresee a very real threat by the modern world; countries with free political, non-theocratic systems of government that enjoy the freedom of expression of all ideas, concepts, and philosophical views. The Qur'an has served Arabs in establishing an Islamic Empire by force and continues today to preserve the traditions of Islam. All free people pray that Islam's repression of peoples' rights through extremist religious views will give way to intellectual freedom so that Muslims can develop their God-given capabilities and respect the religions of other nations.

9.4.1 Muslim Conquests under the First Caliph

The Qur'an's greatest purpose, designed by Muhammad, was the moral elevation and unification of the Arabic tribes that worshiped multiple gods to believe instead, Allah, the one God. After the death of Muhammad in 632 CE, the two sects that evolved were the Sunnah and Shiah in a power struggle for Muhammad's leadership authority. The first three Caliphs were elected by the majority of Muslims.

They were unrelated to the genealogy of Muhammad until the fourth Caliph, Ali ibn Abi Talib, who was his cousin and son-in-law.

The Companions were the first to choose Abu Bakr as their first Caliph. He lasted only one year but accomplished two things: he conducted the Riddah wars, that brought many tribes to submit to Islam; and he united tribal forces to initiate the first organized assault on the outside world. He amassed three armies, totaling 10,000 men, whose ranks eventually swelled to twice that number, and invaded Syria via three separate routes.[1]

9.4.2 Muslim Conquests under the Second Caliph

The second Caliph, 'Umar, served ten years (634-644 CE). While directing the great general Khalid ibn al-Walid, 'Umar altered the destiny of the Near East by capturing the city of Damascus after a six month siege in 635 CE. The Byzantine Emperor, Heraclius, released a 50,000-man force to drive Khalid's army away. But in the smothering heat and dust, an environment Bedouins were used to, he retreated. Khalid won a decisive victory in which Theodorus, brother of Heraclius and general of the Christian forces, was killed. The whole of Syria up to the Taurus Mountains was conquered. The Muslim victories added Jerusalem in 638 CE and Caesarea in 640 CE. The whole of Palestine then surrendered to the Arabs, cutting off Egypt from needed aid; that country too, was conquered after a three-year effort from 639 to 641 CE. The Arabs pushed on into North Africa, subjugating at least half of it, and on the other side of the Mediterranean, acquired Spain. Back in the Near East, the Muslims attacked the fabulously rich cities of Iraq in 637 CE and then subdued Persia from 640 to 649 CE. This conquest took longer because its inhabitants were non-Semitic, well unified, and firmly

---

[1]   **John B. Noss,** *Man's Religions,* **Page 526.**

Zoroastrian. It took a 12-year campaign (640-652) in the northwest to bring the greater part of Asia Minor into subjection.

The success of the Muslim armies was due, in part, to their expert use of the cavalry and the high mobility of Arab horse and camel transport. Muslim warriors were strongly motivated by their Prophet's word that by winning a battle in Allah's cause they could keep four-fifths of the booty, and if they died, would go to paradise. Added to the rich fortunes of war was the wonder and discovery of the earthly paradises of rich metropolitan cities lying ready for their taking in the ancient lands that were the "cradle of civilization." The young Muslims, who had had little exposure to the art and architecture of many beautiful cities, must have been excited by the prospects of learning Greek and Persian arts, philosophies, literature, and sciences. Having thus far been deprived of any formal education, the Muslims were ripe for learning.

The vast amount of territory acquired under 'Umar's rule provided an ongoing stream of tribute money that poured into the treasury at Medina. Muhammad could never have dreamed of so much wealth. 'Umar, who lived simply, determined to distribute this wealth in the form of yearly stipends to Muhammad's widows and dependents,[1] the Companions, and in lesser amounts, the Arab warriors and tribesmen. In order to keep the Arabian Muslims together as a military unit, he forbade any Arab to acquire lands outside the Saudi Arabian peninsula. He did not tolerate people who would not convert to Islam; he dispossessed and drove from Arabia resistant members of other religions, especially Jews, Christians, and Zoroastrians.

---

[1]   Muhammad's favorite wife, Aisha, was assigned 12,000 dirhems, or about $2,400 dollars.

9.4.3 A Muslim Empire by the 4ᵗʰ Caliph

The 3ʳᵈ Caliph, 'Uthman, a son-in-law and close associate of Muhammad, was chosen and served the office from 644 to 656. An Ummayad, he allowed the pressures of his family to appoint so many Ummayads to high office that the ensuing scandals led to his assassination in Medina by dissatisfied Muslims. He was succeeded by 'Ali ibn Abi Talib, another of Muhammad's son-in-laws and father of two boys who were Muhammad's only male descendants. When Ali became the 4ᵗʰ Caliph in 656 CE, the Shiah referred to him as the first Imam or leader of the ummah (Muslim community). Competing for this office was the governor of Syria, Muawiya, an Ummayad who was busily establishing himself as the chief Caliph contender in Egypt, Arabia, and Yemen. 'Ali remained disappointingly passive, and his army, after marching west to confront Muawiya, became disgusted with 'Ali's procrastination to settle the issues by arbitration and had him murdered; an event that would deepen the schism between the Sunnis and Shiites. By 661, Muawiya seized the caliphate and centralized in Damascus. He ruled a Muslim empire that extended itself over an enormous territory, stretching from India to Spain.[1]

In just 29 years from the death of Muhammad (661-632 CE), the Muslims had established an Empire. The first Caliph had been concerned only with spreading Islam among the Arabs in Saudi Arabia. Motivated by power and wealth, by 1300 CE, the Muslim leaders forced conversion to Islam not only in the Byzantine and Persian empires, but as far west as Spain and all of North Africa, including its east coast down to the island Madagascar, and further east to the northern half of India.

A greater schism between the Sunnis and Shiites occurred when the grandson of Muhammad, Husayn ibn Ali, seized the caliphate after

---

[1]   **John B. Noss**, *Man's Religions*, Sections 8.4.2 - 8.4.3, **Pages 526-528**.

the death of his father 'Ali. He refused to accept the Ummayads who held the caliphate majority and was killed by a small band of supporters in Iraq headed by the Ummayad, Caliph Yazid in 680 CE,. All Muslims regard this immoral slaughter of Husayn with horror. As a result, he has become a particular hero to the Shiites.[1] This event ignited the conflict over power and political interests between the Sunnis and Shiites. Even today, it has continued to cause Muslims to kill Muslims in a civil war reminiscent of the split between the conservative and liberal parties of the Jews, which resulted in their ultimate destruction by the Romans.

9.5 The Qur'an, its Beauty and its Flaws

The greatest attribute of the Qur'an is displayed when it is recited. Its Arabic language exudes hypnotic sounds that ring with a poetic rhythm, transporting the listener into a divine state of worship. Muslims say that when they hear the Qur'an chanted in the mosque they feel enveloped in a divine dimension of sound. Yet Muslims also say that when they read the Qur'an for its substantive content, they feel they are reading a different book because nothing of the beauty of the Arabic is conveyed. This is particularly so when the Qur'an is translated into other languages. It contains many repetitive Suras that tend to border on boring, as they seem to go over the same ground repeatedly.[1] A coherent development of its moral code and social ordinances is intertwined with too many passages that repeatedly preach warnings, chastisements, admonishments, punishments, and violence against nonbelievers.

The Qur'an, as does the Old and New Testament, presents a personal God who does everything that a human being does: He loves, judges, punishes, creates, and destroys as people do. The Qur'an creates a *highly personal God* that has passionate human likes and dislikes. As described

---

[1]   **Karen Armstrong**, *A History of God*, **Pages 158 and 159.**

in Subsection 9.3.1, Allah provides (via the intercession between Gabriel, Muhammad, and the *We Group*) warnings, chastisements, admonitions, and commands Muslims to fight and kill unbelievers in His name. The Qur'an further personalizes God by describing His heaven in physical terms. Karen Armstrong eloquently states, in *A History of God*, that when God is referred to on a personal and physical basis by using Him as a model of perfection for admirable human traits, He can also be used in a destructive manner.[2]

"A personal God can become a grave liability. He can be a mere idol carved in our own image, a projection of our limited needs, fears, and desires. We can assume that He loves what we love and hates what we hate, endorsing our prejudices instead of compelling us to transcend them. When He seems to fail to prevent a catastrophe or seems even to desire a tragedy, He can seem callous and cruel . . . A personal God can be dangerous, therefore. Instead of pulling us beyond our limitations, "He" can encourage us to remain complacently within them; "He" can make us as cruel, callous, self-satisfied and partial as "He" seems to be. Instead of inspiring the compassion that should characterize all advanced religions, "He" can encourage us to judge, condemn and marginalize. It seems, therefore, that the idea of a personal God can only be a stage in our religious development. The world religions all seem to have recognized this danger and have sought to transcend the personal conception of supreme reality."

Table 9-2 lists the many human qualities of what God loves and is replete with duplications. In today's world, the very danger described by Karen Armstrong exists—the condemnation and marginalization of people whose beliefs in God, even the same God, are practiced in a different way. Radical, fundamentalist religious leaders have become fanatical men who use the Qur'an to judge, condemn, and marginalize those people who practice another religion. They even teach their children to classify non-Muslims as infidels. Such a low

---

[2]   **Karen Armstrong,** *A History of God*, **Pages 209 and 210.**

Table 9-2. The 'Loves' of God in the Qur'an.

Sura	What God Loves and Does Not Love in the Qur'an
2.195, 3.134, 3.148, 5.13 5.93,	Allah **loves** the doers of good.
2.205, 5.64, 28.77	Allah does not **love** mischief-making.
2.222, 9.108	He **loves** those who purify themselves.
2.276	Allah does not **love** any ungrateful sinner.
3.32, 30.45	Allah does not **love** the unbelievers.
3.57, 3.140, 42.40	Allah does not **love** the unjust.
60.8	Allah **loves** the doers of justice.
3.76	Allah **loves** those who guard (against evil).
9.4, 9.7	Allah **loves** those who are careful (of their duty).
3.146	Allah **loves** the patient.
3.159	Allah **loves** those who trust.
4.36	Allah does not **love** him who is proud, boastful;
16.23	Allah does not **love** the proud.
31.18	Allah does not **love** any self-conceited boaster;
57.23	Allah does not **love** any arrogant boaster:
4.107	Allah does not **love** him who is treacherous, sinful;
8.58	Allah does not **love** him who is treacherous.
4.148	Allah does not **love** the public utterance of hurtful speech unless (it be) by one to whom injustice has been done;
5.42	Allah **loves** those who judge equitably.
49.9	Allah **loves** those who act equitably.
6.141, 7.31	He does not **love** the extravagant.
22.38	Allah does not **love** any one who is unfaithful, ungrateful.
61.4	Allah **loves** those who fight in His way in ranks as if they were a firm and compact wall.

regard for how other people worship their God has resulted in the loss of lives by beheadings and murder of innocent human beings in the name of Allah. Eventually these brutal actions can only bring shame on a people who have been led astray by religious leaders who seek only expansion of power and wealth. This is truly unfortunate, for many Muslims are like all other people; they are inherently loving and good but are taught mistrust and hate.

It would be unfair to cast aspersions on all Muslims; they are a product of the warnings, chastisements, admonishments, punishments, and violence advocated in the Qur'an. Many Muslims desire peace, justice, and truth, and there are many who also believe that all people have a right to worship their God of righteousness. God has created many paths to share His Word and rejoice in the gift of love for all His children—the sisters and brothers of the world. Loving Muslims will eventually be bold enough to attend houses of worship of other monotheistic religions. Hopefully, their religious leaders will be courageous to join leaders of the Judaic and Christian faiths, and together revise their Holy Scriptures.

The Qur'an omits the command given in both the Old and New Testaments, "thou shalt love thy neighbor as thyself." This command only referred to loving your neighbors, but Jesus Christ delivered God's *new* command that encompasses all people—*that ye love one another* (John 15:17). Sura 4:37, stated in Table 9-1, says to be benevolent, but only towards specified people. As *The Qu'ran* is the most recent Scripture, one would expect that God would have repeated to Muhammad His *new* command—*to love one another*. This is an inclusive command that applies to all sisters and brothers from any nation. Religious leaders of every religion should make its highest goal God's *new* command; any religion which fails to do so is a sham.

10.0 God of Future Generations

Dear reader, the author has shared with you a journey that hopefully has provided the grounding to understand more completely the development of our monotheistic God. People from all civilizations have always sought to understand their world. Awed by nature's beauty, they felt moved to acknowledge a creative force which led them to create meaningful forms of worship. For people today, there should be no fear or shame in exploring the past to gain a better understanding of the God they may worship.

Researching and writing this book has been a marvelous journey. This author has learned and now appreciates so much more the achievements of courageous and righteous men covered in this writing. They have led efforts to improve the morality of people by replacing myths and distortions with truth. You can now understand why the image of one of our greatest men appears on the front cover of this book. Ikhnaton, a pharaoh who received the best education in Egypt, had the sensitivity, perception, and fortitude to establish his concept of one God by courageously eliminating the worship of many gods in Egypt. Not long after, the Egyptian Priesthood endorsed his concept and were inspired to write Scripture proclaiming, *"Amon As the Sole God."* After reading this book, it should become obvious that Amon is the name of God that is pronounced at the end of every prayer as *Amen.*

The God many believe in today has been revealed through man's spirit, imagination, and love for the God he created in his own image. The philosophical questions of who created the universe, the first atom, and the enormous amount of matter, galaxies, and stars—lead one's mind to ponder the wonder of it all. The world has become much larger than it was to the minds of men 4,000 years ago. Today, many realize that there may be other intelligent life in the billions of galaxies in the universe. This leads one to not only revere life on this planet, but to eventually love and respect alien life that may come to visit us in the future. Our future depends, first, on how much sisters and brothers, throughout our world, love one another.

10.1 Need to Revise and Improve Religious Beliefs

The evolution of our monotheistic God took thousands of years, and in the process underwent many changes. This should come as no surprise, for each generation has developed concepts that were embraced and improved upon. This has been true in the scientific and technical spheres whereby scientists have learned to substitute and communicate at the speed of light. Change also occurs in our religious heritage. In the past, it has become obvious to many great minds that their Holy Scriptures must be reviewed and updated. Today, many passages are out of date and many that once served to unite a unique people are no longer applicable. One need only to turn to the Torah to see outdated passages dealing with ancient animal sacrifices, specific details for the garments of the priest, and detailed measurements on how to build a place of worship, an altar, and its accessories (Refer to Exodus 23, 25-31).

Many passages from the Qur'an have been presented and one may conclude that its main purpose, as carried out by Muhammad and his followers, was to unite a people that had a multitude of gods and unify them both spiritually and as a nation. But these God fearing people have taken their belief and carried it to an extreme by conquering other people and converting them not by love, but by the sword. Today, the Muslim sect called the Taliban is a disgrace to their people as they murder innocent human beings and restrict their people from developing their God-given capabilities.

The New Testament is also not immune to criticism. One has only to read John Shelby Spong's book, *The Sins of Scripture*. Here, one is apprised of the pain suffered by Jews because of anti-Semitic references in the Bible. This pain has been extended to homosexuals by negative references. Women are still regarded as second-class citizens whereby, even today in Jewish Temples, Catholic Churches, and Islamic Mosques, they are not considered capable of being priests and delivering valuable insights in sermons. Still worse, the fruit tree myth has made women the source of blame for man's fall from the grace of God. Yet, sons and daughters look to their mothers to raise, guide, discipline, and love them.

Change is essential if religious institutions are to keep pace with their worshippers as they acquire more education and the ability to inquire and seek meaning in their lives. If they continue to cling to worn, outdated passages of their Holy Scriptures, they will only become a further embarrassment to discerning and intelligent people. By not acknowledging the need for change, they will find their religious myths ridiculed and their institutions laughed at because their words no longer provide the guidance and spirituality people so much desire. Can our religious institutions, be they of Jewish, Christian, or Islamic origins, afford this outcome that is sure to develop in the future? There are many brilliant minds that would gladly assist in the reformation of their religious institutions and Holy Scriptures. But will those entrusted with the responsibility of religious leadership be courageous and perceptive enough to improve their doctrines? Or are they so indoctrinated that they cannot search their hearts and minds to find the truths and words of love that can truly guide their worshippers?

As a man who has learned to love all people, the sisters and brothers of this world, there is hope for change. Human beings are born with the gift to love; it is the one gift that insures their survival. The following pages offer recommendations for religious leaders and our sisters and brothers of all nations. They are provided as a starting point for many more necessary changes. Surely, there are men and women who have the talent and gifts to help implement the recommendations offered and commend many more to improve the morality and spiritual nature of mankind.

10.2 Conclusions and Recommendations

- ***The Three Basic Religions Worship the Same God.*** This obvious conclusion initiates the recommendation that religious leaders be truthful and loudly proclaim that Jews, Christians, and Muslims all worship the same God.

- ***The Name of God is Amen.*** Men have conceived God in different stages and by different groups of people. The one-god concept was known even prior to Ikhnaton in the form of a creator of all things. But man was so closely attached to and awed by the wonders of nature that he continued to worship the gods of the past. To break away from the past of multiple gods and develop the first one-god concept was a feat that could only be accomplished by a man in power; that man was the pharaoh, Ikhnaton. The Egyptian Priesthood then took Ikhnaton's writings and formalized them into Scripture that defined the god, Amen, as the creator of all things. It is no wonder that his name is still pronounced at the end of a prayer. Even Jesus, in John's Revelation 3:14, acknowledged Amen:

  *"And unto the angel of the church of the Laodoceans write; These things saith the **Amen**, the faithful and true witness, **the beginning of the creation of God."***

Religious leaders of the three basic faiths must put aside their selfish reasons for having their people believe their God is unique to them only. It is the name *Amen* that has survived over 4,000 years and reigns over Jehovah and Allah. As a case in point, Allah is not the name of a god but an Arabic word meaning one God. When the three religions concede that the name of God is Amen—then they will acknowledge truth. The present definition for Amen, "So be it." should be revised and revered as the name of God.

- *The 3 Basic Religions Must Open Their Doors to All People.*
  By having the same God, the leaders of Judaic, Christian, and Islamic religions are obligated to open the doors of their houses of worship to all those who believe in that same God. To restrict their temples, churches, and mosques to only those who subscribe to the practices and rites of their religion is to prohibit the children of God from seeking, inquiring, and learning more about the God they worship. The religious leaders who are proud of their practices and the doctrines they teach will surely welcome the sisters and brothers of any nation. If not, their religion is nothing more than a sham, a cult for arrogant human beings who believe that they are better than their sisters and brothers of other ethnic groups and countries.

- *People Must Go to Each Others' Houses of Worship.* It has been acknowledged that the three basic religions all advocate the same God. God has made Himself known to different groups of people at different times so that they could eventually benefit in accepting God's Holy Spirit of compassion and love. Now, followers of Judaism, Catholicism, and Islam, and their many sects, have an opportunity to visit the different houses of worship. Several benefits will be derived:

1. Worshippers will learn other aspects of their God and how He has revealed Himself to his children.
2. Worshippers will learn why religious doctrines have been received differently for different peoples to serve their needs for moral direction.
3. By attending the services of different religions, people worldwide will be able to learn to appreciate the differences in how they worship the same God.
4. Rabbis, priests, ministers, caliphs, imams, and mullahs of Judaic, Christian, and Islamic religions will be able to teach sisters and brothers from different nations about their prophets and Holy Scriptures.

5. The sermons from the religious leaders will be given more significance because, like businesses in competition with each other, they must reach within their beings to bring relevance from within their Holy Scriptures to their congregations.

6. Finally, the tolerance and respect people give to each other's religions will, in time, cause them to merge with a unified conception of their God and His commandments.

It is inconceivable that any house of God would prohibit the sisters and brothers from different nations, creeds and beliefs, from attending their holy services. However, from a practical view, because arrogance and bias does exist both with religious leaders and their followers, the following approaches are recommended:

- *Sisters and brothers of different nations must attend different houses of worship in groups of fives and tens.*

- *Where a language barrier exists, obtain an interpreter from the house of worship being visited.*

- *Show appreciation for receiving instruction from another house of God by giving an affordable donation.*

People who are proud of their religion will be honored that others are interested in learning more about their religious practices and teachings. Dear people, seek to break down religious barriers of ignorance with the above recommendations so that,—*The sisters and brothers from all nations will love one another.*

- *Religions Must Update and Improve their Holy Scripture.* The revision of outdated dogma is not sacrilegious or blasphemous, as strict religious leaders would like people to believe. In Figure 10-1 it is revealed that the Egyptians evolved the conception of one God, beginning from the 1st Dynasty to the 19th Dynasty. After Ikhnaton introduced the concept of one God about 1370 BCE, the

Priesthood of Amon updated their religious Scripture in 1270 BCE and proclaimed *Amon As the Sole God.* Twenty years later, in 1250 BCE, Moses walked out of Egypt with worshippers that believed in one God. His conversations with God were recorded in the *Book of the Covenant* which initiated the Torah during Solomon's reign around 950 BCE. By 444 BCE, the Five Books of Moses were finalized by the efforts of Ezra and Nehemiah (Subsection 7.5.2).

After the Jewish-Roman war, which caused near annihilation of the Jews throughout Israel and complete destruction of Jewish towns and cities, a sect of Jewish Holy men saw a need to salvage their legacy in the belief in one God. Their writings led to the creation of the New Testament. Therefore, Holy Scripture is not cast in concrete. Rather, it is revised due to critical events. But also, revisions become necessary as mankind grows in intellect, experience, and knowledge of the world around him.

Development of the One-God Concept			
Predynastic	**1st Dynasty**	**5th-6th Dynasty**	**13th-18th Dynasty**
Qustul Incense Burner, Worship of Animal Gods. Osiris and the Hereafter, Righteousness and Truth	Concept of a Son of God. The King as Son of Horus	**The Creation by Atum.** Concept of a Soul, the Ka. The King as Son of Amon-Re	Priesthood compose **A Hymn to Amon-Re**

Development of the One-God Concept Cont.			
18th Dynasty	**19th Dynasty**	**1250 BCE**	**950 BCE**
Amenhotep IV in 1370 BCE wrote **Hymn to the Aton.** First to implement concept of One God	Priesthood of Amon around 1270 BCE wrote Scripture titled **Amon As the Sole God**	Moses leaves Egypt with Concept of One God, Wrote **Book of the Covenant**	**Torah** initiated during Solomon's Reign and finalized in 444 BCE by Erza and Nehemiah

Figure 10-1. Scripture Evolves as Man Gains Knowledge.

When will present-day religious leaders become receptive to the needs of a more civilized world by getting their greatest minds to revise Scripture that was written as long as 3,000 years ago? Religious men have been reluctant to add, modify, or change the revelations of men who were inspired in an ancient world. Where are the courageous minds like those of Ikhnaton, Moses, Jesus and Muhammad who set out to establish doctrine meant to direct humanity on a path of righteousness, compassion, and love? Surely there are inspired, perceptive, and loving people today who have the ability to enhance Scriptures with the needed changes for which the world of the future demands.

- ***Don't Wait for a Prophet for Inspired Revelation.*** Sons and daughters of God need not be prophets to communicate with God. There are highly capable people with loving hearts and brilliant minds who can revise the Holy Scriptures of the Judaic, Christian, and Islamic religions. The man that introduced the concept of one God and made it a reality was Ikhnaton. He was an educated man with sensitivity and creativity who was not inspired from without but from within his own heart and mind. To wait for someone to be informed in a dreamlike state of mind is fruitless and ridiculous. The greatest innovations and inventions in music, medicine, and the technical spheres were conceived by hard work and thought that logically built upon itself until thought became a reality.

- ***Much of Holy Scripture is Valuable—Build Upon It.*** The Scriptures of the Judaic, Christian, and Islamic religions have many common themes and, of course, we must preserve the best to create a more meaningful whole. Moses learned much Scripture from the Egyptians as an adopted son of an Egyptian pharaoh. He condensed many of the instructions and laws that Egyptians followed in order to enter eternal life and, inspired by his one-god belief, wrote the *Book of the Covenant.* By 950 BCE, Jewish priests initiated Scripture that led to completion of the Torah in 444 BCE. Jesus came along and simplified the

Law so that many more sheep could join the fold of the chosen ones. Muhammad, influenced by followers of the Book (Torah) and new Christian faith, created the Qur'an as a new 'Book' of righteousness. He and his religious leaders used the Qur'an as an instrument to forcefully unite the multiple Arabic tribes and people from other countries, into an Islamic nation (Section 9.4). These holy men used the conception of God of the Judaic and Christian religions and made it applicable to their own people. So it is shown, history confirms that inspired men learn from the Scriptures of their predecessors and adapt what they have learned for use by their own people.

Today, there are people who think that the three religions pray to different Gods. This is not just a sad reality; it's a shame that religious leaders have not united the sisters and brothers of our world through love. The religion that advocates terror and the murder of innocent lives has got to take a real look at their Holy Scriptures and see if, in fact, the rhetoric and teachings precipitate violence and hate. If so, they must make an honorable effort to correct what once was well-intended guidance but now an abomination to the Word of God. Of Ikhnaton, Moses, Jesus, and Muhammad, only Ikhnaton and Jesus were men of true peace and love. Let us remember that Moses killed about 3,000 of his own people and invaded Canaan. Muhammad converted many people in the towns and cities within his own country by the sword and his successors, caliphs and imams, conquered other lands with the threat of conversion to Islam or death. The recommendation here is clear; much of Holy Scripture is outdated and religious leaders would better serve mankind by building upon much of what men of peace and love have taught to bring sisters and brothers closer to God.

10.3 Revisions Needed in the Holy Scriptures

The most obvious changes and additions that are required in the Scriptures of religions are:

- **Killing of human beings on a one-for-one or genocide basis is forbidden.** Any leader or person that advocates the taking of life must be immediately put on trial as a danger to the rest of the world. Incitement to kill must be met swiftly with imprisonment. The people of any nation have a responsibility to eliminate murder.

- **Women are to be treated as co-equal with men.** The idea that the man is the authority of a family unit because he emulates God the Father is an infantile notion. Many men do not match the intelligence and sensitivity of many fine women. The myth that Eve is responsible for man's downfall and ushered in the concept of original sin is to be rescinded. A book of Scripture that denigrates our most beautiful counterpart and partner in this world must be corrected. The fruit tree myth was conjured up by inadequate men who tried to explain their loss of immortality by placing the blame on women.

- **Respect All of God's Creations.** This includes not only the mentally and physically deficient, but also those who prefer to love others who are of their own gender. Those who wish to love one's own gender and do not induce others who are meant to love the opposite sex should not be deprived of that love. God has made human beings differently to serve a purpose; to harm those who choose to love their own gender is unacceptable. Human beings who are fortunate to love the opposite sex are blessed with being able to explore the marvelous intimacy of another gender. If a same-gender choice is made by two people who are truly committed to a sincere and loving relationship, allow them to find their own happiness.

- **Education and Science are Essential Elements for Knowing God.** The most wonderful gift with which God has endowed mankind is an inquiring mind. Without it, people could not possibly possess the spirit to come to know Him. The ideas of being all one can be, tapping into one's abilities and creative talents to make your creator proud, is what should be taught in every home and by every religion. It is through education and the sciences that people not only learn to understand themselves better, but also eliminate ignorance by exploring their world. The benefit will be a greater appreciation of how He has created life throughout the universe. Someday, if mankind is truly blessed, they may come face to face with intelligent aliens. It is knowledge that must be sought. Fear and the repression of knowledge can only lead to disbelief in God because the human spirit will be reduced to ignorance. Through exposure of the wonders of God's universe, people are sure to gain a greater understanding of themselves and God. By extending perception of God beyond heaven and earth to the expanse of the universe, all life will be revered and God becomes a greater reality.

- **Recommend a Council for Religious Unity.** The three great monotheistic religions, Judaism, Christianity, and Islam have a responsibility to teach the sisters and brothers throughout the world to love one another. To implement this objective, it is recommended that these three religions form a *Council for Religious Unity*. The leaders from these religions must communicate with each other with sincere and honest efforts to make compromises in their religious doctrines. It is recommended that the leaders of these religions look at their doctrines, list them, and pick out those doctrines that need to be revised or eliminated so that all may start on a course of unification of their belief in the One God. This initiative will require extremely brave and courageous leaders who understand that it is the very roots of religious Scripture that divide people in today's world.

This author believes that people can "see" much more than they permit themselves to "see." Hopefully, this book will lift the veil from the eyes of those who wish to "know God" founded on truth. It provides an opportunity for perceptive and courageous religious leaders to unify their Scriptures and create a path of love for all sisters and brothers. By accomplishing this commandment from God, they will save not only their own religions from eventual decay, but more importantly, they will save the spiritual heritage of the human race.

10.4 Revelation, Jesus Christ, and Amen

The following discourse intimates that through Jesus Christ, God inspired Saint John's Revelation to induce, in future generations, leaders of the three major religions, Judaism, Christianity, and Islam, to come together by acknowledging the same God, Amen. Through God's Holy Spirit, man has learned to conceive a better understanding of God as He progressed from various forms of worship from the creator god Atum (Section 3.3) to Amen—the God Jesus proclaimed in John's Revelation. This progression began with the spiritual nature of the Egyptians.

The gradual development of Egyptian religious beliefs began from animal worship to veneration of a personal god that represented the renewal process of the Nile. In Section 3.5 the reader found that centuries before the 1st Dynasty, Egyptians worshipped Osiris who embodied the Nile process of renewal. This veneration induced the Priesthood to conceive the concept of an afterlife, upon which, they developed a morality based upon truth and righteousness.

Figure 10-2 provides a brief overview of how the original conception of the creator God Atum led to the worship of Amon-Re and then to *Amon as the Sole God*. There is conclusive evidence throughout this book that reveals how the influence of Egyptian religious beliefs led to the creation of the Torah and New Testament. Further conclusive evidence is revealed in Saint John's Revelation. There, the reader finds that through Jesus Christ, God has never lost His hold on the minds of men; for they continue to announce His name in temples, churches, and mosques. This realization is illustrated in Figure 10-2 and is summarized below.

The worship of Atum, the creator God, developed man's first conception of a soul, the ka; the vital force of His creations (Section 3.4). The Egyptian Priesthood further ignited the imagination of mankind by the promise of a hereafter upon leading a righteous life (Section 3.5). To attain immortality and join their gods, the Egyptians were taught to follow a civil and religious code of ethics. To attain eternal life after death, they would repeat a litany of protestations within the halls of Osiris to reside with the gods (Section 3.6). To enforce a moral code of conduct, the Priesthood taught that their king was a Son of God, thereby providing an authority on Earth to enforce conduct to please their God (Section 3.7). By 1370 BCE, a pharaoh, Amenhotep IV, broke with the traditional worship of multiple gods and instituted the belief in a monotheistic god, Aton (Chapter 4.0). One hundred years later, during the reign of Ramses, this progression became centralized and unified as the Egyptians worshiped Amon-Re as their supreme God (Chapter 6.0). Their belief became more universal as they conceived *Amon* as the *embodiment* of the sun-god Re and Atum—*the Maker of all mankind and maker of all that is* (Subsection 6.1.5.2).

The concept of *Amon As the Sole God* was readily received by the people of Palestine and Syria; his acceptance was precipitated at least two centuries earlier when pharaohs led invasions to turn back foreign incursions into Egyptian territory.

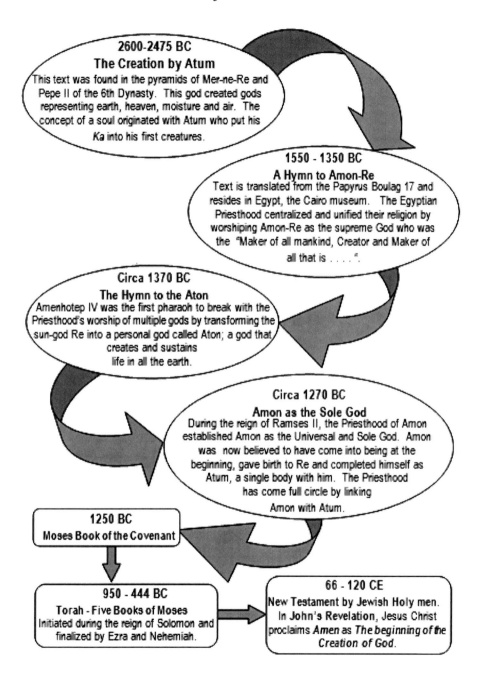

Figure 10-2. Jesus Christ Proclaims Amen as the Beginning of God.

The Egyptian religion crossed the Jewish boundaries of Palestine and Syria as early as 1479 BCE when Thutmose III invaded the threatening Kadesh coalition at Yehem and Megiddo. Thutmose III demonstrated his organizational and political skills by educating the captured sons of kings in these revolting cities. As early as his first campaign, he was astute enough to realize it would be to Egypt's advantage to have these sons replace the kings of the conquered cities. He understood that these sons would have an appreciation and tolerance to inculcate their people with Egypt's religious beliefs and culture. During Thutmose's 5th campaign, he erected a temple dedicated to Amon in a city just opposite Tunip on the northern Phoenician coast of Syria.[1] The exposure of the Palestinian and Syrian peoples to Egyptian religious beliefs was increased by other pharaohs who continued to fend off Asian intrusions into Egypt and build temples to Amon in several other Asiatic cities.

Referring again to Figure 10-2, the reader finds that it was through the efforts of Amenhotep IV that the worship of multiple gods was stopped circa 1370 BCE, and that he was first to establish monotheism with his Aton God. By the 19th Dynasty, around 1270 BCE, Egyptians worshipped Amon as the Sole God. The Priesthood taught that Amon gave birth to Re and completed himself as Atum, the first God of creation. He was worshiped by the Egyptians as far back as 2600 BCE (Subsection 6.1.3).

The worship of Amon was so prevalent, that many pharaohs included Amon and Amen in their throne names as early as 2000 BCE starting with the pharaoh, Amenemhet I. While on the throne in Thebes, where Amon was the principal god, Amenemhet I led Egypt to her second great period of productive development, the Middle Kingdom. Table 5-1 illustrates the frequent use of Amon and Amen in the throne names of pharaohs two and eleven times, respectively. It illustrates

---

[1]   **James H. Breasted**, *A History of Egypt,* **Pages 284-301**.

that the pharaohs used Amon and Amen interchangeably with only Tutenkhamon and Siamon using Amon as a suffix.

It did not take long for the Amon God to materialize into the god of the Hebrews through the efforts of Moses by 1250 BCE. They established a religion of their own with Holy Scripture initiated during Solomon's reign in 950 BCE. After the Hebrew leaders Ezra and Nehemiah added significant changes to their Holy Scripture, the first five books of Moses, known as the Torah was completed in 444 BCE and has remained unchanged. It was the Torah that unified the Hebrews and strengthened their people to resist repression by conquerors from other countries.

Figure 10-2 illustrates how there was a transition of Egyptian beliefs that influenced the writing of Jewish Scriptures known as the Old and New Testaments. The Egyptian hymns themselves may be considered Holy Scripture because they reveal the belief systems of the Egyptians. Much later, around 610 CE, the beliefs of Judaic and Christian Scripture inspired Muhammad to write the Qur'an, which was used to create an Islamic empire by 661 CE.

The above summary reveals that, starting with the Egyptian civilization, God has revealed Himself to different groups of people in stages. As men gained more experience within their world and learned the advantages of religion to employ morality and truth within their growing civilization, greater reverence in the worship of God became dominant in the conduct of their lives. History shows that the belief in God did not spread by peaceful means, but by catastrophic events where people from other countries clashed due to different traditions, beliefs, and economic circumstances.

Section 8.1 clearly describes that it was the near annihilation of the Jewish people that motivated Jewish Holy Men to write the Gospels of the New Testament. Unfortunately, the spread of God's Word was not definitized, or made clear, until the appearance of Jesus Christ who stated God's new command—to love one another. God used His surrogate, Jesus Christ to implement His Word. Later, God's Holy Spirit inspired Saint John to write a revelation that acknowledged Amen as, *'the beginning of the creation of God.'*

10.4.1 The Acknowledgement of Amen by Jesus Christ

It is extremely important that religious leaders and worshippers of the Judaic, Christian, and Islamic religions ponder over the words inspired by God in Saint John's Revelation. For too long religious leaders and scholars have ignored the words of Jesus Christ recorded in Saint John's Revelation, 3:13,14; they are highly significant and are presented below:

3:13 **He that hath an ear, let him hear what the Spirit saith unto the churches.**

3:14 And unto the angel of the church of the Laodoceans write; **These things saith the Amen, the faithful and true witness, the beginning of the creation of God.**

It is noted in 3:13 that Jesus requests all to hear what the Spirit has said to the churches. This statement indicates that Jesus was about to announce what the Spirit of God intends for the churches. Additionally, Jesus entreats those with the ability to hear to listen to what the Spirit of God is about to say. It is in the very next verse, 3:14 that Jesus proclaims Amen as, "the faithful and true witness, the beginning of the creation of God." The following verses, 3:15 through 3:21, consisted of several reprimands for the churches. In a memorable and poignant verse, 3:20, Jesus states the words of the Spirit of God, "Behold, I stand at the door, and knock: if any man hear my voice, and open the door, I will come into him, and will sup with him, and he with me."

The author has heard sermons whereby men of the cloth have informed their parishioners that God stands at the door and knocks, and those who hear His voice and open the door, He will come and sup with them. However, he has never heard a minister, priest, rabbi, imam, or mullah ever mention the words of Jesus that acknowledges Amen as the beginning of the creation of God. Through God's Holy Spirit, Jesus proclaimed Amen as, 'the faithful and true witness,' which means He exists as an entity and not an expression that means, "So be it."

Why have religious leaders neglected the profound words that honor the God Amen and worse yet, do not acknowledge that Jesus Christ spoke those words to the churches? Were they simply ignorant of Egyptian history that Amen was, in fact, Egypt's greatest god? This may not be surprising since it was only 180 years ago that the Egyptian hieroglyphic code was broken and the world has since learned so much from what was written on their temple walls and monuments.

Still, in light of the fact that rabbis, priests, ministers, imams, and mullahs have been thoroughly schooled in Holy Scriptures, it is surprising that not one religious leader has stood up to proclaim that Jesus Christ has acknowledged Amen as the 'beginning of the creation of God.' This observation raises the depressing realization that the religious institutions seek only to justify and perpetuate their own existence at the expense of serving God's mandate to love one another; whereby our brothers and sisters, from every nation, love and support one another. When Judaic, Christian, and Islamic religious leaders redefine "So be it" to a truth revealed by Jesus, that Amen is "the faithful and true witness, the beginning of the creation of God," then God's mandate will truly be realized.

10.4.2 Today's World Needs a Religious Renaissance

The conflict with today's believers, regarding the true meaning of Amen, arises because they have not been exposed to knowledge that has recently been revealed to the reader. In 1799, the French discovered one of the greatest findings in Rosetta, a harbor on the Mediterranean coast in Egypt. The Rosetta stone contained Egyptian hieroglyphics, demotic and classical Greek text. Due to the Greek text, the French scholar, Jean-François Champollion, was able to decipher the hieroglyphics in 1822.[1] It should be noted that the Egyptians and their neighbors to the east, Palestine and Syria, had lost the ability to interpret the hieroglyphics that were carved on ancient temple walls, tombs and monuments. It is for this reason, except for Jesus Christ in John's Revelation, that Abraham, Moses, and Jewish Holy Men were unable to give credit to a legacy of the Egyptian people—their conception of one God, Amen.

Only 83 years from Champollion's achievement, one of the greatest Egyptologists, James H. Breasted, wrote *A History of Egypt* in 1905. This book revealed that Egypt had a spiritual belief in a creator God more than 2,000 years before the Torah was written. Other enlightening books, such as *The Book of the Dead* by E.A. Wallis Budge, first published in 1899, provided many hymns and rituals that revealed that the Egyptian Priesthood had religious rituals and traditions far older than the Judaic religion. More importantly, Egyptian scholars have translated the hymns from Egyptian temples, tombs, and monuments. They found that the ancient Egyptians not only created the first belief in a soul and belief in a hereafter, but also created the concept of one God. One may refer to *Ancient Near Eastern Texts Relating to the Old Testament,* edited by James B. Pritchard, which contains many translated Egyptian hymns, prayers, and words of wisdom. The reader should pause here to be thankful for the efforts of those men that have been able to decipher Egypt's hieroglyphics. The words carved on Egypt's ancient walls of pyramids, temples, and tombs have provided the linkages of human thought that allows one to better understand the development of scriptures and belief in God.

---

[1] **James Cross Giblin,** *The Riddle of the Rosetta Stone,* **Pages 46, 60.** Champollion published his discovery that hieroglyphics consisted of sounds and symbols in 1824.

Considering that the Egyptian hieroglyphic code was broken and translations were made possible by Egyptologists, such as E. A. Wallis Budge and James H. Breasted a little more than 100 years ago, it is understandable that many biblical scholars and religious leaders may not have read that Egyptian religious beliefs have had a profound influence on the development of Judaic, Christian, and Islamic Scripture. Unfortunately, the lack of ancient Egyptian history may have prevented religious leaders from learning about the most wonderful findings revealed by the dedicated efforts of James Breasted and E.A. Wallis Budge.

Could it also be that leaders of the major religions fear that when worshippers learn that God first revealed Himself to the Egyptians as Amen, the integrity of their Holy Scriptures will be weakened? Except for Jesus Christ in John's Revelation, the Scriptures of Judaism, Christianity, and Islam do not honor Amen as the God of Creation. This fear is very real, but it was God who intended for worshippers of the three major religions to consistently remember and announce His name at the end of a prayer, supplication, and in giving thanks and praise. Through John's Revelation, it appears that God foresaw that unification of the three religions will occur when they all accept that it was He, in the name of Amen, that mankind came to know Him. This author asserts that God has used Jesus Christ to reveal this truth in John's Revelation because He knew that His name, Amen, would live on into modern times and would be the bond needed to bring the three religions together.

It is hoped that religious leaders will honor the words God's Holy Spirit had Jesus announce to those "that hath an ear". When religious leaders of Judaism, Christianity, and Islam acknowledge that they all pray to the same God Amen, the human race will then be set on a religious breakthrough based upon truth. Truth was the prime attribute admired and followed by the Egyptians. When fears people have of losing their religious identity are resolved, they can all pray to the same God with pride. There is need for a Religious Renaissance to acknowledge the truths of mankind's spiritual legacy. The ultimate objective of religious leaders is to bring sisters and brothers throughout the world together in peace and love.

10.5 Sons and Daughters of God

The author's journey in the writing of this book has enabled him to grapple with a concept too often overlooked in the many sermons he has heard. It will serve the reader well to revisit John's Gospel, 1:12, wherein he states that anyone can become a Son of God.

> *But as many as received Him, to them gave He power to become the Sons of God, even to them that believe on His name.*

Then in John 14:12, Jesus himself confirms that those who believe in him will do even greater works:

> *Verily, verily, I say unto you, he that believeth on me, the works that I do shall he do also; and greater works than these shall he do; because I go to my Father.*

This is a wonderful statement whereby Jesus makes it known that greater works shall be done by those who believe in him because he must go to his Father. God's Holy Spirit has Saint John and Jesus Christ confirm that there will be other daughters and sons of God. Jesus was therefore a Son of God not genetically but spiritually, for he was the product of the genes of a man and a woman. He was, as he so often stated, the Son of Man. It was through his love of God and the dissemination of His Word that he simplified all the Law and stated in John 13:34, the great *new* commandment:

> *A new commandment I give unto you, That ye love one another; as I have loved you, that ye also love one another.*

There is therefore hope in the world that religious leaders will recognize that Holy Scripture is not encased in concrete. There will be Sons and Daughters of God who will step forward to meet the task of revising and improving the Holy Scriptures of the three basic religions that venerate the same God. It would be so beneficial if all the monotheistic religions, having the same God, jointly form one Holy Scripture that will serve mankind for future generations. If present day religions ignore this challenge, they will eventually fail in conveying the true spirit of God. They will not only stagnate, crumble, and die, but people will no longer believe in the spirit that is a part of humanity. Worse yet, people will see these religions as worn out institutions, and will perhaps laugh at and ridicule what should have been mankind's salvation; something that could have elevated humanity to a higher level of consciousness, righteousness, and truth.

Anyone who searches for the truth and who encourages people to love one another is a viable candidate to update our Holy Scriptures. Scripture has been developed and revised so many times that religious leaders, educated and groomed to guide the spirit of humans, have a responsibility to use their God-given gifts to continue to improve their doctrines. They may need to be openminded to accept recommendations by Daughters and Sons of God who are gifted with perceptions of love and humanity. It is hoped that religious leaders remember that God gave mankind the gift of free will so that their spiritual and intellectual attributes could grow. Religious institutions must heed the call to provide the insights and perception needed to enlighten the spirit of human beings by revealing God's Word—to love one another.

Who will dedicate their lives to becoming the Daughters and Sons of God?

Epilogue

In the course of writing this book, several ancient mysteries have revealed themselves. By examining the historical development of the Egyptian religion, its origin, the beginning of the creation of God has surfaced. No longer a mystery, it was the spiritual nature of man that evolved the concept of one, universal God. This God was conceived by the Egyptian Priesthood as, *"mysterious of form,"* the *"All-Lord, the beginning of that which is."* However, we have also found that the Judaic and Christian Priesthoods extended this belief by conceiving God in the image of man.[1]

The Bible's Old and New Testament has established aspects of belief very different from that of the Egyptians; in particular, the idea that "original sin" was committed by Adam and Eve (Genesis 3:16-19) and initiated the fallen state of human nature, which affects every person born into the world. This doctrine demeans the birthright and nature of man. It has been advocated by Christian religious leaders to give credence to the belief in Christ, as the "new Adam," to redeem us.[2] Religious leaders have inserted the Adam and Eve tree revelation and constructed the idea of original sin that has influenced the thought processes of the human mind. By emphasizing that God created man in His image and promulgating the idea that man is sinful, religious leaders have established a bureaucracy, making their religion the medium of redemption between God and man. These beliefs have the effect of causing man to worship God as His creator and bow down to ask for forgiveness of sins committed. This promotes a sense of guilt and unworthiness that fosters a negative mental outlook rather than a belief that man is like God in spirit and can create great things by believing that he is pure, loving, and a wonderful creature of this world.

---

[1] **Holy Bible,** *King James Version,* **Genesis 9:6.**

[2] **Pope John Paul II,** *Catechism of the Catholic Church,* **Page 890.**

The concept of God is not to be taken lightly as being a fanciful illusion. It was the spirit of man, as he evolved, that has come to conceive the most wonderful concept – God, which has elevated him to aspire to truth, justice, and righteousness. Man has much to be proud of for "we are builders and creators" so aptly put by the author, Dan Brown: *"Since the beginning of time, man has sensed there was something special about himself. . . something more. He had longed for powers he did not possess. He had dreamed of flying, of healing, and of transforming his world in every way imaginable. And he had done just that."*[3]

In *The Lost Symbol,* Mr. Brown has indicated that the Bible contains ancient mysteries and words of wisdom. *Future of God Amen* has revealed one such ancient mystery - how man came to conceive God, namely, the origin of God. Revelation, an apropos title of a book in the Bible, offers wisdom kept secret by Judaic, Christian, and Islamic religious leaders. It should be no surprise that the most revered, honest, and loving human being – Jesus Christ himself - reveals the mysterious secret about the origin of God. In Revelation 3:14, Jesus proclaims Amen as,

The faithful and true witness, the beginning of the creation of God.

Kept secret by religious leaders who have avoided, ignored, and misinterpreted the words of Jesus, few people are aware that Amen was worshipped for more than 2,000 years before the birth of Christ. This pronouncement clearly reveals that Jesus himself is not God but a man of God who acknowledges that God introduced Himself to mankind as Amen.

Another Bible revelation not promulgated to worshippers by religious leaders is the statement made by Jesus Christ in John 14:12 that

---

[3]   **Dan Brown,** *The Lost Symbol,* Epilogue, **Page 507.**

those who believe in him will do even greater works than he. This admission indicates that Jesus was a man who believes there will be others who will do greater works. John 1:12 also clearly states there will be other Sons of God, even to them (which includes Daughters) that believe in His name. This revelation substantiates that there will be others that will acknowledge God's name. The name of God has been announced more than 4,000 years and continues to be praised and sung by worshippers in temples, churches, and mosques - their voices throughout the world reverently announce "*Amen*."

By embracing the two ancient mysteries, the origin of God and that man has within him God's gift to do greater works and thereby create a better world - there is hope that in the near future man will fulfill God's Word to *love one another*. Upon us is the Age of Aquarius, the New Age of Enlightenment, whereby Daughters and Sons of God will stimulate positive initiatives by Judaic, Christian, and Islamic leaders to acknowledge that their common bond is *Amen*.

This book provides the historical background and verified findings by Egyptologists that undeniably conclude that the religion of the Egyptians and their God, Amen, has had a profound effect on the development of the Judaic, Christian, and Islamic religions. The last chapter provides recommendations to religious leaders and worshippers of these religions to preserve a most wonderful legacy – *the belief in God*. A cooperative response to this challenge by religious leaders and their followers will steer mankind into the realm of knowledge where science and faith are compatible in man's quest to know God.

Bibliography

Author	Title	Publisher	Date
Ahamed, Syed Vickar, Dr.	The Quran	Book of Signs Foundation 444 E. Roosevelt Rd, Suite 173, Lombard, IL 60148	2006
Armstrong, Karen	A History of God	Ballantine Books, division of Random House, NY, NY	1993
Breasted, James H	The Dawn of Conscience	Charles Scribner's Sons, New York, NY	1933
Breasted, James H	A History of Egypt	Charles Scribner's Sons, 2nd Ed., New York, NY	1935
Breasted, James H	Development of Religion and Thought In Ancient Egypt	University of Pennsylvania Press, Philadelphia, Pennsylvania	1972
Brown, Dan	The lost Symbol	Doubleday, a division of Ranom House, Inc. New York and Canada	2009
Bruno, Giordano	Giordano Bruno, His Life and Thought, with Annotat. Provides translation of—On the Infinite Universe and Worlds	Henry Schuman, New York, NY	1950
Budge, E.A. Wallis	The Book of the Dead	Published by the Penguin Group, London, England; Published by Arkana	1923 1989
Clayton, Peter A.	Chronicle of the Pharaohs: The Reign-by-Reign Record of the Rulers and Dynasties in Ancient Egypt	Thames and Hudson Inc., 500 Fifth Ave, New York, NY 10110	1994
Dimont, Max I	Jews, God and History (10th printing)	Signet Books, paperback Simon & Schuster, Inc., (hard cover) New York, NY	1962
Freud, Sigmund	Moses and Monotheism	Vintage Books, division of Random House, Inc. New York, NY	1967
Giblin, James Cross	The Riddle of the Rosetta Stone – Key to Ancient Egypt	Thomas Y. Crowell Junior Books, 10 East 53 St., New York, NY 10022	1990

Author	Title	Publisher	Date
Grimal, Nicolas	A History of Ancient Egypt	Blackwell Publishing Co., Williston, Vermont	1992
Jacobs, Louis	The Book of Jewish Belief	Behrman House, Inc., Publishers & Booksellers, Springfield, New Jersey	1984
Jones-Wake, Bible, N.T. Apocryphal books	The Lost Books of the Bible, Being all the Gospels, Epistles, . . . to Jesus Christ his Apostles	Bell Publishing Company, New York, NY (Distributed by Crown Publishers, Inc.)	1979
Khan, Muhammad Zafrulla	The Qur'an (1st printing in Great Britain by Curson Press, Ltd in 1970)	Olive Branch Press, An imprint of Interlink Publishing Group, Inc., Brooklyn, NY	1997
King James Version	Holy Bible, King James Version (Red Letter Reference Edition)	Regency Publishing House, Nashville, Tennessee	1978
La Barre, Weston	The Ghost Dance	Dell Publishing Co., Inc. New York, NY	1972
Manji, Irshad	The Trouble With Islam	Random House Canada, Saint Martin's Press, NY. NY	2004
Massey, Gerald	Poems by Gerald Massey	Ticknor and Fields, Boston, Mass.	1895
Noss, John B	Man's Religions (5th Ed.)	Macmillan Publishing Co., Inc. New York, NY	1974
Preble, Robert C	Britannica World Language Dictionary	Funk & Wagnalls Company, New York, NY	1958
Pritchard, James B Edited by	Ancient Near Eastern Texts Relating to the Old Testament	Princeton University Press, 2nd Ed.	1955
Pope John Paul II Promulgated by	Catechism of the Catholic Church	Libreria Editrice Vaticana, 2nd Ed.	2000
Rohl, David	The Lost Testament	Century (Random House), London, UK	2002
Sagan, Carl	Cosmos	Random House Inc. New York, NY	1980
Smith, Homer W	Man and His Gods	Grosset & Dunlap, NY	1957
Spong, John Shelby	The Sins of Scripture	HarperCollins Publishers, New York, NY	2005
Vermes, Geza	The Dead Sea Scrolls in English	Penguin Books, Ltd. Middlesex, England & NY	1982
Whiston, William, Translated by	Antiquities of the Jews by Flavius Josephus	Lighting Source Inc.; Paperbackshop—US, Elk Grove Village. IL	2001

Index

Figure Ending. Nefertari Receives Truth from Isis.

∞

My very best wishes for the success of our

Daughters and Sons of God

who assist perceptive and courageous

Judaic, Christian, and Islamic Religious Leaders

to

work together and teach our

sisters and brothers, from every nation,

to

love and support one another.

Nicholas P. Ginex

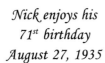

*Nick enjoys his
71st birthday
August 27, 1935*

Photographer: Jennifer Schwartz

Nick Ginex is a retired Electrical Engineer with an MBA in Finance. He worked in design and distinguished himself in the support disciplines of Maintainability and Configuration Management (CM).

As CM Manager of software and hardware products at top aerospace and commercial companies, his planning and organizational skills were applied for the successful operation of entire engineering projects.

While writing this book, Nick sang and played his guitar at senior care centers and nursing homes for their enjoyment. The smiles on their faces and joy in their eyes has been his greatest reward.

His love for his children and desire to inform them about the God Amen and His influence on the Judaic, Christian, and Islamic religions - has motivated him to write this book. A book he hopes others will benefit by learning more about God and their purpose in life.

CPSIA information can be obtained at www.ICGtesting.com
Printed in the USA
243513LV00002B/35/P